The Book of David

Beverley Eley was born in Sydney and now lives with her husband John on a small holding at Gleniffer in Northern New South Wales. She was publicity and advertising manager for Angus&Robertson's Bookshops in the 1970s, and was later marketing manager for the publisher Cassell Australia Collier Macmillan before becoming marketing manager and spokesperson for the Australian Consumers Association for several years. Her biography of the Australian writer Ion L. Idriess was published in 1995.

The BOOK of DAVID

BEVERLEY ELEY

HarperCollins*Publishers*

HarperCollins*Publishers*

First published in Australia in 1996
Reprinted in 1996 (twice)
by HarperCollins*Publishers* Pty Limited
ACN 009 913 517
A member of the HarperCollins*Publishers* (Australia) Pty Limited Group

HarperCollins*Publishers*
25 Ryde Road, Pymble, Sydney, NSW 2073, Australia
31 View Road, Glenfield, Auckland 10, New Zealand
77-85 Fulham Palace Road, London W6 8JB, United Kingdom
Hazelton Lanes, 55 Avenue Road, Suite 2900, Toronto, Ontario M5R 3L2
and 1995 Markham Road, Scarborough, Ontario M1B 5M8, Canada
10 East 53rd Street, New York NY 10032, USA

National Library of Australia Cataloguing-in-Publication data:

Eley, Beverley.
  The book of David.
  ISBN 0 207 19105 0.
  1. Helfgott, David, 1931–   . 2. Pianists—Australia—Biography.
  I. Title.
786.2092

Cover photograph courtesty of Ray Peek
Printed in Australia by Griffin Paperbacks, Adelaide

9 8 7 6 5 4 3
99 98 97 96

ACKNOWLEDGMENTS

Permission to reproduce, and quote from, David Helfgott's letters to Sir Frank Callaway, and from Sir Frank's letters to David Helfgott, is gratefully acknowledged. (David's letters are quoted as they originally appeared.) Permission to quote from Mrs Luber-Smith's letter to me is also gratefully acknowledged.

Permission to reproduce an extract from *Duet for Three Hands*, by Cyril Smith, first published in 1958 by Angus & Robertson Ltd, London, is gratefully acknowledged.

The search for ourselves is indeed a complex and difficult one. The biographer's task, from this point of view, is fraught with many perils and pitfalls. The introduction to this book tells the story of how it all began, but here I must record some special thanks.

My thanks to David's sisters, Margaret, Suzie and Louise, for the time and care they took to provide photographs and details of David's early years and the Helfgott family background. David's brother Leslie has also been of great help. I would like to record my appreciation of the warmth with which the Helfgott family received me. Especial thanks to David's wife, Gillian Helfgott, for her assistance and for 'sharing the joy' of the eleven years since she first met David.

My grateful thanks to Dr Chris Reynolds, with whom I have had many lengthy and often humorous conversations.

I cannot sufficiently thank Emeritus Professor Sir Frank Callaway for his time in putting pen to paper and for our several telephone conversations, and also for providing his musical expertise in reading the manuscript. My thanks also go to Lady Callaway for her useful conversations with me.

I would like to thank Mrs Luber-Smith, now ninety-four, for

the hours she sat at her typewriter recording her memories of David in his early and late teens.

My sincere thanks to Madame Alice Carrard, now ninety-nine years old, a warm-hearted lady who filled in many details of David's life which were generally unknown.

I would like to thank my son-in-law, the Hon. Harry Denison-Pender, for research at London's Royal College of Music and for providing other written material, also my daughter Vanessa, who helped with descriptions of various locations in and around London.

There are others who deserve mention, among them the music critic James Penberthy, and Kirsty Cockburn and George Negus, who know David well. Last but not least is David himself, who over the years has enchanted me while giving me some great one-liners.

Thanks also to Chris and Lou Underwood, who provided the printer that printed most of the manuscript. Finally, I must thank my husband, John, for his ceaseless support and invaluable assistance.

*To my husband, John, who believes
in friendship, loyalty and justice.*

CONTENTS

Phoenix: A fabulous Egyptian bird, the only one of its kind, according to Greek legend said to live a certain number of years, at the close of which it makes in Egypt a nest of spices, sings a melodious dirge, flaps its wings to set fire to the pile, burns itself to ashes, and comes forth with new life.

Brewer's Dictionary of Phrase and Fable

The Promised Land

In the corner of a room in a house in the Promised Land, a hunched and mumbling figure sat at an upright piano — his nose mere centimetres from the keyboard. With raised eyebrows, he peered intensely at the keys through very thick-lensed glasses. Later I would discover that his eyes were sky blue. Oblivious to the festivities of the birthday party going on around him, his long sensitive fingers moved randomly across the keys, as if searching for sounds unknown.

'David, darling, come and meet John and Beverley,' said Gillian Helfgott, a vibrant woman with blonde hair and heavy, colourful earrings. She had just been introduced to us by Kirsty Cockburn, our friend and neighbour, whose gathering in the Promised Land we were attending.

David Helfgott, slight, fair-haired and balding on top, red-gold curls brushing the back of his shirt collar, jumped off the piano stool and made his way towards us. It was difficult to tell how tall he was because he was so stooped. He ran with a crouched and ungainly gait to immediately reach behind my knees and press his head into my groin. To say it took me aback is scarcely an adequate comment. It was a most unusual introduction to a man I was to become very fond of.

'David,' Gillian said firmly, 'don't hug Beverley like that, stand up, stand up straight.'

David, taking absolutely no notice, was muttering, 'Got to treasure these times ... is that the idea, darling? ... got to be grateful, got to be sociable, even if it kills me ... got to be grateful, got to be grateful.'

'There's no need to be grateful,' I said, completely bewildered.

'Stand up, David,' said Gillian again.

Taking him by the shoulders, I tried to get him to stand up straight, only to be rewarded with a vigorous, determined and spasmodic jerking of his arms behind my knees.

'David, why don't you play something for Bev?'

David released me and I heard for the first time his distinctive laugh, ack-ack-ack, as he ran back to his piano.

'What'll I play, darling ... what'll I play?'

'Oh, why not play the Tchaik ... darling, the Tchaikovsky.'

David, who had previously been tinkering around at the keys, burst, without hesitation, into a passionate rendition of Tchaikovsky's Piano Concerto No. 1 that, at such close quarters, was quite overpowering.

My husband John moved away and went over to the piano to listen, and when he came back to me exclaimed, 'That man is incredible.'

'Yes,' I said.

The Promised Land was opened up in the early eighteen hundreds. It was not long before the giant cedar trees were all taken and dragged, by bullock team, down to the waiting sailing ships tied up on the Bellinger River. The land then came to the notice of several dairy farmers with Scottish ancestry and the valley became known as the Glen of Iffer. To this valley also came one Angel Gabriel Capararo, a farmer of Italian descent, who exclaimed upon his first sighting of the rolling green hills, and the crystal-clear waters of the river that wound through the valley, 'This is the Promised Land.' That's the story, anyway, and today we have the community of Gleniffer residing in the Promised Land.

When the Capararo property came up for subdivision, there were two large holdings of some 300 to 400 acres, and several five-acre blocks. Purely out of interest, John and I attended the auction at the cottage of old Mrs Capararo, who had recently died.

Gillian Helfgott was there and we spoke again. The whole subdivision had been bought by a single developer. Gillian said to us, 'I think I'll go and ask him if he will sell me the block by the river.' It transpired that the block she was interested in was too expensive for her and she inquired if there was another block available. There was a five-acre block with a creek running through it, and a large, very nicely grassed, level area on which to build a house. It was not long before a house was under way. The inevitable house-warming party followed.

In this way we came to know and love David. His childish enthusiasm, his open-hearted love for anyone and anything, was most bewitching, and of course it was his delight to play for us. The friendship grew and it soon became routine to have David and Gillian to dinner; David inevitably jogged off down the road and back to his piano after he had eaten. Gillian would stay and we would share a little more wine. In the same vein John and I would dine at Gillian's, often with other friends she would invite. So we came to know David and Gillian very well.

In November of 1994 Gillian approached me, as a friend and biographer, asking me if I would consider writing David's biography. David is such a lovable and complex character that it was a tempting thought. I realised that from what I knew of

David's tortured background, the work would prove to be an emotional challenge. As at that time my youngest daughter and her partner were coming home to Australia, together with his parents and some of her English friends, to be married in the garden at home, I declined.

The subject of David's biography came up again in March and April and later in July, 1995, when my biography of the Australian author and chronicler of early Australia, Ion L. Idriess, was released. The idea of writing the biography of such a mercurial, confounding and gifted individual as David Helfgott captured my interest and I agreed to write *The Book of David*.

The 1 a.m., 2 a.m. nights began again — almost before my other biography had hit the bookshops. And once again I abandoned my garden and my peaceful lifestyle for the emotional business of digging into other people's lives and generally prying into the human condition.

The biography of David was well underway, in fact almost complete, when the acclaimed movie *Shine* received a standing ovation at the US Sundance film festival. Overnight he had captured the interest and affection of the masses.

When I first undertook my research prior to writing this biography of David Helfgott, I naturally began where most biographers begin — at the beginning.

Without attempting some understanding of his family background, and key figures in his life, it would have been impossible to gain insight into David's complex personality. As my research and writing progressed it became evident that David's biography was, up to a point, also a biography of the Helfgott family. David's brother Leslie and his sisters, Margaret, Suzie and Louise, shared with me many important details about their sibling and their own childhood. All of them are talented and highly intelligent. Margaret, it was said, could have achieved a musical recognition that would have rivalled that of her genius brother, had she had David's opportunities. Leslie, while decrying his talents with the violin, enthrals his fans at bush dances with Australian, Irish, English and Scottish folk music. Suzie, a social worker, is an accomplished pianist with an associate music diploma. Louise, who has a graduate diploma in English, is also a musician, a published poet, a prize-winning playwright and a piano teacher. Gillian Helfgott, David's wife and a renowned astrologer, has contributed generously to our understanding of David.

With so many people involved, research became tricky territory, made more so by the fact that David — who appears to have become less coherent over the years, and basically communicates with the world in riddles — was unwilling to talk about those times and incidents in family history which he identifies as 'too painful'. These communication problems made the writing of this biography extraordinarily difficult. Sorting out stories and information from sources other than David, material often presented as first-hand accounts when it could only have been second- or even third-hand, made the task more complex. The passing of time, in some cases of decades, since the events recalled has perhaps also led to what Clive James might call some 'unreliable memoirs'.

When I went in search of David I never presumed to find or provide definitive answers to questions which psychologists and psychiatrists have been unable to answer. I have tried to give everyone in the story a voice, including David.

Beverley Eley, 1996

1

David: Chaos in Action

When confronted with David, the incessantly babbling, mumbling jumping-jack, the cricket on the griddle, the man who furiously hugs everyone he meets while sounding his own peculiar ack-ack gunfire laugh, most people mentally pin a label on him. But just when you think you've read him right, categorised and neatly pigeon-holed him, he produces an exceedingly clever comment. With boyish enthusiasm, he accurately rattles off the answer to your question about who first conceptualised the atom. 'Leucippus of Miletus in 440 BC,' he says and then adds, 'People think it was Democritus, but he stole it.' Not only is his memory phenomenal, his wit is dry and clever. One day he walked in on a conversation about homilies, proverbs and adages. After patting and kissing those close at hand, he walked away with the comment, 'Preach speech ... it's preach speech.'

By what yardstick do we measure someone like the eccentric, yet greatly gifted, David Helfgott?

Surely not by our own presumption of, so-called normality, which raises the very frightening question, 'Who is normal?'

Why label him at all? Is it because he confounds us? Certainly we cannot understand, with our self-assessed rational intelligence, how someone like this desperately near-sighted, internationally acclaimed pianist can be on the one hand, a genius virtuoso, a man who expresses his quick, wry wit in clever alliteration, a person with a phenomenal memory, who speed-reads and recalls all that he reads to the last detail, even to the page number; and on the other hand a childlike forty-nine-year-old who babbles, clings, kisses, pats and strokes everyone he meets, a person who seemingly lacks stable mental coordination or any visible sign of ordinary concentration.

Anyone who has heard David play Tchaikovsky's First Piano Concerto, or Beethoven's Fifth Piano Concerto (the 'Emperor'), or his 'Appassionata' Piano Sonata; or the Polonaise in A-flat Major by Chopin (Popolski, as David calls him because of his Polish ancestry); or Rachmaninof's romantic Second Piano Concerto; or Scriabin's complex Etude in E-flat Minor; or Rimsky-Korsakof's furious 'Flight of the Bumble Bee'; or melodious, contemporary music such as Gershwin's 'Rhapsody in Blue', will surely be transported by the man and his music and, for a brief interlude, experience an exhilarating assault on the senses. Lost in the state of rapture and awed wonderment which David's playing evokes, one doesn't mind just who or what he is, just so long as he keeps on playing. However, the spell he fashions quite often dissolves when he stops playing. Then some listeners may appraise him with a jaundiced and socially conditioned eye, from behind their own protective facade of conformity.

Searching for the real David is like investigating theory chaos, which demonstrates that in apparent chaos there exists not only order but unimaginable, exquisite patterns which are manifest within other unimaginable, exquisite patterns ad infinitum, but none of which are discernible to the naked eye. The further we go in this search for David the more complicated and chaotic it becomes, for every conclusion is at risk of being set at naught: just when you think you have the answer there is a parallel contradiction which seems to be equally true. If, in our estimation, David's personality is an expression of chaos, then we must at least consider the possibility that the inexplicable patterns within patterns chaos theory tells us exist in natural phenomena also exist in David's mercurial mind.

And further, if we accept another premise of chaos theory namely that that a butterfly flapping its wings in Tokyo may ultimately help create a tornado in Chicago, then we must at least consider the possibility that while an emotional disturbance would only be the flap of a butterfly's wings to a 'normal' person it could manifest as a traumatic tornado in a person with David's finely tuned sensitivities.

According to Gillian Helfgott, some psychologists have labelled David as psychotic, while others have ventured the opinion that perhaps he suffers from an acute anxiety neurosis. Dr Chris Reynolds says, however, that when he consulted with the psychiatrist who had handled David's case during the time he was hospitalised in Perth's Graylands Hospital, he was told that David's condition was unclassifiable. It is his personal opinion that the genius David showed for the piano as a child and teenager was not fully understood and that the consequent mismanagement of that genius led to frustration and his eventual breakdown.

David did, however, suffer severe depression and complex mental illness for ten years, and as a result was institutionalised for much of that time. During those lost, agonising years he was treated with of various psychotic drugs. Gillian Helfgott says there have been unsubstantiated rumours that he also received the now infamous deep sleep treatment, which had lasting and destructive effects on those who were subjected to it, but there is no evidence to support this. David also received electroconvulsive therapy (ECT).

Recent medical research shows that many people who present as depressive carry a gene which, given the right trigger, will pitch them into severe depression. Further, psychiatrists generally agree that all depression, no matter how it starts, will ultimately become chemical, as long-term depression creates biochemical changes in the brain.

Current medical research into depression indicates that creative people, high achievers, obsessive personalities, along with meticulous or sensitive personalities and people who demand a lot of themselves, are more prone to depression, whose causes may be genetic, environmental, chemical, or a combination of all these. It seems that when David first became obviously disturbed his was a personality which fell squarely and unavoidably within this ambit whose causes may be genetic. Clearly it is impossible for anyone to say whether his long-term depression led to or revealed an underlying mental illness, or whether he did in fact suffer from mental instability, one of the many manifestations of this being depression.

David received ECT during the early 1970s, when the therapy was in its experimental stages. It is thus possible that doctors, as Gillian says, made 'mistakes' when treating him for his depression, which had been building slowly until some pivotal event triggered the reaction that pushed him into a world of his own. It is possible, even probable, that the electric shock therapy, which some clinical trials indicate depends on the timing of re-applications for its effectiveness, reinforced his anxieties instead of removing his depression. Perhaps the combination of drugs and ECT was responsible for sending David Helfgott into the depths of that inner world, to emerge with those very things which are now most important to him. These are now demonstrated in his towering musical talent, his incredible memory, and a love for the world and everyone and everything in it.

Anyone who encounters him would agree that the David we see is a conundrum. Is he a man with superior intellectual capacities who has unconsciously disposed of all that learned psychological dross which, for most of us, is fused into our personalities? Or is he ultimately a superb game-player who deliberately maintains the unworldly and impractical stance which allows him to pursue his extraordinary musical talent unhindered, using it to avoid performing those boring daily tasks which ordinary people are pleased to undertake for him? Or does he simply hide in confusing conversation and brilliant playing from a world which he knows he is still unable to cope with? Or is it possible to accept the conjecture that perhaps he is the end product of drugs and medical treatments which, by sheer accident, heightened and enhanced the brilliant intrinsic genius of this sometimes wilful child–man who appears to be the personification of Parsifal, the eternal innocent child who, according to legend, glimpsed the Holy Grail, a sight denied to ordinary mortals?

Perhaps there is another explanation, certainly not as exotic as the Parsifal comparison but more understandable. I believe the answer is a combination of all these perhapses. Recently David was overheard saying to himself, 'It's alright to be different, it protects you.' Protects him from what? Only David really knows and I suspect that he is now, in his own way, asking himself if he can come out of hiding and cope with facing the truth. Whether he does or not should be important only to him.

There is no mistaking, however, what is important to David. It is his music. Music is his life and his only reason for being, it is the breath and fibre of his being, it is all he lives for. Music was established in David's life by his father when David was still virtually a toddler. A myth persists that when it came to music Peter Helfgott was an unyielding fanatic, David's Svengali, a man who had an immense, if not overwhelming, patriarchal, musical and psychological impact on his son's life, and that it was this influence which ultimately made David 'different'. Apart from David's comments about his father there is no hard evidence to support these claims. The Helfgott family, the people who knew Peter best, emphatically deny that there is any truth to the 'malicious' and 'judgmental' statements which have been made against him, saying that Peter was a loving and much-loved father and further that David was born 'different'.

As David's eldest sister Margaret wrote in her father's obituary in 1975, 'The truly great are often misunderstood.' In order to understand what may appear to have been Peter's complex and driven personality, his desperate need to maintain absolute control of David's life and the lives of his other children, and to understand his conviction that he and he alone was capable of protecting his family, it is necessary to have some knowledge of Peter's background and of what it meant to be a descendant of the persecuted Jewish generation which reached adulthood in Poland during the years of Hitler's rise to power.

The simple phrase 'Polish Jew, born under the Russian flag', the throwaway line Peter used to describe his origins, embodies all the pathos endured by generations of Jews since the final destruction of the Temple of Jerusalem at the hands of the Romans led to the scattering of the Jewish people throughout the lands of the Roman Empire.

The Holocaust is perhaps the most potent symbol of the persecution of the Jewish people. This systematic genocide, carried out against the Jews throughout Europe and in Nazi concentration camps, those infamous places of horror, was not however an isolated incident. In western Russian provinces Jewish suffering was appalling through the centuries. According to Max Wurmbrand and Cecil Roth in their work, *The Jewish People: 4000 Years of Survival*, the suffering reached a climax during the Russian Civil War between 1917 and 1921. The Communist 'Red' troops and the 'White' troops, while waging war against each other, mounted monstrous pogroms against the Jews in many places. It is estimated that some 60 000 Jews were murdered during this period. After the war Jewish rights were nominally guaranteed by the peace settlement of 1920. However, the Minority Treaties were to a great extent defied, except by Czechoslovakia, which strictly observed Jewish minority rights until the German occupation in 1939.

For the population of about three million Jews in Poland, equal rights existed only on paper. Ingrained Polish anti-Semitism revealed itself in universities, where Christian students and their professors did all they could to ostracise Jewish students from the lecture halls. In tandem, the government-supported anti-Jewish boycott on the economic front gradually expelled all Jews from their academic positions, thereby reducing a substantial section of the Jewish community to appalling impoverishment.

It is not difficult to imagine the consternation which overtook European Jewry when Hitler came to power with his appointment as *Reichskanzler* in January 1933. It was an apprehension which escalated to panic during this first year of the Third Reich as German Jews were systematically excluded from public office and civil service positions, and removed from journalism and radio broadcasting. The discrimination extended to farming, teaching and the performing arts. By 1934 the reign of terror was well established; all Jews were expelled from the stock exchanges, doctors and lawyers were prohibited from practising. Throughout Germany, organised 'spontaneous' demonstrations of indignation were waged against the Jews, but the most ominous of the Nazi regime's actions was the construction of a series of concentration camps, ostensibly for the internment of 'political prisoners and enemies of the Third Reich', including devout Christians who had opposed Hitler. However, the reality was that soon the overwhelming numbers of these people would be Jews.

The Polish Jews had suffered throughout history, shot at by Russians one day and avoiding Polish boots and bullets the next. But by the spring of 1933, it became clear that the worst was yet to come, with the persecution of German Jews, Communists, Socialists, Gypsies, homosexuals and other minority groups openly accelerating in Nazi Germany.

It was against this historical background of enforced endemic poverty and persecution, of sudden but not unexpected violent death, that Peter Helfgott reached young adulthood — at a time when invasion of his homeland by Nazi Germany was imminent.

2

From Whence They Came

David's father, Elias Peter (Pinchas) Helfgott, born in 1903, was a classic survivor. As a young teenage boy he was fiercely independent in spirit and mind; by 1917, when he was fourteen, he was already developing into a progressive, radical, freethinker who rebelled against the religious mores of his family. He ran away from home on three occasions, only to be caught and brought back.

Apart from his strength of will and individuality Peter had music in his blood. It was the joy of his life — to live without music was unthinkable. The vital and soulful music of the Slavic peoples, the passionate full-blooded outpourings of Gypsy music, the works of the Romantic composers such as Borodin, Tchaikovsky and the great Rachmaninof, filled his soul. A self-taught musician, Peter conferred this intense love of music on his children and gave them their early musical training.

Peter's father, a religious disciplinarian, believed that religious veneration was the only acceptable form of musical expression. Ivan Rostkier, who knew Peter Helfgott well, says that Peter told him Helfgott senior adhered to Chassidism, a type of specific Jewish mysticism. In his work *The Unknown Sanctuary: The Story of Judaism, its Teachings, Philosophy and*

Symbols, Rabbi Rudolph Brasch explains how Chassidism, literally meaning 'pietism', taught a world-accepting kind of piety. Israel Ben Eliezer, the founder of Chassidism, was born in Poland in 1700. His pupils preserved Ben Eliezer's legends and teachings, further expanding them and their message. Chassidism teaches that man can find God's divine fire everywhere and in everything. Yet he must release it from its prison. Without man's conscious effort, God will remain unredeemed. Thus Chassidism pronounced the principle of man's responsibility for God's fate on earth.

Peter, who did not share his father's religious views, believed in socialism and the equality of man. He was also passionate about music. Determined to learn to play an instrument, at fourteen years of age, he bought himself a violin with the few precious roubles he had managed to save over many months. Possibly shocked by this act of independence, his father seized the violin from him and smashed it. This confrontation between Peter and his father destroyed more than the offending violin; it shattered the family. Soon after this painful incident in 1917, Peter ran away for the last time from his father's house in Kamyk, a Polish *shtetl*, the Yiddish description of a small township or village. His will and his determination to play music were not weakened but strengthened by his father's display of patriarchal power. Sadly, Peter would never again see his parents or his brothers Zelig and Abraham, or his sisters Miriam, Rivka and Na'acha. Apart from his mother, who died before the Holocaust, they were all murdered by the Nazis. His other sister, Hannah, was reunited with him in Melbourne, Australia, in 1938.

The year 1917 saw not only the continuation of the 1914–18 war but also the beginning of the Russian Revolution. Certainly not the best of times, possibly the worst of times, for a young

Jewish boy to make his bid for freedom. Exactly what he did, where he went, or how he managed to survive wandering, alone, in a Europe devastated by World War I and in the East by the Russian Civil War (which began a year before the last shot had been fired in 1918 and continued until 1921), is unknown. How did this boy survive one of the bloodiest periods in history? It was a time when Communist reactionaries annihilated defenceless Jewish communities. Where was he when the 'White' armies mounted the inhuman pogroms said to be responsible for the slaughter of over 60 000 Jews?

It was at this time, 16 March 1917, when the provisional Russian government published a decree declaring that all Jews living under the Russian flag were equal citizens of the empire. This decree gave rise to unprecedented opportunities for Jews, leading to a good number of Jews playing a conspicuous role in the early Communist leadership. Many Jewish young men and boys took the opportunity to join the Russian army as a result of the provisional government's decree. Perhaps Elias Peter Helfgott was amongst them.

It was later in that same year, on 2 November, that the then British Foreign Secretary, Arthur James Balfour, signed the famous declaration, known by his name, which viewed with favour the establishment of a 'national home for the Jewish People' in Palestine. Peter's journey from Poland to the Promised Land took nine years, for family history tells us that Peter was in Palestine in 1926, where he lived for a year.

Once again, it was not the best of times. The Balfour Declaration had been endorsed by other Allied powers and by the Supreme Council of the Peace Conference at San Remo. The Mandate, assigned in 1920 by the League of Nations to Britain to implement, was soon to crumble. Arab leaders made known their opposition to the establishment of a Jewish national home in Palestine almost instantly by attacking a number of Jewish settlements. After further attacks in 1921, the British Administration became acutely sympathetic to the Arab population's objections to the Balfour Declaration and all it embodied.

When Peter came to Palestine in 1926, Transjordan had been detached from Palestine for five years. The loss of the Transjordan had drastically reduced the territory designated for the Jewish national home. Jewish political rights and Jewish immigration were very restricted and Palestine was struggling economically. Although Peter lived there for a year, he was unable to find work. It is recounted that complex laws and administration made it as difficult to leave the country as it was to enter it, which must have compounded Peter's problems. Whatever events brought about Peter's difficulties in leaving Palestine, they were most likely solved by his obtaining a British passport.

Peter later told his family that he joined a travelling circus, departing from Palestine as a circus hand. In later years he showed his children a scar on his hand which he said he had received from a tiger. He also told them how he had been crushed into a corner by an elephant, and how, if a trainer had not passed by and saved him by pulling the elephant away, he would not have lived to tell the tale.

Peter's eldest daughter, Margaret, also relates that he joined the navy, assumed to have been the British merchant navy. This was an unlikely career for a Jewish boy from Kamyk, which is famous not for its seamen but for making matzo, the Jewish unleavened bread eaten during Passover. Just when Peter joined the British navy is unclear. Given his youth and the lapse of time between 1917 and 1926, the year he spent in Palestine, it seems more likely that he joined the navy in 1927, after he left

Palestine. At that time he would have been around the age of twenty-four and joining the British merchant navy could have been a well-considered move, one which would ultimately provide him with transport to Australia, where he could begin a new life. At that time passages to Australia were not government-assisted and working as a seaman was probably the only way he could have migrated to Australia, which he did in 1934.

Other Europeans seeking refuge from persecution, and there were many, either had to pay their own way, or were assisted by already resident national or religious groups. Many Jewish migrants, after settling, obtaining work and setting up homes in their chosen cities, kept in touch with other immigrants from their area through the social network provided by the *Landsmannschaften*. This could be described as a loose brotherhood of any Jewish people from the same locality. Relatives and friends still at home were urged to come to Australia, where many more found safe haven.

Peter is believed to have come ashore in Melbourne when he was about thirty-one years old. Margaret says he chose to live in Melbourne because many Jewish people from Czestochowa, the large Polish town close to Kamyk, had already settled there.

At approximately the same time, Polish Jews living in Germany were being deported to Poland, only to find the Polish authorities refusing to allow them entry at the border. Although turning the dispossessed Jews away would seal their fate, the Poles and Russians took advantage of the situation, covertly giving the Germans free rein to continue the continual Polish and Russian pogroms on a grand scale.

Despite the fact that Peter had escaped the coming Holocaust, his early experiences in Australia were not easy. The restrained economic conditions endured by the Melbourne lower middle classes and indeed by the majority of Australians at the close of the 1930s Depression were easing when he landed. Conditions were still not affluent, but the opportunities for him to make a good life were manifold when compared to those he had left behind in Poland. However, continental refugees fleeing from the impending European war were often viewed with disdain and suspicion, and contemptuously labelled 'reffos'. Despite all the propaganda promoting a vision of Australian society as egalitarian, Peter had not escaped social stigma. He was still, in Australian eyes, a second-class citizen.

However, it was never Peter's nature to kowtow. Calling upon his natural pride and obvious personal strength he quickly settled down, appreciating the freedom he had found for the first time in his life.

Knowing that war was imminent, Peter wrote to his father in Poland, at the same time sending money to pay the passages for his brothers to join him in Australia. It was Peter's hope that once the boys arrived they would be able to work and save enough money to bring the rest of the family to Australia. In the belief that Hannah, his mentally fragile sister, would not be able to withstand the rigours of war, Peter's father sent her in place of the boys telling Peter 'God would take care of the family.' Peter was furious. In Peter's radical but firmly held view, this was nothing more than a grotesque and unfounded platitude.

On 1 September 1939, Nazi Germany attacked Poland. Although the Poles fought fiercely, their out-of-date army, based mainly on cavalry and field guns, was briskly obliterated by a paltry tank force supported by an overpoweringly superior air force. Soviet Russian troops crossed Poland's eastern frontier on 17 September, dealing Poland a death blow to the back. The garrison of Warsaw held out until 28 September despite massive bombardment from air and ground, and the remaining sizeable

Polish segment surrendered on 5 October. Guerrilla resistance continued into the winter, but Poland lay crushed between Russian and German jaws. The pocket-size country had been conquered in approximately twenty-eight days. It was abundantly clear by the close of the month that Polish Jews, sharing the fate of other 'enemies of the Third Reich', trapped in Poland were to be used, persecuted or annihilated. Over the next six years, six million Poles were killed, and three million of these were Jews.

Czestochowa, the large town a short distance from Kamyk where Peter had lived and where his family still lived at the time of the invasion, about 250 km south-west of Warsaw, lay directly in the path of Reichenau's 10th Army Group. Reichenau had been given the bulk of the German armoured forces for the purpose of delivering the decisive fatal strike at Poland's heart.

Peter's scepticism proved correct: God did not take care of his family. The fate of Peter's father and his brothers and sisters is unclear; they may have been killed in that first attack or worked to death in the labour camps. However, it is generally believed that they were murdered by the Nazis in the Treblinka concentration camp and consumed in its ovens.

Naturally the loss of his family had a huge and terrible influence on Peter. Suzie, one of his daughters and one of David's sisters, feels that this loss contributed to Peter's over-protective attitude toward his children. 'I remember I was nine years old before I was allowed to go to the shop alone. That shop was only three doors away. I was so excited that I had been allowed to go alone and that I had come back safely that, in my excitement to let him [Peter] know I'd got back without any misadventure befalling me, I dropped the bottle of milk I had gone to get and cut my arm quite badly. I guess, in effect, I had fulfilled his fear.'

Peter's youngest daughter, Louise, also feels that he was over-protective. She believes this stemmed not only from the loss of his family in the Holocaust, but from a deep, almost genetic fear of loss, which most Jewish people must have deeply buried in their subconscious as a result of their history of persecution.

Margaret Helfgott, who is two years older than David, disagrees. It is her opinion that Peter was no more protective of his children than any other father. It is not surprising that his children, in particular Margaret and Louise hold differing opinions. Margaret being the eldest, and fourteen years older than Louise, had the advantage of knowing Peter when he had every reason to believe that his dreams and hopes would be fulfilled, while Louise knew a very different man, one who had become disillusioned by people and who felt he had been betrayed by life.

In 1944 Peter married Rachel, a Polish Jew and a beautiful girl, also born under the Russian flag. Rachel was born in 1920 in Klubutzka, which, like Kamyk, was a *shtetl* close to Czestochowa.

From the early nineteenth century the Jewish community of Czestochowa played an important role in the industrial and commercial life of the town. At the social level they established a number of Jewish educational and charitable institutions. Also in Czestochowa is the Jasna Gora Madonna, celebrated as a centre of Catholic pilgrimage. Every Easter Catholics from all over Poland would make the pilgrimage to worship at Czestochowa. Every year many among these folk sought absolution of their sins by howling abuse and hurling stones at Jews.

Rachel and her friends had suffered these insults on numerous occasions. Rachel's mother, Chaya, had died when Rachel was only two years old, leaving her father, Mordecai, with Rachel and her brother Morry (Maurice) to care for. As was often the custom amongst her people, her mother's sister, Bronia, took up residence in Mordecai's home to care for his motherless children. Eventually she married Rachel's father, and the couple extended Mordecai's first family by adding three children of their own: two girls, Gutka and Henya, and a boy, Johnny.

In 1938, with the invasion of Poland merely a matter of time, Mordecai and Bronia did not have enough money to take the entire family to to Australia. These two unhappy people were compelled to make the harsh and difficult decision to split the family. Bronia, her two daughters and her son would stay in Poland, while Mordecai, Rachel and Morry, all able to work, went to Australia in the hope of earning enough money to bring the others to join them before the outbreak of war. According to plan, Mordecai, Rachel and Morry left Odessa for Australia on one of the last ships able to leave Poland in 1938.

Mordecai and Bronia, just as Peter's father had, placed their faith in God for the survival of Bronia and their children. Indeed, with the exception of a few who questioned the validity of throwing themselves on God's mercy, a whole people facing uncontrollable disaster unquestioningly reaffirmed their religious beliefs.

The German army entered Czestochowa on 3 September 1939. The next day, later called 'Bloody Monday', a pogrom took place and several hundred Jews were murdered. On 25 December, Christmas Day of all days, a second pogrom took place and the Great Synagogue was set on fire. In August 1940, 1000 young Czestochowa men between the ages of eighteen and twenty-five were sent to the forced labour-camp in Lublin province. Few survived.

When many Jews from other provinces of western Poland

came to Czestochowa in 1940–41, the city's Jewish population swelled by several thousands. In April 1941 a ghetto was established; it was sealed off on 23 August. The population inside that intensely crowded and awful place suffered severe hunger, while inadequate sanitation brought killer epidemics. But the worst was yet to come. On 23 September 1942, the day after the Day of Atonement, the Jews' holiest day of the year, a large-scale *Aktion* began. By 5 October 1942, two weeks later, 39 000 people had been deported to Treblinka, while 2000 were executed on the spot.

This was not to be the end of the horror which had befallen Czestochowa. The ghetto, by then greatly diminished and within new borders, was now referred to as the 'small ghetto'. The 6500 Jews remaining were transferred to the two slave labour camps organised by the city's two HASAG Metal Warenfabrik factories, privately owned by the German companies Hugo Schnider and Aktiengesellschaft, manufacturers of armoury.

On 20 July 1943, 500 prisoners from these camps were executed at the Jewish cemetery. Before leaving the city on 17 January 1945 the Germans managed to deport 6000 prisoners from the HASAG camps to the three concentration camps of Buchenwald, Gross-Rosen and Ravensbruck. The 5200 prisoners who succeeded in hiding were liberated by the Soviet Army.

Aside from some heroic rabbis who, in total faith, continued to preach until their death, there were many who questioned their faith and raised ancient debates. One, Rabbi Kalonymus Kalmish Shapiro, referred to a talmudic legend which tells of angels querying the Lord as to whether the martyrdom of the Ten Martyrs, executed in the days of Emperor Hadrian, was proper reward for the unflinching devotion of these scholars of the Torah. The Lord is supposed to have promised that if such an event were to happen again, the universe would return to chaos. At this point, as Salo W. Baron recounts in *The Russian Jew Under Tsars and Soviets*, the rabbi, himself to become a victim of the gas chambers in 1943, cried in anguish:

> *And now innocent children, pure as angels, as well as great and holy men in Israel, are being killed and slaughtered only because they are Jews ... and the world's space is filled with their heart-rending shouts: 'Save us, save us!' They too cry, 'Is this the reward for devotion to Torah?' Yet the universe is not destroyed but remains intact, as if nothing happened.'*

For Bronia, the two girls and Johnny, the universe was shattered, not by the hand of God, but by the hand of man. They were sent to the Treblinka extermination camp, where each of the ten gas chambers disposed of 200 people a day. In this, however, it was only one-third as efficient as Auschwitz, where in 1944, by conservative estimate, 6000 bodies were cremated each day. Even today there are no accurate figures as to the numbers killed at Auschwitz, but it is known that there were times when the ovens proved inadequate to dispose of them. On those days many were shot in mass executions, their bodies thrown into ditches, burned, and a blanket of earth bulldozed over the charred mass. That Auschwitz extermination camp was a more efficient killing machine than Treblinka there is no doubt; it was purpose-designed to achieve that objective. Aside from the number of people the Nazis were able to dispose of each day there was one other traumatic difference between Auschwitz and Treblinka: at Auschwitz, the victims were sent to gas chambers concealed under mounds of lush lawns fringed with flower beds, while all-girl orchestras played gay selections from light operettas. These victims were led to believe they were merely going to delousing showers. At times they were given towels and soap to complete the sadistic charade. But at Treblinka, the victims almost always knew that they were to be murdered.

The two little girls, Gutka and Henya, who are reported to have been talented pianists, died in the Treblinka camp. Bronia and her son Johnny survived, and a very strong bond was forged between mother and son. At the end of the war the pair were released, to be reunited with Mordecai, Rachel and Morry. Rachel and Peter Helfgott were to meet in Australia.

3

In the Beginning

Peter was fairly well established in Melbourne by the time Mordecai, Bronia, Johnny, Rachel and Morry were reunited there after the war. Peter had become a member of Rachel's family when the pair married in 1944. Their first child, a girl, was born in 1945. Peter and Rachel named her Malka, for Peter's mother, which in Hebrew means 'queen', and Chaya, which means 'life', for Rachel's mother. Apart from the traditional names customarily used to perpetuate the memory of departed close relatives, her birth certificate also carries the anglicised 'Margaret'. Their son David, named after Peter's father, was born in 1947; his name is both Hebrew and English. David's only brother, Leslie, was born in 1951 and a sister, Suzie, was born in 1953, all in Melbourne. Louise, the youngest of the Helfgott family, was born in Perth in 1960.

Although Mordecai, Rachel and Morry had been living in Melbourne for approximately eight years before they were joined by Bronia and Johnny, Peter is said to have taken the whole family under his wing and, according to Louise, 'got them on their feet'. When Peter first arrived in Melbourne he settled in what has been described as a little cottage in Pigdon Street, Carlton. Before too long he established his own tailoring factory in Little Bourke Street. Given the fact that his schooling was incomplete, Peter had come a long way, both in terms of distance and in achievement, since he left home in Poland.

As a settled member of the Melbourne Jewish community and part of the *Landsmannschaft*, Peter gave accommodation to people newly arrived from Poland, in particular those from Czestochowa. He fed and clothed them, while assisting them to find work. Naturally Peter thought of these people as friends, but although many of these 'fair weather friends' became very wealthy as time passed, very few stood by him when he in turn experienced tough times. Aside from one or two steadfast friends who did not turn away from him when he went bankrupt, losing his tailoring factory in the process, the majority of people he had helped in the early days somehow disappeared from his life when he needed them most. They just didn't want to know him. Not surprisingly, their disloyalty and indifference, combined with other factors, contributed to the disappointment in human nature which he was to feel keenly in later years.

While there may be some disagreement between his children over some aspects of Peter's character, no one argues that he was other than extremely intellectual, perhaps bordering on brilliant, and that he loved his children to a fault.

It is true that Peter acquired all his extensive knowledge through his own motivation and through reading. He obviously had a natural ability to understand and put into practice much of what he read in technical journals and scientific literature, for he designed and sold to the clothing trade the Helfgott pressing machine. As the inventor, patent holder and sole distributor, Peter sold through his own company the 20th Century Patent Pressing Machine, which was claimed to eliminate all heavy lifting, halve electricity bills, and iron all materials including knits and velvets all with equal efficiency and ease without scorching — all without the tiring need to hold a steaming iron above the garments. Aside from its practical attributes, one of which was to eliminate the need for a boiler attendant, the patented press carried a five-year guarantee.

Music was Peter's grand passion. Margaret says, 'He would have loved to have become a musician but because of his family and Poland he was unable to fulfil his dream. That is why he gave us the gift of music, and he gave it to all of us. We all absorbed this love of music and this was due to my father.'

There are two basically similar stories of how Peter learned to play music, differing only as to whether he learnt as a child in Poland or as an adult in Australia. One story tells of how Peter, denied the opportunity to learn to play the violin, realised his dream, by going to the homes of his more privileged Polish playmates, who passed on to him the benefit of their music lessons. The other tells of how he learnt to play the piano by visiting the homes of his Melbourne friends whose children were learning the piano, and how, sitting beside the young students, he memorised all he heard from their music masters. In this way he not only learned how to play the piano but acquired enough musical expertise to enable him to teach his children, in particular Margaret and David. This was not simple, rudimentary musical knowledge, but a knowledge that advanced their studies to public performance standard, without either child ever receiving a professional lesson until David began his first formal music studies at the age of ten and Margaret at twelve.

Margaret recalls, 'My father took us to Sue Tilley with a view to having her teach us piano. She recommended we see Frank Arndt, who subsequently took us both as pupils without any payment whatsoever. He did this when my father explained that he couldn't afford piano lessons but "the children will make you famous".'

The Helfgott family do not know when Peter learned to play the violin, or how he acquired this complex skill. David's brother Leslie, himself an accomplished violinist taught by his father, and who makes his living from music, says, 'He just did it.' And from what is known about Peter, who was demonstrably a natural musician and a very determined man with the ability to persevere against all odds, that is probably exactly what happened.

The differences between Peter and Rachel were fundamental. Apart from the seventeen-year age gap, their maturity had been gained at much emotional expense. While Peter chose to leave his family and Poland, Rachel had been forced by the coming war to leave both. Peter's maturation had been achieved through self-reliance as he progressed alone through the 'school of hard knocks'. For Rachel, growing up in Poland meant she had endured the Jewish experience as had Peter, but at a different level.

The memory of her distress when she had been taken to her mother's grave at nineteen to say goodbye, before she and her father and brother escaped from the looming Nazi invasion, stayed with her throughout her life. Additionally, driven by fear for the safety of her stepmother and aunt, Bronia, the only mother she had known from the age of two, her half brother Johnny, and her half sisters Gutka and Henya, she had worked with her father and brother to save enough money to deliver them from the Nazis before the frontiers were closed. To no avail. However, despite the fact that Rachel had never had to survive alone, she would have been emotionally scarred and uncertain. She would have had to find her own way of coping with her past and facing her future. Obviously, if Rachel had learned one thing, it was the futility of fighting when the odds were against her.

When Rachel married Peter at twenty-three years of age, she could perhaps be said to have, in effect, traded a father for a father figure. Her life had encompassed a series of traumatic losses including the death of her mother, the loss of her homeland, and the death of the two little half sisters whom she often spoke about with much affection and nostalgia.

It has been said that when Rachel married Peter she surrendered all her self-confidence. Rachel, the Helfgott family and Ian Rostkier, who also knew Rachel and her family, the Graneks, testify that this is not true. Rachel says that she had no self-confidence before her marriage and further, that at the time of her marriage she was exhausted and physically depleted. Both Ivan and Rachel state that her own family were not supportive of her and that, after their marriage, Peter contributed to increasing her self-esteem and helped her to regain her health.

When Rachel and Peter's youngest daughter, Louise, speaks of her parents she recalls that 'Although they cared deeply for each other, they were different in every way you could imagine.' Perhaps Rachel did not fully understand Peter, the rebel, revolutionary and progressive thinker who believed in humanity. Perhaps, while she appreciated their abilities, she didn't understand her intellectually gifted children, who had had the opportunity to develop their potential through advanced schooling as she had not.

It should be remembered that Rachel was probably a victim of her era and her provincial birth. Given the fact that she was a woman and virtually unschooled, she would not have had the opportunity to participate in the intensive discussions and reading which had formed Peter's attitudes and ideas. And she certainly had no access to the level of education enjoyed by her children. Just as her lack of education precluded her from taking part in family and social discussions involving the credos of the well-known intellectuals of the time, such as George Bernard Shaw and the many French left-wing thinkers, her lack of education had the effect, only in an intellectual sense, of also isolating her from her children.

Margaret says, 'Peter did not discuss concepts of socialistic doctrine with Rachel. Rachel is not an intellectual! She can be described as having a guileless, ingenuous, natural, childlike and honest character. The fact that our mother didn't participate in discussions was not because she was isolated or excluded. Not everyone is an intellectual, or interested in such discussions, but she certainly appreciated her family's ability to hold such discussions, even though they were of no interest to her.'

David says that his mother 'only ever obeyed Daddy's orders'. Suzie also observes, 'Mum was always a background figure. Dad made all her decisions for her, even to which apples to buy, green or red. If she brought home the wrong ones he would go on at her for hours.'

Suzie says of her mother: 'I wouldn't say Mum was backward. She was very simple in her outlook, very tolerant and uncomplicated, with her own simple wisdom … I mean she was not educated … not sophisticated in any way.' When speaking about family relationships at that time, Suzie recalls, 'David's closest association was with Dad. Mum tried to protect David from Dad if she thought Dad was being hard on David, pushing him too hard.' She adds, 'To our shame we all shouted at Mum, poor Mum, but we couldn't shout at Dad! Terrible, isn't it?'

Margaret speaks of her mother with great warmth: 'Her character is gentle, tolerant, understanding and non-judgmental. She has the ability to accept life on its own terms, whether good or bad, and to get on with the business of living. She does not dwell on the past, nor on the difficult times. She has great staying power. From my mother I learned acceptance of life's conditions, tolerance, to swim with the tide when necessary, and not to criticise unduly and without cause.'

By the time Margaret and David were born, Peter and Rachel were living in a flat in Glenhuntly Road, Elwood, a Melbourne suburb. By the time Leslie arrived, Peter had installed a swing between the dining room and the lounge room, which were separated by double doors, so that the children could enjoy themselves and have the added bonus of indoor physical exercise. Peter was fanatical about exercise and keeping fit. He spent some considerable time teaching both Margaret and David to walk on their hands, a feat it is assumed he learned, or taught himself, when he was with the circus.

Friday night was 'party night', says Margaret. 'Dad would arrive home with sweets, cakes and drinks and all sorts of goodies; I used to think of this as party night, but in retrospect it was probably because of the beginning of the Jewish Sabbath, which is always celebrated on Friday night, a very special night.'

For transport Peter had an old three-wheeled motor bike with what Margaret describes as 'a box at the back'. This Mazda, with its 1500cc twin Indian motor and gearbox, was a marvellous contraption. It was in this that Peter used to take the family for hair-raising rides around Melbourne. Perched in the box on the back, cruising along the tram tracks as they often did, the terrified Margaret was convinced that a tram would, sooner or later, run them down.

While the children might have had fun, life at Glenhuntly Road was not easy for Rachel. For a period of almost eight years, Rachel was either pregnant or recovering from a birth, while at the same time caring for babies and toddlers in the small flat.

Margaret was seven, David was five and Leslie was a two-year-old toddler when Rachel found herself pregnant yet again, this time with Suzie, who was born in 1953. To say that Rachel had her hands full is an understatement. It seems that she found it difficult to cope with her brood and that it was her frequent habit to telephone the factory, asking Peter to come home to help her with the children. It is believed that Rachel 'couldn't cope' because she lacked the strength and the will to do what society expected of her as a woman, to care for her children selflessly and without complaint. Obviously she was physically and mentally overtaxed and desperately in need of some respite from the demands of her young family. Although the family say there is no evidence to suggest that Rachel was suffering from some form of postnatal depression, it is possible, given the frequency of her pregnancies and subsequent births, that she may have endured this over a protracted period. This disruptive, even dangerous, condition not only affects the mental and emotional stability of the mother, but can also affect her children.

Assuming this to have been the reason why Rachel kept calling Peter for help, she must have been extremely distressed. It would also be true that Peter, despite all his reading and enlightenment, would have had no chance, forty-five years ago, of understanding her condition and neither would Rachel's father, Mordecai. or her stepmother Bronia, to whom Peter repeatedly turned for help in his predicament: help which the Helfgott family say was refused. It is also not hard to imagine that Rachel would have been made to feel even more unstable, useless and inadequate and perhaps worst of all, guilty, because Mordecai and Bronia would probably have insisted that she was being foolish and that she should, in essence, straighten up and get on with it, none of which would have facilitated her recovery.

The Helfgott children say that Peter's approach to anyone who was ill or helpless was to tend to their needs with great care and gentleness and to do most of the necessary daily tasks himself to reduce their burden. Given his need to be absent from his business on a regular basis to care for his family, it is not surprising that during this period Peter fell into bankruptcy and lost his tailoring factory. The blame for this economic disaster seems to have been apportioned to Rachel, for it is presumed to have occurred because Peter was forced to neglect the business in order to assist her with the children. Blame is also apportioned to her family, who allegedly refused Peter their help when he needed them most. Whether Mordecai and Bronia deserted him only by refusing to help him with Rachel and the children, or whether they only refused him monetary assistance to save his factory, or both, is not known. Either way, from that time on the Helfgott family believe that, in view of all the assistance their father is said to have given Rachel's family both when they first arrived in Melbourne before the war and after the war, they repaid his kindness by betrayal.

After the loss of his tailoring business, Peter, ever able to adapt to changing circumstances, turned the factory into a successful coffee shop and bar. This was a little European haven, something of a nightclub, which offered its patrons the opportunity to dance and to be entertained by Peter's violin playing. However, the strained relationship between Rachel's family and Peter deteriorated still further until in 1953 Peter decided to move his family to Perth. David was six years old.

4

Perth

The sea trip from Melbourne to Perth was no great joy for any but Peter. The whole family was seasick. Despite Peter's urging and assurances that the seasickness would pass if only they would come on deck, all stayed in their cabin except Margaret, who eventually joined him to take the fresh air.

For Margaret, leaving Melbourne was tinged with mixed emotions. On the good side she had been able to sneak out early one night before they sailed for Perth to throw a skirt, which she hated and which Rachel insisted that she wear, into the canal that ran close to the Elwood flat. On the bad side, she had to leave behind her loved collection of 115 comics because there was not enough room for them in their luggage. Even so, Peter could have freighted them over by train at little cost. Saying goodbye to The Phantom, Li'l Abner, Superman, and Archie and Veronica broke her young heart.

While it may have made Peter happy to have the width of the Australian continent between himself and Rachel's family, the move did not improve his financial position. In fact he was almost penniless. Desperate for accommodation, the family took up residence in a warehouse in West Perth for a few weeks while searching for suitable housing. The warehouse provided shelter from the elements and very little else; all the family slept on one double-bed mattress surrounded by lustrous white, new refrigerators. Rachel cooked on a radiator turned on its side, not ideal conditions for a mother with young children and a baby to care for.

One has to wonder how Rachel coped under these severely reduced circumstances, indeed how she continued to cope over the many years ahead, for it seems that the Helfgott fortunes never really improved to the point where there was enough money for anything other than the bare necessities.

During this period when the family had no home, no furniture, no decent cooking facilities, in fact nothing at all except food, Peter bought a piano. Margaret, somewhat fondly, cites this as a perfect illustration of what kind of man her father was and how music was his prime and only motivation in life. She doesn't mention how Rachel reacted to what many would consider to have been, under the circumstances, a rash and selfish purchase. Did she accept this as a reasonable thing for Peter to do? Was she happy, or unhappy, when Peter brought the piano home? Or did she simply accept it in silence because she knew that to complain was useless?

When Peter decided he, or his family, couldn't live without a piano, did he ever give a thought to the possibility that, instead of buying a piano, he could have made Rachel's lot a little easier to bear? Knowing Peter's obsession with music, I doubt it. If Rachel stayed silent, there were those who didn't. People from the Jewish community who were helping Peter to find a house to rent were aghast at what they obviously viewed as his reckless irresponsibility. When they asked him, 'How can you go out and buy a piano when you don't even have a place for your children to live?' Margaret says he replied, in all seriousness, 'You can't live without a piano, you can't live without music.' Although

Rachel never played an instrument, she always adored music. Despite her musical appreciation it is not easy, however, to picture Rachel dancing and singing around the warehouse in a delirium of delight because Peter had bought a piano in preference to, say, an inexpensive but effective pump-up kerosene cooker.

The Helfgotts moved house on three occasions, and the piano remained their single most important piece of furniture. Their existence seems to have been hard going all along the line. The first house Peter rented was on the corner of Harold and Beaufort Streets, in Highgate, a Perth suburb, where they lived for two years. The house was situated on two levels, a shop in the front and living quarters at the rear accessed by several steps from the shop. Peter decided that they should run a cafe, selling tea, coffee and cake; a dream, perhaps, of the European life he had left behind him. To this end they made curtains for the windows and decorated the tables, but the pleasant and welcoming surroundings failed to entice sufficient customers from which to make any kind of a living.

From Beaufort Street, Peter moved his family to a housing estate in Maniana, where they lived for approximately two and half years. Maniana later became part of the suburb of Queens Park. The house, one of many duplex homes, constructed from asbestos, was 'bleakly functional', with walls so thin that neither their neighbours' conversations or their own were private. There was no garden or lawn until Margaret planted grass and flowers. Margaret says, 'I took great pride in this garden. It was a raw housing estate recently begun and there were hardly any gardens, consequently it was a very dusty area.'

David and Margaret attended the Queens Park State School. Margaret recalls, 'After I started at Armadale High School in 1958, Dad announced that we would be leaving Maniana and going back to Highgate. I remember thinking how relieved I was to leave Maniana, I always felt so poor there, but I also wondered what attracted Dad so much to the suburb of Highgate.'

In 1958 Peter moved his family to 13 Bulwer Avenue, Highgate. Here they lived for five years, during which period his health continued to be a problem. The house was directly opposite the Highgate State Elementary School, which the Helfgott children attended. The house was of brick and asbestos construction, with two big front rooms off a short passageway. Margaret recalls that this was a house where they felt very comfortable: 'It wasn't a big house but it was cosy. I remember when Dad had one of his frequent heart attacks, he lay on a mattress on the floor in one of the front rooms and we were all terrified he would die. Thankfully he recovered, eventually.'

Margaret was very happy there. In her letter about that time, she describes everything on the block including a short stone wall in front facing the street; the tall wooden fence 'picketed at the top' separating their neighbours' house from their own; the small shelter to keep the wood dry; the short path to the outside toilet and how people walking by the house would hear the music coming from the house when she and David were practising. However, she was most delighted with the garden: 'There was a long, big garden at the back, the grass was a bit overgrown. There were gladioli in the garden and a big bush at the side which sprouted small blue flowers. There was a wooden garden bench under a big tree in the backyard and another tree in the garden near the back of the house where we would often sit with the black cat which David loved.'

Once again the family moved, returning to Beaufort Street, Highgate, this time to take up residence at number 460. This house, on a busy main street, didn't have the same seclusion and feeling of 'suburbia' as the one in Bulwer Avenue. The house was not in pristine condition, far from it, but it was very spacious. Margaret's room was at the front, and there she practised on her Concord piano. The Rönish was at the other end of the house, so that when two people were practising they did not disturb each other. The bathroom, with its peeling paint and 'big bath' with 'curvy legs' was at the back of the house, not far from the copper where the water was heated for the bath. Here they had screen doors to keep out Perth's myriad of summertime flies.

Margaret recalls that while these houses may have flowed with music, the plumbing did not flow with hot water. The Helfgott children, like many postwar working-class children, grew up in houses which did not have either gas or electricity. The weekly bath in the Helfgott household was a grand event which required wood to be chopped and a fire to be lit under the laundry copper and kept continually stoked, a procedure which took hours before the whole family had enjoyed the luxury of a steaming hot bath.

Beaufort Street, Highgate, was literally the 'wrong side of the tracks'. All the suburbs in which the Helfgott family lived in the 1960s were peopled by immigrants from countries such as Italy, Latvia and Estonia, including small numbers of Jews. All were displaced people who were tough survivors from a Europe torn apart by war.

Basically these families were under the patriarchal thumb. The majority of males demanded subservience from their women and got it. According to Linley Christiansen, a schoolfriend of Suzie Helfgott when they lived as young girls in the Highgate area, many of these women were not even allowed to learn English. The lack of English as a second language had the effect of isolating them from the mainstream of Australian life and contributing to their continuing loss of self-respect and self-determination. Stripped of the ability to confront their men and unable to become integrated into the new social structure, these migrant women stayed victims of old patriarchal dominance which perpetuated the favouring of male children.

While Peter didn't fraternise with these patriarchal dinosaurs, he retained, either consciously or unconsciously, their outdated, strict European attitudes to family life. When the family moved from Melbourne to Perth nothing changed for Rachel. In fact life for Rachel was a continuation of all that had gone before. Peter refused to allow the neighbours to visit. In fact, so opposed was he to outside influences he would not allow her to speak to the Italian neighbours over the backyard fence. While Peter and no doubt the other European men in the district obviously loved and adored their children, they did not have the foresight to recognise that, when exposed to the heady air of egalitarianism, their previously obedient little subjects would burst out of orbit.

Suzie says: 'When Margaret knew Dad he was all the things she said he was: positive, a giver, enthusiastic, warm. He was wonderful to all of us until we reached the age of around fourteen. This all changed when we began to show signs of becoming independent. Margaret doesn't understand that he found it difficult to deal with the teenage transition to adulthood.'

Both Louise and Suzie, who hold psychology and social work degrees respectively, have given much thought to why Peter found it almost impossible to come to terms with his children's maturation. They conjecture that Peter, who left home at approximately fourteen and did not experience the phase when a teenager becomes autonomous inside a family environment, was unable to comprehend this process in his children. Perhaps it might be closer to the truth to say that it was not the transition to adulthood which changed Peter's attitude to his children but the fear that their growing independence foreshadowed their separation from the family and as a consequence the termination of his parenting role — his reason for being.

Growing up was not easy for the Helfgott children. While there was always enough to eat, there was never enough money. Finances were always a problem. However, while there were very few, if any, material comforts, their life was enriched by Peter, who taught the children about such things as astronomy, natural science, nuclear physics, politics, religion, physical fitness, chess, and of course music.

There is no question that Peter had a passion for music which went beyond a personal obsession. He had a vision of himself teaching his children music, a vision which came to fruition, fulfilling itself in David's genius for music, in Margaret's more than considerable talent, and to a lesser degree in his other children. This fixation could never have found its expression had the children not all been born with inherent ability and a love of music. Margaret says that, when asked why Peter had taught them music above all else, he replied, 'If I had given you money or other material possessions, these things are transitory and can be lost or frittered away. However, if I give you the gift of music, I have given something that will always be a friend to you. If you are ever alone in the world, without a friend, without possessions, you will never be completely alone while you have music as your friend. It will always be an inspiration and comfort and companion to you.'

However, Peter gave his children more than music. He also gave them a liberal upbringing and, through his abiding belief in socialism, a platform of thinking and personal values not commonly found in the average Australian home.

Margaret says that some people concluded Peter was a

Stalinist and that Stalin was the closest thing to God in his home, the implication being that Peter must have been a monster like his idol. Margaret says this is not true and asserts that Peter was not a Stalinist and was never a member of the Communist Party, and further that all political discussions were conducted only on a philosophical level. She says Peter lost all faith in Communism and in particular in Stalin after the so-called doctors' plot, supposedly hatched by nine eminent Moscow physicians, six of whom 'happened' to be Jewish. It was alleged that these doctors conspired to poison Stalin and other Soviet leaders in order to create an internal upheaval.

Nikita Khrushchev's secret report to the Twentieth Congress of the Communist Party of 24–25 February 1956– stated:

> *He [Stalin] personally issued advice on the conduct of the investigation and the method of interrogation of the arrested persons. He said that the academician Vinogradov should be put in chains, another one should be beaten. Present at this Congress as a delegate is the former Minister of State Security, Comrade Ignatiev. Stalin told him curtly, 'If you do not obtain confessions from the doctors we will shorten you by a head.'*

After Stalin's orders to 'beat, beat and, once again, beat' were followed, not surprisingly the confessions were obtained.

Evidently the doctors' plot was intended to serve as an excuse for new violent purges, with the Jews marked for particular retribution. Those Jews who had managed to survive the nightmare of Nazi extermination a few years before were saved from further terror by Stalin's death, after which the maligned doctors were discharged and the proposed terrorist purges cancelled.

Following that potentially devastating incident, Peter became totally disillusioned with Russian socialism, turning instead to

Chinese socialism in the belief that it was, in essence, pure and correct. Although, for Peter, there had been a subtle change of emphasis from one socialist credo to another, he and the children continued to occasionally buy magazines and books from the Communist Bookshop in Highgate. It was a household where many heated debates took place about true socialism, debates in which David, as a teenager, opposed Peter, with David supporting Russian communism in its pure form. As a consequence Peter endowed his family with a lasting legacy which perhaps transcends his gift of music; for they are particularly non-racist individuals who have a deep belief in the equality of man and possess a great understanding of minority groups.

At that time the writer Katharine Susannah Prichard, one of the founding members of the Australian Communist Party, was an outstanding figure on the Perth scene. Like Peter, she too was committed to the belief in the equality of all mankind, for she too had seen the social and economic void between the rich and the poor, in London, where she lived and worked as a journalist between 1908 and 1916. In later years David would make the journey to Greenmount, where Katharine lived, to have dinner and play for her each Friday evening.

In his biography of Katharine, *Wild Weeds and Wind Songs*, Ric Throssell, her son, writes:

> *Through her love of music, Katharine became interested in the work of a young Perth pianist, David Helfgott. Each week or so in the years before he left to take up a scholarship in London, David, an awkward, unassuming young man, caught the bus to Greenmount, ate the dinner that Katharine specially prepared for him and played to her for hours.*

A strange and touching friendship, this intimate understanding between a young man on the threshold of his all-absorbing vocation and an old woman in whose sympathy he found encouragement. When David speaks of Katharine today his memories of her are warm and he refers to her with affection as 'lovely Susie', or 'my wonderful KSP'.

Life wasn't entirely a serious business for the Helfgott children. The backyard offered more opportunity for exercise than the flat at Elwood and Peter built himself parallel bars, on which he would swing himself around with all the agility he had had when he performed in the circus. Apart from gyrating in furious somersaults and cartwheels, Margaret and David, who didn't use Peter's parallel bars, walked on their hands, because Peter believed this was better than any other exercise to strengthen a pianist's hands. David, who was and still is exceptionally physically strong, and has excellent balance, used to confound everyone by walking up and down the backyard on his hands, non-stop, for a half-hour or more.

Like the majority of children they had pets, in fact six cats. 'We all loved the cats,' says Margaret. 'I was crazy about them. David loved the cats as well.' David recently had this to say about cats: 'I love cats because they never press you and are independent.' Perhaps David envies cats because they are free, independent and bullied by no-one.

It would appear that, apart from the fact that the Helfgott children had above-average intelligence and that they were mentally stimulated by being presented with subjects beyond the prosaic range of most adults' interest and comprehension, they enjoyed a relatively normal early childhood.

Certainly Peter was not the average father; those were the days when he was positive, warm and enthusiastic. Suzie says, 'If he had a fault it could be said that he sacrificed himself for his children, he lived for his children. However he expected all of his children to follow his dream that we should all have musical careers. We were, and we are, musical but Margaret and David were the most brilliant and David was a genius who couldn't be kept away from the piano.'

5

David

Margaret remembers David as an introverted child, a 'late starter' who didn't begin to talk until he was three years old. From an early age, the idea developed in the Helfgott family that David was 'different', extremely sensitive, withdrawn, lovable but quiet, somehow not able to socialise properly with other children. Perhaps this idea itself had a powerful shaping influence on him. Margaret also recalls, with a great deal of compassion and sensitivity of her own, what she feels to be evidence of David's extreme sensitivity, nervousness and anxiety, when, as a five-year-old, he failed to control his bowels when he first attended Elwood State School, Melbourne.

Neither of these examples, however, provides conclusive proof that as a child David was fragile, or slow, or that these problems were the early manifestations of emotional or mental instability. Both talking and bladder or bowel control are determined by maturation and learning; indeed, both are involved in the development of most behaviour.

David was within the average range when he began to speak at three. Being an introverted child, and one with a sister two years his senior, he was probably not 'a late starter', as Margaret suggests, but a reticent communicator who was very happy to allow his older sister do his talking for him. It is most probable that his failure to control his bowels was the result of the new and, to him, stressful school environment. After all, it is known that even the great Russian bear suffers from a similar problem: a good fright will turn his bowels to water.

It should also be borne in mind that when David began school in 1951, Leslie was approximately one year old. David was in effect the 'middle child' at that time, and competing with a baby for attention. In addition to finding himself in the alien school environment, he possibly also experienced a sense of rejection, a threatening combination for any small boy but also an extremely painful one for a highly sensitive child such as David.

Both Suzie and Margaret say it was also clear from a very early age that David would never be able to take care of himself. Both say he was totally impractical and that, as a child and a teenager, he couldn't tie his own shoelaces. However, David's response when recently asked about this was clear and to the point: 'Daddy wouldn't let me tie my own shoelaces or cross roads … I was just obedient to Daddy.'

This answer brought forth a cry of protest from the Helfgott girls: 'This is *not* true! Peter, Rachel and Margaret used to spend an inordinate amount of time trying to teach David how to tie his laces, but he seemed unable to learn!' Perhaps 'seemed' is the key word here.

David can and does tie his shoelaces, which doesn't stop him asking the unwitting newcomer to tie them for him. (I have been caught a number of times.) It is not feasible to believe that a person with the exceptional manual dexterity that David possesses would not be able to accomplish such a mundane act as tying his laces. This forces us to consider whether, at an early age, David was either showing signs of being perverse, or was prepared to get the attention he craved, albeit unconsciously, by seeming to be unable to take care of himself.

When questioned about David's 'fragility', his lack of practicality, and the claim that he would 'never be able to take care of himself', his brother Leslie says: 'Nonsense. Dave was not fragile. We played together a lot when we were kids and there was nothing wrong with him then.'

There is no reason to doubt that the recollections and the assessments of David by Margaret and Leslie, the two people who knew him best when he was a child and a teenager, are equally correct, the only difference between them being that each arises from a different perspective which is influenced by gender and their places in the family hierarchy.

Margaret protests that her view of David was never influenced by Peter or Rachel. 'I never saw, nor do see, people, or siblings through anyone's eyes but make my own assessment or observations according to what I see.' However, as a highly perceptive child, she could not have avoided assimilating some of her parents' concerns, for, whether she consciously recognises it or not, she must have overheard discussions between them over what appeared to be David's developmental delay.

Leslie, the epitome of uncluttered basic common sense, being only four years younger than David and certainly unswayed by the views expressed by the Helfgott sisters, saw David as a brother and a playmate who, aside from his musical brilliance, was no different from any other little boy or teenager.

Suzie, however, being six years younger than David, is only in the position of being able to repeat what she has been told by the family, for it is highly unlikely that she would be able to call upon accurate memories of David as a very young child.

David's life-long love affair and obsession with music began with his first tentative tap on the keys of the old Rönish piano which Peter bought when they moved to Perth. He was six years old, and although the sounds he produced were meaningless to the other members of the Helfgott family they bewitched, seduced and ensnared David and were, to him, as harmonious as the music of the spheres. David couldn't stay away from the piano; before school, at lunch time and after school he kept returning to it day after day. He was completely enchanted by it.

David's fascination with the piano held for Peter the promise of the realisation of his dreams. When he came home from work each evening he would sit at the piano with David, showing him pages of music and pointing out to him the various notes, trying in vain to get David to recognise them. But, despite all Peter's efforts, and David's yearning to learn, he failed to meet his father's expectations; he simply could not tell one note from another. The sessions always came to an end with David in tears. It was at these times that Rachel's mothering instincts overrode Peter's and domineering but inadequate attempts to have David master the music. David recently said, 'My little Mummy would come and comfort me when I cried and take me away from Daddy.' He also commented, 'Daddy's methods were very suspect,' but would say no more.

Between the ages of six and eight it seemed David was unable to recognise or memorise a note, yet for those two years Peter, with infinite patience, repeated the nightly lessons. On David's part it was as if he was totally devoid of comprehension.

And then, in one of these evening lessons, the incredible happened. Without any indication of what was to come, David burst into Chopin's Polonaise in A-flat, playing it note perfect, performing without fault the difficult two pages of repeated octaves contained in the score. Margaret says, 'It was as if he had gone from nothing and won the Olympics.'

I have heard many stories about David and his ability, many of which border on the unbelievable. To believe this one was a test of faith. How could it be that a boy eight years of age, after two years of not playing a note, was able to burst into a piece as complex as the Polonaise? My first thought was that Margaret, who was only ten years old when this occurred, must have been a highly imaginative child. Perhaps what she had heard was not in fact the accomplished rendition of the Polonaise she recalled. And yet, from a member of such an acutely musical family, a musician herself, this memory was unlikely to be faulty.

When I asked David if he remembered that mysterious event, he was surprised and mildly vexed that I sounded a little sceptical.

'Of course I remember,' he answered simply. 'My fingers suddenly got hot.'

David's reference to his fingers getting hot reminded me of the times when I have stood behind him while he plays the work of one of my favourite Romantic composers, 'especially for you darling'. He asks me to put my fingers on his temples, saying, 'Feel the heat, can you feel the heat?' And sometimes I do. On these occasions David plays like a man possessed, his sensitivity to the music heightened beyond normal comprehension. He surpasses even his usual interpretation. Under the powerful influence of the music it is not unusual to become a little intoxicated and overcome by the moment and take off on a flight of fancy, imagining another presence, vaguely feeling that perhaps David is not playing alone.

Could it be that at the moment when David's fingers 'got hot', as he says, his gift, his rare and incredible talent, was bestowed on him by something which defies explanation? Perhaps.

The mystery remains, however, of how David Helfgott

learned to play the piano and emerged overnight as a prodigiously gifted musician. Perhaps the key to the mystery lies in his difficult and unusual childhood. The paramount desire of this somewhat nervous, anxious and introverted child was to play the piano, a desire frustrated by his inability to distinguish one note from another. No doubt the tension generated by this failure created a mental block. His frustration would have continued to build each day and as evening approached, bringing with it the prospect of another lesson which he desperately wanted to understand, he would have become increasingly anxious that he would fail, yet again. Had he not been such a sensitive and highly intelligent child, with such a burning need to learn to play this instrument which was at once his delight and his torment, he could not have forced himself to endure the misery which he faced each day. Even so, locked in this vicious circle, this Catch-22 situation of anxiety and frustration, without any positive progress, he continued fighting day after day to overcome the block. This in turn made it impossible for him to meet his own and Peter's expectations.

Whether he actively recognised it or not, he was also locked in a terrible unspoken competition with Margaret, who even then had considerable keyboard expertise. Hard on his heels was his younger brother Leslie, who was also beginning to show signs of musical ability. To compound this insecurity, he was contending with his baby sister Susanna for his share of attention.

If nothing else, during those two years he received from Peter the attention he craved, but the anxiety to comprehend the music, and the frustration at his inability to understand the rudiments of the instrument he was drawn to, remained unrelieved. Given that David was at that time a very sensitive child who perhaps did not have effective communication skills, no-one would have recognised his distress, or his sheer panic. Perhaps all the pressure building in his psyche became so unbearable it literally exploded, his musical genius, liberated at last, finding expression in Chopin's fiery Polonaise. Who can say with confidence what triggers genius?

The mystery is still a mystery, for there are questions which remain unanswered, questions which even David could not, or probably would not, answer. David, by his own account, is a game-player. He is the master of the 'red herring'. When asked serious questions which he doesn't wish to answer he will say, 'I reckon it's all a game, darling. You can do anything you like, is that right, darling? Up to a point, up to a pun fun!' Unless you know David, it isn't easy to recognise that a game is afoot and that what seems to be a stream of unconscious conversation on his part is in fact his way of telling us he does what he likes, and that he plays games with all of us. As George Negus, a neighbour of the Helfgotts' who has known David for over six years, says: 'David plays us all off the break.' David doesn't play hurtful games but personal, one-sided games which he finds amusing. More importantly, these games also have the effect of protecting the real David and allowing him to do exactly as he wishes.

Was David playing games with Peter by deliberately maintaining an innocent facade of ignorance which lasted two long years in order to keep his father's attention focused on him until, with instinctive cunning, he changed the game before Peter lost interest? Did he replace the charade with a monumental performance which transcended all credibility? Was he such a consummate player that he knew a dazzling, dramatic display of previously unforeseen and unexpected brilliance would capture Peter's undivided attention and keep it forever focused on him? Or, in that instant when he began to play the Polonaise, was he touched by some blinding, inexplicable power which unlocked the floodgates, endowing him with the ability not only to remember all that Peter had taught him but to interpret the complexity of Chopin's music? Possible but not probable. Playing any of Chopin's works is no easy task, even for the experienced pianist, much less an eight-year-old child who appeared unable to distinguish C from G or E from F, and had no concept of chords, minor or major.

While David successfully astonished the family, he hadn't foreseen the outcome of the game, assuming that was what it was, for his performance intensified Peter's resolve to have him achieve a career on the concert platform.

Genius is not chosen by its possessor, instead it chooses a vehicle for its expression and in doing so banishes the possibility of a modest, uncomplicated, private life. The price of genius comes high, for it demands the spotlight and will not reside in obscurity. It must bask in the comfort of familial adoration and affection; this insidious thing called genius also draws to it many who would luxuriate in its reflected glory. It requires others to love, nurture and cosset the chosen vehicle, ensuring that genius, like evil, lives on in the memory of generations.

When genius claimed David, he found himself not only in competition with his brother and sisters but catapulted into the highly competitive public arena, an arena where success is measured against the relative successes of others and where one is subject to critical acclaim or critical destruction. This led to even greater pressure and anxiety. David was nine years old when he was awarded a special prize for his exceptional performance of Chopin's Polonaise in A flat at a country festival. It was astonishing that a nine-year-old child should achieve commendable mastery over music such as Chopin's when he had never had a formal music lesson in his life!

Did David, at nine, make the piano 'sing' as Chopin had done? Did he have the smooth touch required to play the accents of phrasing? Did he employ the rhythmic freedom known as *tempo rubato* (literally, robbed time), for which Chopin became famous? Was he aware then that, in *rubato*, the melody notes are not played exactly as written? Did he know they are deliberately hurried or slowed down while the accompaniment maintains strict metric time? It is hard to believe that he did, especially when he had only been tutored by Peter, a self-taught musician who had no knowledge of musical theory. But whether he did or not, to this day David seems to have a deep affinity with Chopin's music and in particular with this Polonaise.

Because it is difficult for David to freely express himself in conversation, or because he does not choose to communicate, he does not become involved in lengthy, technical explanations of the intricate structure of Chopin's music. Assuming that it is common knowledge that some of Chopin's music is not played as written, he demonstrates the differences between three variations, the last of which he identifies as the correct, or better, interpretation of the music. With me beside him on the piano stool as he plays these differing phrases, he explains: 'This is how it is written; this is how other people play it; and this is how I play it.' And the way he plays it is sheer magic.

Chopin made much of the left hand, as does David, and mastered the use of the sustaining pedal to provide a rich background to the melody. Many well-known concert pianists do not have a strong left hand, and neither have they become entirely proficient in the intricate use of the sustaining pedal. Today, David's powerful use of his left hand is described as being as strong as that of the famous Russian-born pianist Sviatoslav Richter. He does, however, have a tendency to overuse the soft pedal. When asked why, he says his left foot 'gets tired, darling'. What better place to rest it than on the soft pedal? How can you argue with logic like that? On occasions during performance, he is also known to take his foot right off the sustaining pedal and thump the floor. Perhaps this is because he has given up being concerned about what the critics say, or perhaps it is a display of a slight touch of arrogance. At any rate, 'They don't build monuments for critics,' David says.

For David the journey from eight to forty-nine has been long and tortured, beginning when, as a brilliant, nervous child, he first climbed on the competition treadmill — a sorry step which increased his anxiety to gain self-esteem though prestige and applause. And, of course, there was always Peter, ever-present at his elbow, encouraging, pushing the pace, setting ever higher goals for him to achieve, giving him music to master which by normal standards was too complex for one so young but never too complex for David.

6

Survival

David has very little to say about his early childhood or his school days except to complain bitterly, to 'cretch', as he says (which might be taken from the Yiddish *kvetch*, meaning to complain), that he was not allowed to play tennis. This is simply not true, according to other family members. David was not interested in tennis or any other activity: he was obsessed by the piano. It is as if he has no recollections of ever being a child, or ever doing anything other than play the piano. Maybe he doesn't. When he is asked about his childhood his answers relate not to friends, his brother or his sisters but to music and his father's driving need for him to become an outstanding concert pianist. David neglects to mention his passion for the piano or that his own goal from a very early age was to become an internationally recognised concert pianist — a desire which matched and perhaps even transcended Peter's.

A number of musical giants through the ages have been the victims of parental aspirations and the focus of their parents' displeasure. Most of these musical geniuses were born with a gift for music and were child prodigies. Each of these remarkable children was subjected to varying types of stress. Some were pressured to perform, while others were denied an outlet for their creativity at an early age by parents who wished them to follow in their father's footsteps and become doctors, lawyers, military or naval officers. A number appear to have had in common fathers who were also exceptionally musically proficient but who had not achieved greatness and whose driving urge was to have their sons realise their own dreams, as in the case of Mozart and Liszt, or fathers who desired that their progeny attain greater social standing through a profession which they had been unable to achieve for themselves.

Musical talent often seems to be inherited, if not directly from fathers or mothers, from grandfathers and grandmothers on either side of the family tree; the famous Bach family of musicians is a case in point, where the brilliant musical gene ran through generations.

Many of the great musicians and composers have suffered from emotional instability. Among these are Tchaikovsky, whose addiction to music amounted to a neurosis; Modeste Petrovich Mussorgsky, whose passion for music was matched by his passion for alcohol; Franz Schubert, who endured frequent bouts of 'melancholia', a mental condition which manifests as a great depression, sadness and foreboding; Robert Schumann, a depressive, who, two years after throwing himself into the Rhine, was confined in a mental asylum, where he died aged forty-six; and the ultramodernist Anton Bruckner, constantly haunted by terrifying fantasies, who suffered a nervous breakdown at the age of forty-three which heightened his lifelong fears and his obsession with morbid stories from which he sought escape in music and God.

It is tempting to assert that genius must be hereditary and that environment plays a minor role in its expression. It is also possible, however, to advance the theory that without the necessary environmental stimulation the inherent genius may not find expression at all. There can be no doubt that specially gifted people are greatly affected not only by their immediate environmental conditions but also by the cultural conditions that exist at that time.

In his engrossing psychological biography, *Mozart: A Life*, Maynard Solomon shines a revealing light on Wolfgang Amadeus Mozart, perhaps music's most talented genius, who did not fare well in his immediate environment. Constantly under the supervision of his relentless father, Leopold, throughout his childhood and adolescence, Mozart developed a lasting fear of him which kept him a mental hostage to the man for the rest of his life. He was unable to escape the terror of his father, who is sometimes referred to as the 'fabulous monster Leopold', a notable example of a 'stage father' possessing all the aggressive attitudes of that unappealing twentieth-century phenomenon, the ubiquitous 'stage mother'. Leopold, himself a gifted court composer and violinist of no mean talent, was quick to capitalise on his son's brilliance and his daughter's precocious gifts for singing and keyboard expertise by launching the children, Wolfgang, six, and Nannerl, eleven, into a series of extended European tours which made the family, especially young Wolfgang, internationally famous.

The cherubic Wolfgang, with his translucent skin, frail constitution and startling ability, was the jewel in the musical crown which Leopold was unable to fashion for his own head; a jewel which he hoped would ensure the family's fortune but one which proved a great disappointment when its lustre did not bring the money Leopold had expected. Although young Wolfgang was eventually able to free himself physically from his father by living freelance in Vienna, his lifetime fear of the man allowed Leopold to retain his emotional hold on his son, for Leopold, refusing to accept that his son had matured, constantly attempted to emasculate him.

It seems that Wolfgang, as David may also have done, took refuge in the image of the eternal child, his mutual devotion to music the ultimate refuge, ensuring that the musician survived. However, unlike David, Wolfgang did not suffer a debilitating breakdown. Instead, he see-sawed emotionally back and forth between struggling for his freedom and, driven by his fear of Leopold, perpetually surrendering to his father's dominance.

Wolfgang slid into an identity crisis which lasted throughout his short lifetime. His fear of Leopold created a schizophrenic escape hatch which allowed him to be two people. One was the eternal child desired by Leopold, a persona which not only pleased Leopold but provided Wolfgang with an excuse for his famous risqué and childish behaviour. In it he took on a frenetic but comfortable mantle of mental instability which permitted the child genius to run rampant and to indulge in the tolerance of others and the confirmation that he was still the loved charmer he had been as a boy. The other Mozart was the real Wolfgang, the hard-working master musician dedicated to his work. Did Mozart retain his childlike role in order to survive Leopold and the punishing life of the performer and composer?

The comparison between David and Mozart is, of course, at best tenuous. David is not known as a composer, nor does he particularly like Mozart's music, claiming that much of it is mechanical. And of course he does not have the stature of Mozart. However, there are interesting similarities between these two, the most obvious being their fathers. Leopold, like Peter Helfgott, did aspire to achieve his dreams through his son's ability. However, Leopold exploited his son for his own prestige and the added benefit of substantial financial reward. Indirectly and perhaps unconsciously, Peter did much the same.

When I tried to discuss the relationship David had with his father when he was a child, and in particular what he thought motivated Peter's intense desire to have him achieve as a virtuoso, I met with the usual diverse answers.

'Daddy wasn't very wise. I love my little Daddy and my Daddy loved me, but Daddy was jealous, Daddy was jealous!' It was impossible to get him to clarify what he meant by 'jealous'.

In Peter we see a very complex personality: a prideful man but one who, in a personal sense, saw himself as a born loser; a man who was determined at all costs to see his children, especially David, achieve the success which had eluded him throughout his life.

Undoubtedly Peter loved his son, but he allowed himself to be blinded by the boy's genius. Peter believed that his care of David's physical health was all that David required to withstand the merciless pressure of constant competition. Peter, who measured strength using himself as a yardstick, did not have the knowledge, or the wisdom, to see that between himself and David lay a vast difference. Peter was self-motivated and didn't have to meet anyone's expectations, he played music for the sheer joy of it. David, who began playing for the same reason, was pressured on every side, not only by his father, to perform and to excel.

Leopold is said to have 'emasculated' Wolfgang by refusing to accept him as an adult. While Peter is said to have tried to help David to become more independent, it seems that, indirectly, he also did much the same, by using David's impracticality as a reason to stop him leaving the family to further his studies in the United States in 1961. Peter appears to have robbed David of the opportunity to develop his own social and survival skills, but did he? It is difficult to say whether Peter, like Leopold, created the image of the eternal child which, in effect, kept David tied to the piano and to himself, unable to be divorced from either. Or did David, like Wolfgang, choose the persona of the eternal child, taking cover in mental instability which in turn allowed him to be feted and fussed over, loved and indulged, excused from all mundane tasks, freed to do nothing except play the piano?

Liszt, who would come to be recognised as the greatest pianist of his generation, perhaps of any generation, had a father who, although he was an accountant in the service of Count Esterhazy, was also a talented musician. He played the piano, violin, guitar and flute with equal expertise. When Liszt senior saw young Franz showing signs of an interest in music beyond his years, he gave him his first piano lessons, much as Peter Helfgott fastened on David's early two-finger exploration of the keyboard. Although both fathers transferred all the pent-up dreams of the frustrated virtuoso to their sons, Lizst's father did not, or could not, keep his son tied to his side.

Liszt, like David, was just nine years old when he first played in public, at the Esterhazy palace. Liszt won instant acclaim from his audience, the adoring aristocracy, who contributed to a bursary established to enable him to go to study in Vienna. David was awarded a special prize, not however a bursary, which, had one been available, might have freed him, as Liszt had been freed, from the constant influence of his father. After a period of three years Liszt concluded his studies in Vienna, moving at the tender age of twelve to Paris, where he was to spend much of his life. Not only did Liszt effectively escape the influence of his father, but by the time he reached fifteen he was undertaking advanced musical study in a strange country.

David spent his childhood and teenage years until the age of seventeen under Peter's watchful and overwhelming supervision. The harmonious relationship between Peter and his children appears to have been maintained while ever the youngsters remained malleable, accepting without question his authority to direct their lives, particularly when they responded to his musical ambitions.

David claims that his childhood was a happy one and that Peter's demands on his children were not overtly overbearing. All the children testify to this; but Suzie states that the prevailing felicitous atmosphere disintegrated when each reached the age of about fourteen.

For Louise, who was born when Peter was fifty-seven, the break came much earlier. She says, 'I was seven when I first told him that I wanted to be a writer, and he turned away from me at that point. He couldn't accept that we were not all born to be musicians.'

David's brother Leslie, while denying that his father was perhaps something of a dictator, says, 'He was arrogant and domineering, but I didn't have any problems with him. I remember when I wanted to switch from the piano to the violin, I just told him I didn't want to play the piano any more. He was alright. He didn't argue, and that was that.' Of course, while Leslie may have been turning his back on the piano, he was not turning his back on music, and the instrument of his choice, the violin, was one his father also played and loved. It is also probable Peter didn't argue because he welcomed the prospect of a violinist to join Margaret and David, who were both already brilliantly proficient at the keyboard.

Margaret, who knew her father when he was 'positive, warm, enthusiastic, a giver, a big personality with a big heart', the wonderful Dad who used to take her on his knees and rock her to sleep when she was three years old while crooning an old plantation song, 'Ma Curly Headed Baby', makes no mention of experiencing any problems when she began to exhibit signs of burgeoning independence. However, it would be some years, and many fine performances, before Peter was called upon to come face to face with David's rebellious attempt to establish himself as an independent adult.

7

Adolescence

David did not begin his formal music training until he was ten years old. Prior to that time, and while still under Peter's tutelage, David and Margaret had played before the public on several occasions, both winning a number of competitions. After hearing David perform, Frank Arndt was so impressed with his ability that he offered to give him a year's free tuition. With reluctance Peter loosened his control over the selection of David's music, music which Frank Arndt believed to be far too complex for one so young.

Peter had already taken both David and Margaret to various competitions and eisteddfods in Perth. Margaret recalls one competition in particular in which the music was a set piece, and where she competed and won against thirty other children, all of whom she thought played incorrectly. It was not until she looked at her music after arriving home that she discovered she had played the music out of sequence. Instead of playing pages 1, 2, 3, and 4, she had played pages 1, 3, 2 and 4. She also recalls another occasion when, as a child of eleven, she played Liszt's Hungarian Rhapsody No. 2 in the North Perth Town Hall, deliberately leaving out a few of the difficult middle passages. No-one realised that she had cheated; in fact she was vigorously applauded and congratulated on her ability to handle such a difficult piece. Margaret says it all goes to prove that 'It ain't what you do, but the way that you do it.' Both incidents, however, are indicative of Margaret's expertise at a very early age and glaring examples of the lack of professionalism on the part of the examiners, who should have been familiar with every note.

James Penberthy, the Perth composer and music critic, and David's long-time friend, who often visited the family, says with marked emphasis, 'If that girl's career had not been set aside in favour of David's, she could have become a brilliant concert pianist. At an early age she had the potential to be better than David inasmuch as she was steady. David was the genius, but she had the far greater capacity for lasting success.' Margaret's sisters both believe that Margaret could have become an acclaimed pianist had she been given the same opportunity as David. In Suzie's words, 'Although Margaret was exceptionally talented, Dad nurtured David's talent.' She added that David and her father, 'They were an item.'

What was the bond between father and son which kept Peter's attention focused on David? Was Peter solely devoted to David because he was convinced that David had the greater talent of the two? Or did he harbour the belief that it was a waste of time and effort encouraging a woman to pursue a career when her place was in the home? Was a career for Margaret never a serious possibility because, as the eldest child, it was taken for granted that she would leave school as soon as possible to begin work and contribute financially to the family?

Whatever the reason, by the time David reached his teenage years the pressure on him and on his siblings, especially Margaret, was beginning to bite. Margaret states that during his preadolescent years David was 'a wonderful, giving, caring little boy who couldn't do enough for you'. But was this really his nature, or had he adopted a policy of compliance, conformity and self-effacement? Was yielding, moving with the tide, placating and appeasing, always being the 'good' boy, his survival strategy? Was this his way of coping with a growing anxiety to measure up to the perfection which was expected from him?

By 1959 the pressure for David to perform at ever heightening levels came not only from within the family but from the public, who were becoming aware of his genius through his public appearances in various competitions. Now he was coping with the added stress of competing to win, not just for his personal satisfaction but for his music teacher, his father, his family, his school friends, and the impersonal, fickle, critical 'public'.

David was twelve when he entered the Australian Broadcasting Commission's Western Australian Concerto and Vocal Competition and for the first time he progressed through the heats to become a State finalist. He impressed the judges by playing J. S. Bach's Concerto for Piano and Strings in D Minor.

The following year David gained second place when he performed Ravel's Concerto in G Major. (Whenever David mentions Ravel he finds it impossible to resist repeating his standard Ravel joke. 'Poor old Maurie,' he says with a laugh, 'he might unravel.') Ravel, like Debussy, made much use of medieval church scales, pentatonic scales, rich chords and chords with vibrant dissonances. Ravel's harmonies are often quite complex in construction but traditional in use none the less. While Ravel was often regarded as an impressionist, he could be severely classical, none of which troubled David.

During this period, between the ages of twelve and fourteen, David's personality began to change, which is to be expected, given that he was teetering on the edge of puberty. Margaret and Suzie both say that he became arrogant and rather cruel at this time, kicking the neighbourhood dog, Bitzi, when it came to visit. Leslie, implying that females overreact, says this is nonsense. 'He probably lifted the dog with his foot, which is quite different from laying in the boot.' Whether David 'kicked' or 'lifted', or just pushed the dog aside with his foot, I doubt that it was an action calculated to hurt the dog, for David loves all animals.

Like Margaret, David loves cats. 'I love dogalers but cats are best,' he says, 'Cats don't press you.' David's affection embraces all the cat world from domestic cats to the big cats; he knows them all by name, knows their approximate weight, speed, habitat and country of origin, and can tell you which of the big cats are in danger of becoming extinct.

'Poor mummy cheetah, it's sad, it's sad,' he says in a tone of commiseration and pulling a mournful face. 'She sacrificed strength for speed so she can hunt best, the poor mummy cheetah, she just wants to feed her babies, poor mummy cheetah.' Given the Helfgotts' love for animals it is not surprising that his sisters remember the Bitzi incident.

To be fourteen, fifteen or sixteen is a painful, forlorn experience for most of us. In fact adolescence itself is an ordeal which most teenagers are convinced they suffer in isolation, believing that no-one in the world has ever gone through or understands their distress. They are right; most people are not sympathetic, as they have forgotten groping through their own terrible teens in search of someone they cannot comprehend: themselves!

For Margaret, David's teenage travail, overlaid on her own transition from childhood to adulthood, made life very difficult. In truth, growing up with David was hard on all his siblings.

Because he played so brilliantly, they were subjected to marked discrimination by Peter, who saw to it that David got the extra chop, sometimes eating six chops at a sitting, and the extra pint of milk. The reason Peter gave for the extra food was that David needed it to keep his strength up in order to play well. If there was any money for clothes, David got the new clothes. Margaret recalls, 'I remember I was denied a petticoat. It wasn't considered important that I had a petticoat because any extra money had to go for David's clothing for his concerts.'

Under normal conditions favouritism of one member of a family over the others creates distress and resentment. However, given that the Helfgott children had been reared to believe in socialist principles and the inviolable rights of the individual, they would have had every right to be confused, angered and jealous of Peter's continuing preferential treatment of David. As the eldest child, who had been displaced by David almost from the moment of his first tentative two-finger exploration of the keyboard, Margaret had a right to be deeply disturbed by Peter's double standards. Try as she might, it was impossible for her to accept that David was entitled to receive anything extra simply because he played the piano; to her it wasn't ethical that all things were not shared equally amongst the other children.

Although there does not appear to be an undercurrent of rancour when Margaret recounts the memory of how hard it was for her and the other children to grow up with David, the musical genius, it must have been particularly taxing for her, especially as she was an exceptionally gifted pianist herself.

David was twelve and Margaret fourteen when Louise, the youngest Helfgott sister, was born. The arrival of Louise created both joy and distress for Margaret. Until that time the house had been full of cats. Margaret, who, like David, loves cats, had one which she was particularly fond of. This little cat was also very attached to Margaret. It waited each afternoon at the front gate to run to meet her when she turned the corner on her way home after school.

This special bond came to an abrupt end when Louise was born. Peter, fearful that the cats might suffocate the baby, gathered them up and took the lot to a local timber yard, telling the children that there the animals would be happier and free to catch mice. Although Margaret adored Louise from the moment she came home, she was saddened that her birth had meant the loss of her wonderful cat. Margaret's childhood seems to have been peppered with a series of losses. Perhaps life is nothing but a learning curve, but for Margaret the lessons were unnecessarily painful, especially when Peter was also practising the politics of exclusion. Both Margaret and Suzie tell of how David became 'very arrogant' and 'very selfish' between the ages of fourteen and fifteen, demanding all the attention.

Under the circumstances it is not surprising that David's nature seems to have changed. Here was a youngster who, for most of his young life, had been the apple of his father's eye because of his precocious musical ability and his potential to become a renowned pianist. Everything that he had been given at the expense of his siblings and everything that had been done for him had been done to foster his pianistic brilliance, not for his personal happiness, not to assist him to achieve for himself, but to gratify Peter's driving obsession to have him attain perfection.

Margaret says that David was never denied the opportunity of learning to become self-sufficient by anyone in the Helfgott house. 'The truth was he wasn't interested in becoming more independent.' Given that life in the Helfgott home was geared to caring for David's every desire, it is not surprising that, under the circumstances, he took advantage of the situation — it would have been impossible for any teenager so treated not to believe that the world was his.

However, although being 'useless' relieved David from the boredom of daily tasks and left him free to indulge in his own passion for music, it would have seriously eroded his sense of self-worth. All the positive reinforcement David received confirmed not who he was but rather what he was. Life for any teenager is difficult, but for David his search for his own identity was impossible. The piano was David's security. His music was his security, his reason for being, the reason why he was cosseted and shielded. Without music he would have felt that he had nothing, and was nothing. To survive this first painful identity crisis, he had no choice other than to continue to strive for musical perfection, his alter-ego identity. With nothing except music with which to protect his position, he resorted to what appeared to his sisters to be arrogance and callous competitiveness.

Although his hostility wasn't specifically directed towards Margaret, it was she who suffered most when David is supposed to have told Peter that 'There should be only one star in the family.' Meaning himself, of course. David denies making this statement. Whether he did or not, to have told Margaret this seems unfair of Peter. Margaret, however, says Peter told her what David had said purely because 'they were close and talked frequently.' David's words confirmed for Margaret 'simply what I knew along — David was not interested in having any competition in the household!'

Margaret, who had 'visions of David, my younger brother, and I performing together, playing together, participating in music in the world together', was upset by David's attitude, but she continued to play. David did not choose to become involved in healthy competition with Margaret, whose musical ability represented the greatest threat to his security. Instead he became a compulsive unfair competitor, ultimately forcing Margaret to give up the unequal fight. 'He didn't want me to play the piano. We used to play duets so that we could enter various competitions but David began to play very loud and very fast and I just couldn't keep up with him. When I asked him to play a little slower or play a little softer he just wouldn't. Instead he would play very, very fast, so fast it was impossible to play with him after that.'

David denies that he sabotaged Margaret's playing by playing the duets loud and fast. When he read what Margaret had written he was quite aggrieved and not a little upset.

'I love Santa Margarita, I never did that to her! I love my Santa Margarita!'

8

A Mixed Year

David was thirteen in 1960 when he passed the Australian Music Examination Board's Fifth Grade Musical Perception examination, gaining a credit with a mark of 77 out of the possible 100. This was not an exceptional result but it was theory that was being tested, not performance, his real love. At that time he was still studying music under Frank Arndt, a teacher David describes with affection and a total lack of modesty as 'the unknown professor who produced a star'.

In the same year he played in the Australian Broadcasting Commission's Concerto and Vocal Competition. The composer and critic James Penberthy was astounded by his dexterous handling of Ravel's Concerto in G Major, writing in the *Perth Sunday Times*: 'This is the first sight of a rare and prodigious talent, startling from one so young and so small.' Penberthy, who obviously found the selection of competition winners a chancy process, had placed in the audience three unofficial 'judges'. These independent judges were asked to give their opinions on the contest and on the performances given by the young artists. In addition Penberthy put a man in the audience with a meter to accurately measure the applause. As it transpired, the independent judges favoured David over the winner, Pauline Rowe, while the audience favoured Rowe.

Before the year closed David was rehearsing Brahms for a solo appearance at His Majesty's Theatre, Perth, for the Western Australian Government's Choral Festival.

In tandem with his musical studies David applied himself to his education, successfully completing his first year of high school in fine form, gaining very acceptable marks in those subjects which count: English, 74, Spelling, 94, Social Studies, 87, Arithmetic, 80, Algebra, 80, Geometry, 92, General Science, 83. He did not achieve well in Art, Technical Drawing or Woodwork. It seems that the thirteen-year-old David, in his singular pursuit of a career on the concert platform, did not or could not apply his creativity and manual dexterity to subjects, even artistic ones, which did not contribute immediately to the realisation of his musical ambitions. His attendance was marked as 'satisfactory'. General comment: 'David has worked quite well throughout the year. He is a good class member, quiet and of pleasant disposition.'

In 1961, at the age of fourteen, David won the ABC Western Australian Concerto and Vocal Competition state finals when he played Mozart's Concerto No. 24 in C Minor, which qualified him to compete in Melbourne as Perth's only representative in the competition's Commonwealth finals. David is believed to have been, at that time, the youngest pianist to reach the finals.

The growing publicity surrounding the competition embarrassed David, making him uncertain and concerned that his comparative fame as a classical pianist might cause his Forrest High School classmates to think of him as a sissy. A letter from one of David's old school mates recalls:

I remember David when we both attended Forrest High School, Mount Lawley. It was an 'industrial' type of boys' school so music or the arts was a rare thing; however there were two musicians in the

school, David and me. David was, of course, David, this skinny,
energetic, happy kid who played amazing piano with such energy and
joy.

However, whether music was a 'rare thing' or not, the majority
of the boys found no difficulty in hailing David as their hero, if
not in sports then in keyboard gymnastics. It was his
schoolmates who took up a collection to purchase the luggage he
needed for his trip to Melbourne.

David flew with Peter to Melbourne, where he again played
the Mozart Concerto No. 24 in C Minor, this time accompanied
by the Victorian Symphony Orchestra under the baton of
Georges Tzipine. Sidney Harrison, Professor of Music at the
Guildhall School of Music, London, visiting Australia at the
request of the ABC to act as one of the adjudicators in the
Commonwealth final, described David as among the best and
most talented artists he had seen in twenty-five years. Harrison,
who was unstinting in his praise, said David possessed a most
extraordinary talent and that his rendition of the Mozart
concerto was 'faultless'. David exhibited a special sensitivity to
Mozart's music.

Despite his outstanding performance, David did not win. Mr
Harrison felt the need to explain the adjudicators' decision,
which he said they had arrived at after the predictable 'long and
difficult deliberation'. Harrison said the only reason why David
had not won was that the other contestants attempted higher
'pianistic mountains and succeeded in conquering them'. This
was his way of saying that a good performance of an
overwhelming work beats an equally good performance of a
smaller work any day! In other words, Mozart, 'faultlessly'
performed by a fourteen-year-old, didn't stand a chance against
the majestic Rachmaninof Concerto No. 3 in D Minor

performed by an older musical athlete.

However, while David went from success to success, Margaret is reported to have 'stepped aside' in deference to David's career. When speaking of this period David says that Margaret 'was a victim', and that she went through a 'tragic time'; which seems to be a fairly accurate assessment of her situation. David also says that she was jealous of him. All of Peter's praise and attention seems to have been focused on David. Oddly enough Margaret mentions only how hard it was to live with a talented child, never that her father's favouritism of David contributed to the difficulties experienced by the family.

So complete was Peter's passion for David, his 'Prince', so indifferent was he to the achievements of his other children, that when Margaret, excited and proud, raced home with the news that she had passed all nine subjects of her Junior Certificate, he responded with total lack of interest, saying only, 'Shhh, David's practising.' Margaret's bitterness is evident when she speaks of the following day. 'The next day at school all the other children had been given radios and clothes and other presents for passing their Junior Certificates and all I had got was, "Shhh, your brother's practising".'

This lack of a token of parental pride could have been interpreted as disinterest or financial inability, both reasons being equally painful and embarrassing for Margaret. Under the circumstances Margaret would have had to be a saint not to have been jealous of David. Youngsters they were, musicians they were, but saints they were not.

Margaret, who 'stepped aside' or was pushed aside, couldn't wait to leave school when she obtained her Junior Certificate. If David was the 'good son' then Margaret was the 'good and selfless daughter' who took a job, as was expected of the eldest child, to bring into the home the extra money the family needed. It never occurred to her at that time to seek higher education. That would come much later.

Taking a position as a clerk with a Mr Alec Breckler, then the owner of a shoe store chain in Perth and a well-respected member of the Jewish community, meant that after Margaret had paid board to her mother and father, she had the delight of buying for herself the clothes she craved, a delight which had been denied to her for so many years.

Breckler, who had been known to the Helfgotts from the time of their arrival in Western Australia in 1953, had helped Peter to find and obtain housing for the family. Peter had been ill during that initial period, so ill that Breckler had suggested that the four children be cared for in a private home until Peter was well enough to resume his responsibility. Naturally Peter's pride would not allow this, and David says that as time passed Peter became firmly convinced that Breckler had been motivated not by concern for their welfare but rather by the desire to 'steal' his family. If this was so, it is surprising that he allowed Margaret to work for a man he viewed with such suspicion.

The international celebrities Isaac Stern, violinist, and Abby Simon, pianist, both visiting Australia in June 1961, had heard David play in the Concerto and Vocal Competition. These renowned musicians were enthusiastic about David's work, agreeing that he already had natural poise and maturity in his technique of the kind most musicians never acquire in a lifetime. Abby Simon, an American in Western Australia as a guest of the ABC to play a series of concerts, asked to meet David. After listening to him play a number of pieces, Abby was quoted in the press as saying he 'immediately recognised the boy's great powers', and further, 'There is no doubt the boy is gifted and has a promising future.' David says that Abby called him (David) 'the pianist's pianist'.

Isaac Stern, who was also impressed with David's interpretative ability and musicianship, joined Abby in urging him to further his studies at the famous Curtis Institute of Music in Philadelphia. The musicians suggested that David would be ready to make the transition to the institute in approximately eighteen months, at which time he would have been approaching fifteen and a half.

Neither musician would have had any idea that their suggestion for David to leave Australia, which in essence meant leaving Peter, would have been anything other than positive encouragement for a young artist to further develop his already formidable talent. Yet that encouragement was to precipitate the first crack in the close relationship which had previously existed between father and son.

For James Penberthy, a man who had been committed to helping David's talent from the moment he heard him play the first and third movements of Ravel's Concerto in G Major, the praise from Stern and Simon was enough to set his pen working at a furious pace. He wrote an article which appeared in the *Sunday Times* in June 1961, under the heading 'He'll bring honour to Perth' and subtitled 'Papa wouldn't sell the piano'. It began with a recap of David's amazingly strong performance of the difficult Ravel piano concerto the year before. According to Margaret, Penberthy's description of David at that performance, in which he mentioned that David's trouser legs were too short, 'terribly upset' David. She says David was 'mortified' and that the family 'felt rather humiliated'. David denies this, saying he was only upset by Penberthy's mention of the home-made piano stool.

The article was intended to start a public fund to raise the money for David's tuition at the Curtis Institute after he had completed his Junior Certificate. Penberthy interviewed Peter at the Helfgott home. Peter told him that a short while before, he had fallen ill and at that time had 'lost every stick of furniture in his humble home'. Peter went on to say, 'We wanted to maintain some life in the house so we managed to keep up the payments on the piano.' Apart from the appeal for funds, Penberthy wrote: 'Even now there is something that can be done for the boy . . . his piano needs a complete overhaul so badly it must be a nightmare for him to practise on it.'

The publicity built when *Woman's Day* magazine published a full-page article about David and the Helfgott family in the 10 July 1961 issue. The article, which can only be described as a heart-wrenching 'human interest' story, had all the right ingredients to tug at the heartstrings. It was a fairy story that sent a message to the average Aussie mum, the wife of the 'Aussie battler', that everything turns out right in the end. It couldn't convey, however, that the happy ending was a long way off.

Like the Penberthy article, the *Woman's Day* story also endowed all the Helfgott brood with a musical ability which Leslie says was overrated, especially in relation to himself. 'That article they printed,' he says, 'said something like, "Leslie, 10, untaught, plays Paganini on the violin." What they should have said was, "Leslie, 10, untaught, struggles to play Paganini on the violin . . . perhaps he might get it right in ten years' time"!' In Leslie's opinion, the two articles' assessment of their talent placed a great deal of stress on the Helfgott children. He said they felt pressured by strangers who expected them to have David's musical genius and couldn't accept that they didn't.

The article in *Woman's Day* also repeated Stern and Simon's recommendations, as well as reporting that 'Perth's Lord Mayor,

Sir Harry Howard, and a group of citizens are planning a fund-raising campaign and a group of Sydney businessmen has offered to match any contributions pound for pound. The estimated cost of a five-year course for David would be £5000.' The article closed with, 'For David, a lonely decision may lie ahead. If the money is raised for his studies in the United States he will be forced to leave a family which is closer together than most. The parting may be a price he will have to pay for the ultimate fulfilment of his parents' dream.'

I asked David if he could remember the nature of Peter's illness which had led to the loss of 'every stick of furniture' and/or the 'family's savings'. He answered cryptically and out of context, as only David can: 'Daddy wasn't clever, he forgot, he forgot Lord Jim' an answer which at first made me think he was in playful mode yet again. Becoming somewhat exasperated, and because I have heard David repeatedly refer to 'Lord Jim' and say 'Lord Jim says' for the last five or more years, I became sidetracked, demanding to know the identity of this mysterious individual.

'Lord Jim, Professor Penberthy, Lord Jim!' he replied with equal exasperation.

David's past references to 'Lord Jim' came flooding back, each now making perfect sense! Was this the fleeting opening of a window into his consciousness? If so, how long would he leave it open for me to talk with him before it slammed shut, returning as to the boulder-strewn and convoluted conversations of the past?

'Why wasn't your Daddy clever? What do you mean he forgot Lord Jim?' I asked.

'Dear little Daddy told stories. Daddy wasn't clever. He forgot Lord Jim.' For a moment I thought we were back playing games again, then he said, 'Daddy was robust. Daddy was robust as a lion.'

'Your Daddy wasn't ill, is that right? I am talking about the time when Lord Jim wrote about you and your Daddy, the time when Stern and Abby Simon thought you should go to the States.'

'To America!' he sharply corrected me, and I thought the window was firmly open, for the time being at least.

Questioning David is always a problem, not only to elicit the right answer but to avoid asking a question which might produce not the correct answer, but one you can be seduced into thinking is. On this occasion I had every reason to worry.

I asked him if he meant that Peter had forgotten what he had told Penberthy when he was interviewed by *Woman's Day* and if in fact his father had not only not been ill but never lost either the family savings or the furniture. Was it all just a good story for both Penberthy and *Woman's Day*, to account for the fact that the family really had very little in the way of possessions?

'Daddy wasn't very clever. I reckon it's all a game, it's all a game, is that right, darling?'

In fact, Peter was not 'robust as a lion'. Royal Perth Hospital records testify that at that time he had been so seriously ill from a heart attack that the doctors feared he would not live through the night. Where I had initially thought that perhaps Peter had manipulated the truth, it turned out to be David who was mangling it on this occasion.

Margaret, who has been elected by the Helfgott family as their spokesperson, says: 'Our father was *not* a manipulator of the truth in any shape or form. If anything, he was almost too direct and honest.' About the article in *Woman's Day* she says: 'It is quite common for reporters to embroider their stories to make them sell. This I know from personal experience.'

There are differing accounts as to what really took place

relative to the money raised by the *Sunday Times* and what is supposed to have been the reason why David did not go to America.

Margaret says Peter told her that when he went to the *Sunday Times* to find out how much money had been raised he was informed that the sum was very small, certainly not enough to provide fares and to support David in the United States. However, having said that, Margaret also recalls that Peter refused to let David go because he believed David was 'totally incapable of looking after himself'. She says Peter told those involved in the fund-raising project that he would have no objections if they sent the whole family to the United States to be by David's side to care for him, and that as a father he couldn't let such a young boy as David go on his own to fend for himself in a strange country. Margaret totally agrees with Peter's decision, still holding the opinion that David was already 'manifesting rather strange behaviour' at that time. She speaks of David's 'arrogance, his inability to tie his own shoelaces, to light gas burners, and also his exhibition of cruelty'—kicking the dog, Bitzi.

David says that Peter arranged for the money received by the *Sunday Times* to be returned to its donors. He maintains that his father refused to let him go to New York because Alec Breckler had made arrangements for him to live with a Jewish family; this angered Peter because he believed Breckler had seized the opportunity to steal at least one of his children. Had David gone to New York, he would have been closer to sixteen, not fourteen, and he would not have been alone, 'fending for himself', but living with and being cared for by a Jewish family.

An interview with David by James Penberthy which appeared in the *Sunday Times* in 1966, just before David's departure for the United Kingdom and some four years after his proposed trip to America, mentions that if the sum of $10 000 which could have been made available to David for his study at the Curtis Institute were still able to be called upon, his forthcoming period at they Royal College of Music, London, would have been made far easier.

If this report, which appears to confirm that a sum of $10 000 had indeed been raised, is correct, why would Peter have told David and the family that the money available was far too little to cover his New York expenses?

Perhaps Peter really did believe that David was not capable of looking after himself. Who will ever know? Whatever the reason, David bitterly resented the fact that he hadn't been allowed to go to New York.

Margaret says, 'I think that the relationship between him and my father deteriorated after that. As far as I can remember, David blamed Dad for not being allowed to go. There were two factors. The first factor was that there wasn't enough money from the *Sunday Times* to send David and the second was that David was such a young boy that my father was very worried and couldn't allow him to go to America without proper provision being made for his welfare and his care.'

Margaret continues, 'When he tried to explain this to David, in a tactful way of course, it didn't really get through to David and he was very, very upset with Dad because of this.' On two counts, Peter's refusal constituted the first major frustration David had experienced. He was used to having his every wish granted, and his ambitious plans for his career were thwarted. In his shock and disbelief that Peter had crossed him, he would have been more than 'very, very upset', rather a bundle of seething fury.

David still harbours this resentment. Even now he says, showing a most uncharacteristic degree of anger, 'I should have gone to America, I should have. But I reckon we must cherish these times together, Bev. Got to stay positive, is that the idea, darling? Is that the idea? Mustn't talk about the bad times, is that the idea?'

9

Sweet, Heady Wine

The year 1961 was a very crowded one for fourteen-year-old David. Peter and he were flown to Sydney in September for an appearance on the nationally televised 'Bobby Limb Show'. The day following his arrival in Sydney he recorded Chopin's Fantaisie Impromptu with the Bobby Limb Orchestra, which had been increased to twenty-five musicians for the occasion. At the time David was believed to have been the youngest performer, as well as the first from Western Australia, to appear on the show.

An article about the Bobby Limb engagement also mentioned the fund and reported that David 'considered he was too young to leave his family and that the fund was postponed'. David says Peter had told him to say that the decision not to go to the Curtis Institute had been his own. Doing so was the same as denying himself and his dreams and must have added fuel to his anger.

It should be borne in mind that David was still only fourteen when he became public property, a position which in itself created tension, throughout 1961, a year in which one new and emotionally charged event followed hard on the heels of another. The pressure continued to mount. Although winning the state finals of the ABC Concerto and Vocal Competition had relieved Peter's immediate fear of a loss, it brought new and even greater tensions, some of which were exciting for a young boy. As the state finalist he flew to Melbourne for the first time, the only Western Australian representative in the prestigious competition's finals.

Peter accompanied David to Melbourne. His father's presence in the audience would have been a comfort, but knowing that Peter's thoughts were focused on his success, David's fear of losing the competition overshadowed what otherwise would have been an exciting event.

The unyielding pressure on David to perform well and to win came from all sides. David demanded perfection from himself. He wanted to win for the honour of the family, which in truth meant Peter's honour. In addition he felt he was upholding the honour of the state as its sole representative.

Were Peter's thoughts, as he sat so proudly in the audience watching and listening that night, focused on anything but winning? Was he so driven by his own obsession for music and his desire to have David achieve his own dreams that he was oblivious to what independent observers believe to have been almost unendurable stress for David?

The Helfgott family state emphatically that 'David never manifested any symptoms of "unendurable stress" To the contrary, he loved performing.'

Did Peter really believe that David was mentally fragile? I doubt it. No loving father, as his children profess him to have been, no father who believed his son to be extremely sensitive, would subject his child to such intense prolonged stress if he believed there were even a remote possibility he might crack under the strain.

When I asked David about this period he cleverly answered

all my questions with one of his succinct, profound one-liners, such as 'God help the under-achiever in the Jewish family!' Which, despite the fact that he delivered it with a laugh, held all the pathos of a Shakespearean tragedy.

I believe that David, although he was obsessed by his music, was at that period of his life more stable and better conditioned psychologically to cope with pressure than most youngsters of the same age. And I believe Peter knew this. I also believe that Peter was so blinded by his vision of David (and himself) as musical geniuses that, while he would never have done anything to harm David, he became obsessive in his pursuit to maintain and glorify what for him had become the all-important triumvirate: Peter, David and music.

The pressure on David intensified when the pair returned from Melbourne. While David's defeat in the competition was offset by the very public praise of two major musicians, the resulting publicity exposed him to additional stress. In addition to this he suddenly came face to face with public pressure to advance his musical studies in another country; a cup of sweet, heady wine for a fourteen-year-old!

For Peter it was to prove a bitter cup. For the first time, he was confronted with the possible destruction of the triumvirate. Although Peter had created an eagle he did not have the wisdom to foresee that his golden bird might not wish to be forever restrained in a colonial, suburban cage. The sudden realisation that he could lose David, his alter ego, must have been greatly disturbing if not devastating.

Peter's refusal to allow David to take advantage of the opportunity which had unexpectedly opened out before him, apart from frustrating him, must also have confused David. How could he possibly understand why, when for most of his life he had been pushed into the winner's circle, the same hand that had pushed him now pulled the rug right out from under his feet, just when what he had been led to believe was a joint goal appeared to be within reach?

Peter's entrenched and authoritarian stance was to set up a corrosion that would ultimately lead to the disintegration of his relationship with his 'Prince'. It would also bequeath a bitterness that, even today, David is unable to resolve. He refers to this period in his life as the time when 'the fog started' in his head. This confusion, this 'fog', would intensify and haunt him until 1985.

David, who appears to have been remarkably adept in adopting and employing several survival strategies, became arrogant around this time. What better way was open to him to reinforce his ego? Arrogance would also have helped him to cope with the confusion caused by his father's conflicting signals, which, while loving and supportive, at the same time effectively blocked achievement of his desire. Concealing his anger and humiliation, David thumbed his nose at the world in a show of arrogant indifference.

Of that period Suzie, who was eight at the time, says, 'His attitude was, "I'm better than anyone." Photographs before that time show him to be a very nice, ordinary-looking little boy. However, after that the photographs show the change to an arrogant young man. It's very plain to see that he developed a very big head.'

Margaret, in spite of, or because of, Peter's dismissive attitude towards her talent and her needs, tends to worship her father. Her focus at that time may have been not on the humiliation she endured when Peter consistently refused to allow her friends, especially boyfriends, to visit her at home, but on David and his ungrateful and arrogant rejection of his family.

She recalls, 'When we went to the Capitol Theatre, when the

Concerto and Vocal Competitions were held, David, around this age, didn't want to walk with us, with Dad or with Mum or me. We felt that he was ashamed of us. He just didn't want to know us.' I suspect David wasn't ashamed of his family — just maintaining a rage concealed by what appeared to be arrogance.

By sixteen, the young men of Margaret's acquaintance had begun to notice that she had blossomed into a remarkably attractive young woman, and Peter found his daughter's attention turning away from the home. In turn he refused to let boys visit her. Once again she was supposed to do as she was told without complaint.

Then Margaret, who says she received positive encouragement to continue with her musical studies, gave up playing the piano. She gives a combination of reasons for this. 'Part of the reason was teenage rebellion and I wanted to explore. Also I felt intimidated and inhibited by David's remarkable genius. I just felt that I couldn't actually play when David was around, certainly between the ages of fourteen to nineteen.'

Apart from the fact that David did possess overwhelming musical talent, Margaret had felt for some long time that she was 'playing second fiddle' to David. In fact, she was only allowed to practise after David had finished. Under the circumstances it is understandable that she resented all the attention and favouritism shown to him by Peter. It was only natural that Margaret, who craved some demonstration of her father's affection, or at the very least some real appreciation and recognition from him, would subconsciously find in the boys' attentions an endorsement of her self-worth and her femininity.

David, who was still under the tutelage of Frank Arndt, moved from strength to musical strength. After returning to Perth from his television appearance he put the excitement behind him to briefly settle down before sitting for the Australian Music Examination Board examinations in October 1961. He successfully gained his certificate of Associate in Music, Australia (A. Mus. A.), receiving a mark of 184 out of a possible 200, a remarkable result for a fourteen-year-old sitting his first performance examination. He was also awarded the J. B. Vincent Prize for outstanding results in the yearly examinations conducted by the board.

The following year, in June 1962, David played in the ABC Concerto and Vocal Competition finals again. The *Sunday Times* music critic, James Penberthy, wrote:

> *The 1962 ABC Concerto and Vocal Competitions developed into an absorbing contest between the imaginative, intelligent artistry of Suzanne Maslen and the magic in the brilliant fingers of David Helfgott. Suzanne played the first movement of a very interesting, but quite unknown concerto by Vaughan Williams and David chose the Concerto in E flat by Liszt. Both these young pianists deserved to win, but after considering the qualities I have mentioned the judges gave the decision to the boy.*

Perhaps, despite David's brilliance, had Ms Maslen chosen a known, impressive work such as the Liszt she might well have turned the decision in her favour. If David's defeat in Melbourne the year before had taught him anything, it was to choose a difficult masterwork if he wanted to be noticed and win. Liszt's Concerto No. 1 in E flat is such a work.

Liszt, who was recognised as a master of the mid-nineteenth-century school of 'Music of the Future', a term coined in Liszt's own home, is said to have once declared, 'My sole ambition as a composer is to hurl my javelin into the infinite spaces of the future.'

Approximately a century later David Helfgott would catch

that javelin when the Liszt Trust accorded him the privilege of playing on Liszt's piano in Liszt's Budapest home, shortly after it had been turned into a museum.

10

All That Beckons

The three young winners of the Western Australian Concerto and Vocal Competition for 1962 were featured, with the Western Australian Symphony Orchestra under the baton of John Farnsworth Hall, in a videotaped hour-long program on Channel ABW on 7 June. Once again David played the Liszt.

After his television appearance many Perth viewers telephoned ABW to say that his hands were the most beautiful they had ever seen. While David now uses the need to protect his hands, in addition to feeling lazy, or 'lazos' as he says, as an excuse to avoid raking grass, he made no special effort to protect them when he was a teenager. There are days when David claims to have loved playing tennis, telling of how he could have been a great tennis player. He sometimes enlarges on this story to make it more believable, telling of how he refused to give up tennis despite being repeatedly warned that the sport could harm his hands. Other times he will say that 'Daddy wouldn't let me play tennis,' even managing to become a little misty-eyed when he rattles on about 'the *dommage* . . . the *dommage*'.

His sisters find this story amusing. Suzie, after searching her memory, managed to dredge up only one instance when David did in fact play one game of tennis with a friend. According to the family, the truth is that Peter wanted David to play tennis and take up more general exercise but David refused to do so. David never did have the inclination to be a sportsman, he didn't have the time and further, his eyesight was too poor (he wore glasses from around the age of four).

One newspaper report quotes David as saying he refused to maintain a daily regimen of piano practice and that he only played when he felt like it (which according to his family was every minute he could find), and then rarely for more than two hours a day. It cites Peter, no doubt pushing David forward into the public spotlight, as saying, 'He plays better in front of a large audience.' In that same article David says that the only time he was nervous when playing was when he was not a complete master of the work.

Obviously he was not the 'complete master of the work' when he played the Ravel G Major Concerto with the Western Australian Symphony Orchestra under the baton of the Dutch conductor Willem van Otterloo on 24 July 1962. His performance drew adverse criticism from his long-time champion James Penberthy. In his article, entitled 'Ravel's Ghost Just Shrugged', Penberthy wrote:

An enormous talent, said Dutch conductor Willem van Otterloo of David Helfgott, the 15-year-old Perth pianist, after they had run through Ravel's G major Concerto with the WA Orchestra at the youth concert this week . . . and the ghost of Ravel merely shrugged its shoulders.

The brittle, bouncy light-hearted first and third movements of his concerto got speed and a measure of dexterity, without control or dynamic force from the young soloist, and the orchestra relinquished its customary esprit de corps.

When Helfgott was 13 he startled Perth with his performance of these same movements, but then the orchestra was coherent and Ravel's music lived and glowed. This time he played the second movement as well.

After further criticism the article closed with:

Van Otterloo amplified his remarks about Helfgott by strongly stressing his need of musical education and study overseas.

I would simply repeat the fact that David Helfgott is a prodigiously endowed piano player. Until he opens the doors of musical understanding he will never be anything else.

David was obviously considering the possibility of doing something other than play the piano, for he sat for the University of Western Australia public examinations. His results were: English, 76, French, 73, Geography, 80, Arithmetic and Algebra, 76, Geometry and Trigonometry, 67, Science A, 75, Science B, 70, Music B, 90. It appears from this that David was capable of achieving academically without a great deal of fuss. Aside from being in the top five of his class in all subjects, he enjoyed and had an aptitude for science.

It is not unusual for a scientific bent and pianistic ability to go hand in hand. The Russian-born composer and musician Alexander Borodin, who as a boy showed an interest in playing the piano, had a driving urge to become a scientist. After spending several years in medical school he began concentrating on chemistry and while still young became an authority in the field. Borodin's output of musical compositions was not large because he was always juggling between his two loves, music and lecturing and writing his papers on chemistry.

That same year David, around fifteen years of age at the time, was presented with a Citizenship Diploma Award, 'for diligence, assiduity and integrity in the fundamental tenets, principles and characteristics of true citizenship', by the Parents' and Citizens'

Association. In November he received a diploma from the Alliance Française for written and oral French. David even now quite often resorts to using the odd French word or phrase. This is also a game designed by him to test others' ability with the language.

The following year, 1963, was not a memorable or remarkable year. David reached sixteen and went to study with the prominent teacher, Stephen Dornan.

By 1964 David had changed tutors yet again. This was to prove a fortunate transition, for it began his long and lasting liaison with Madame Alice Carrard. Madame Carrard has taught David since 1964 and continues to give him advice to this day. This wonderful lady, who is now (in 1996) ninety-nine years old, is perhaps the only person who has been constantly supportive of David throughout the years, standing by him during all his ups and downs. When David visits Perth, as he often does, he visits Alice. Naturally a great affection exists between them.

Alice was born in Budapest in 1897. As a youngster she was auditioned by Istvan Thoman, a pupil of Liszt and a teacher of Béla Bartók. In addition to his later fame as a composer, Bartók was also an accomplished pianist. After her audition with Thoman, Alice subsequently studied with Bartók himself and embarked on a concert career which was to take her through Europe, the Dutch East Indies and to Australia in 1941. It is thus possible to make a tenuous connection from Liszt, through Thoman, to Carrard and David himself.

Under the firm guidance of Alice Carrard, David entered the 1964 ABC Concerto and Vocal Competition. His chosen work was the first movement of Rachmaninof's Concerto No. 3 in D Minor. Sergei Rachmaninof idolised Tchaikovsky, and his music has been criticised for the occasional outburst of undue

Romanticism. As a master pianist he knew how to bring forth all the nuances and rich sonorities and how to make the most of the instrument's flexibility. Making scale passages and arpeggios glitter and melodies sing, his work shows his fondness for extensive singing melodies which surge up and down. Rachmaninof wove rhapsodic piano parts around the singing melodies of his concertos, allowing the piano at times to take over completely and sing its own melody to its own accompaniment. Rachmaninof was the master of music for its own sake. He wrote: 'Melodic invention, in the proper meaning of the term, is the real aim of every composer. If he is incapable of inventing melodies that endure, his chances of mastering his material are very slender.'

Rachmaninof's D-minor Third Concerto is a towering masterpiece and one which, it is reasonable to believe, could be much too difficult for a young pianist to accomplish. Even the composer himself is said to have muttered, under his breath, as he departed the stage after one of his performances of this great composition: 'I don't know why I ever wrote such a difficult work.' David says of the concerto, 'The same melody keeps coming in all the time, over and over. It's the hardest concerto in the world, stupefying and rigorous . . . it's a whopper!' He follows this up with one of his oft-repeated sayings, 'It's only a game, mostly a game, a great game, if you don't weaken.'

Alice Carrard none the less had faith in David's ability not only to perform the work but to win the competition against steep opposition. On 16 June 1964, accompanied by the Western Australian Symphony Orchestra conducted by John Farnsworth Hall, David lived up to everyone's expectations by carrying off the prize. Columnist Sally Trethown wrote:

> A performance of magic, excitement, colour and continuity,' said
> judge Frank Hutchens.

*He was speaking of David Helfgott, who last night won the piano
section of the ABC Concerto and Vocal competition in the Capitol
Theatre with his reading of the first movement of Rachmaninof's
Third Piano Concerto.*

*Under his talented hands this work exploded in a display of aural
pyrotechnics that brought long and enthusiastic applause from the
large audience.*

This time it was Rachel who accompanied David to Melbourne
for his second appearance in the Commonwealth final of the
competition, on 4 July 1964. David performed, once again, with
the Victorian Symphony Orchestra conducted by Georges
Tzipine.

David says he doesn't recall why Peter did not go with him to
Melbourne but he does remember it was very cold and that,
prior to the competition, Rachel left him waiting for her on a
street corner for some long time while she shopped. Cold is the
pianist's natural enemy, seizing up the muscles. David's account
of the events of that night is somewhat disjointed, but from what
he says it seems that he was very, very cold and that his hands
were nearly frozen by the time Rachel returned. He implies that
he lost the competition to Roger Woodward, albeit by only half
a point, because of this.

Writer Adrian Rawlins questioned the decision in favour of
Woodward, which was handed down by the visiting Belgian-
born conductor, and in this instance adjudicator, André
Cluytens:

*The finals of this year's ABC Concerto and Vocal Competition were
held on Saturday July 4. Two of the placings adjudicated by André
Cluytens are dubious.*

*He awarded first place to Roger Woodward, 23, a New South Wales
teacher, for a fiercely technical performance of Prokofief's Concerto*

No. 3 in C major. This seems ill-advised: the work is showy and pleasing but by no means a test of mature musicianship.

Another contender, David Helfgott, from Western Australia, played the far more sensitive and demanding Rachmaninof D minor Concerto with great sensitivity and insight. As this is a more difficult work, making greater demands on understanding, though of a less demonstrative sort, it would seem more appropriate to have given Helfgott the prize.

Given that Roger Woodward won the competition by only half a mark, it would seem that André Cluytens may have experienced some difficulty in reaching his decision and that he, too, was impressed, although only slightly, more by spectacle and less by sensitive, melodic interpretation.

The loss of the Commonwealth final, rather than being demoralising, had the opposite effect on David. He threw himself into his music with one purpose: to become a concert pianist. Just exactly what, or who, had given impetus to his determination is unclear. Whether he had come to his own decision that music was all he wanted from life or whether other influences outside the home had convinced him that he must study overseas to fully develop his potential, David doesn't seem able to remember. Whatever the reason, although playing the piano had always been part of his reason for being, he now became obsessive in his dedication to it.

Suzie Helfgott's friend Linley Christiansen gives a rather poetic description of David at around that time. She recalls: 'The house had a long hallway and was always dark. Suzie and I sometimes crept in, even though we were not supposed to, because we might interrupt David, who was always playing and practising. I remember this particular day, David was at the piano and the light from the window was shining on his golden curls. I remember his curls. It looked like he had been touched by the hand of God.'

Gaining nine subjects in his Junior Certificate did nothing to influence David to take his Leaving examination, or Higher School Certificate as it is now known. Margaret says, 'David didn't go on to his Leaving Certificate, although at the time we thought he should, but I guess his whole being was involved in the piano. It was enough for him to be playing the piano, so he didn't go on and complete his matriculation.'

That September David devoted himself to full-time musical study, setting himself a rigorous routine of more than five hours a day at the piano, starting at 4 a.m., then sitting in on selected music lectures at the University of Western Australia. The following month, he sat for and passed his Licentiate in Music (L. Mus.) examination. The L. Mus. was then the highest performing diploma given by the A.M.E.B.

His studies progressed under Alice Carrard and the following year, 1965, he once again entered the ABC Commonwealth Concerto and Vocal Competition final. For this event he played the first movement of Tchaikovsky's Concerto No. 1 in B-flat Minor. This time, the competition was held in Adelaide, where he and the other contestants performed in the Adelaide Town Hall, with the South Australian Symphony Orchestra under John Hopkins as its guest conductor. Sir Bernard Heinze, together with John Hopkins, were the adjudicators.

The presenter of ABC's Classic FM program 'Adventures in Good Music', Karl Haas, recently observed: 'If you cannot stand up and cheer at the end of the first movement of Tchaikovsky's No. 1 Piano Concerto, then you don't have a soul.'

David received rave acclaim for his performance of this mighty work, which was written for and dedicated to the pianist Nicholas Rubinstein. Unfortunately Rubinstein chose at first to receive the work with a shrivelling silence and later with a tirade of caustic abuse. Deeply hurt, Tchaikovsky erased Rubinstein's name and replaced it with the name of Hans von Bülow. Later Rubinstein was to become perhaps the work's greatest interpreter.

The *Sunday Times* carried yet another a piece about David by James Penberthy, which opened with, 'It is now time that Perth's inner musical circles stopped conjecture about the merit of young pianist David Helfgott.' Penberthy continued: 'His performance was of concert pianistic standard.' The article notes that although David made a few mistakes, 'his interpretation, spirit and command would have been acceptable from a visiting celebrity.' The article asked: 'What is young Helfgott's future? He seems to be in good hands. Let his present mentors decide. One thing is certain, it should not be difficult to find assistance if it is ever needed. All the world loves a pianist and this one has a natural public appeal.'

Now, many years later, James Penberthy is still right, David does have a natural, warm communication with his audience. David's Tchaikovsky No. 1, performed in his own home, on his own piano and playing his own *tutti*, is still electrifying; so much so that the orchestra is not missed. In fact, given David's treatment of the 'Tchaik', to again quote David, one would be hard-pressed to make a choice between Sviatoslav Richter with an orchestra under the baton of the great von Karajan and David playing the piece on his own!

11

The End of an Era

Two days after his appearance in the Commonwealth finals in Adelaide, in July 1965, David received a letter from the 'Music Council of Western Australia (Inc.) Administering the WA Music Bursary Trust'. The contents of the letter were hinted at by James Penberthy in the *Sunday Times* of 19 September 1965. Under the heading 'Pianist Undecided on London Trip', Penberthy wrote:

> David Helfgott, the brilliant 18-year-old Perth pianist, has not decided yet whether to accept a scholarship to England offered to him in July. The WA Music Bursary Trust offered him a scholarship to study at the Royal Academy [sic] of Music, London. Details of the offer are secret. It is believed that the schoolboy pianist will have to pay his own living expenses. Professor Callaway, Professor of Music at the University of WA, is in London now making arrangements for David Helfgott if he accepts the scholarship.

Sir Frank Callaway told me that he had taken a hand in putting together the application for David's entry into the Royal College of Music. Sir Frank said that later, when he was visiting the College in London, he asked the late Sir Keith Falkner, then director of the college, who on the staff would be the best teacher for 'this brilliant young pianist from Western Australia' if he were to come to the College. The subject was discussed and David did eventually become a pupil of Mr Smith.

The letter to David containing the 'secret details' read:

Dear Mr Helfgott,

Your application for the Bursary from the WA Music Bursary Trust was considered at a meeting of the Executive Committee of the Council on Tuesday night.

As a result of their discussions on their behalf it is now my pleasure to offer you:

(a) A bursary to the value of 500 pounds in the first year towards living expenses and tuition fees in a course of studies at an institution overseas approved by the Council.

(b) Subject to Council receiving satisfactory reports from the authorities of the institution of your progress during your first year of study consideration will be given to a renewal of the bursary for a further year or years, possibly at reduced rates.

(c) Unless a travel grant can be obtained from other sources an additional grant to enable you to travel by sea at tourist rates to the approved place of study and at expiration of your studies a corresponding grant if necessary for your return to Australia.

These offers are conditional on your satisfying the Council that you can raise the balance of the amount necessary to enable you to complete the first year of your course of studies at the approved institution.

The Music Council of Western Australia (Inc.) was chaired at that time by Professor Fred Alexander who had succeeded its foundation chairman, Professor Frank Callaway. Its offer of a bursary, even though David had applied for it himself, added yet more stress to his already stressful life.

Making the decision to accept the bursary was further complicated for David because he knew from experience that Peter would oppose the proposal. Peter's opposition was not only based on keeping David from leaving the country and his side but was also influenced by his dislike and jealous distrust of those members of the Jewish community who had become David's champions. These were the people Penberthy referred to as David's 'mentors'.

Margaret and Leslie, who best remember this period, both resent what they refer to as 'outside interference'. Margaret harks back to Peter's refusal to allow David to study in America, citing David's continuing resentment as the basis for his determination not to be deterred when 'people outside the family suggested that he be sent overseas'.

When David and I spoke of the events of 1961, when Peter had refused to let him go to the United States, I asked him if his relationship with Peter had been strained from that time. He told me: 'Daddy said, "You put yourself on the hook when you stopped talking to me." ' I believed this to be one of David's encapsulated responses, intended to describe Peter's attitude toward him at that time, telling me that he had withdrawn himself from Peter and stopped speaking to him.

Then he said, 'Daddy was awful to Margaret, until I argued with him, then it was like the Romans, first I was the favourite son, then Margaret was favourite. The Romans were double-crossers. Great game-players.' He added, laughing his ack-ack laugh, 'Great game-players, playing one against the other. Daddy and I played games, mind games.' Assuming that David was trying, in his own way, to relate what was happening at that time, one can only conjecture that as far as he was concerned Peter had switched his attention to Margaret in retribution and in an attempt to bring him to heel by playing Margaret against him, playing 'mind games', as David said.

As usual Leslie was a little more direct when he spoke of Professor Callaway's involvement and the Jewish community's effort to support David's further musical education. It is his belief that David did not need to go overseas to polish his few 'rough' edges. Leslie says: 'There was nothing wrong with David. All he needed was some fine-tuning and he could have got that without going overseas. He would have been alright if those busybodies hadn't interfered and filled his head full of ideas.'

Both Margaret and Leslie have overlooked the fact that it was *David* who applied for the bursary and that it was offered to him to develop his outstanding musical talent to its full potential. All the 'interfering busybodies', well-meaning though they may have been, could never have influenced the Music Council of Western Australia to offer David a bursary if it had not been obvious that he had great potential.

Frank Callaway, then Foundation Professor of Music at the University of Western Australia, had at that time been a man of great stature in the Perth musical community for over ten years. (He was knighted in 1981 for his services to Australian and international music.). Initially appointed to the university's faculty of Education in 1953, he would guide the development of music studies at the university for thirty-one years until his retirement. In the foreword to a published Symposium in honour of Emeritus Professor Sir Frank Callaway on his seventy-fifth birthday in 1994, Frederico Mayor, the Director General of UNESCO, Paris, referred to Sir Frank as 'one of the great pioneers and ambassadors of music education in our time.'

Sir Frank knew David from the time he was nine years old and even then recognised him as uncommonly gifted, doing his utmost to have that talent nurtured.

David, who sometimes cheekily refers to Sir Frank as 'Frankie-boy . . . I don't mean Frank Sinatra', often speaks of him with great affection and admiration, saying, 'Professor Callaway was like a father to me. Frankie-boy said I was a rare prodigy and he was smiling all the time . . . all the time.'

When Professor Callaway presented David's application to the Director of the Royal College of Music in London, the usual entrance examination was waived and David was accepted as a student on Callaway's recommendation. However, a number of paper and emotional hurdles had to be overcome before David sailed for the United Kingdom. On 6 December 1965, David received a letter from Professor Callaway:

> Dear David,
>
> Would you please let me have as soon as possible a statement covering your musical accomplishments to date. I want a list of any awards you have achieved, including the number of marks in the L. Mus., your successes in the ABC Concerto Competitions and so on. Would you also include the details of concertos you have played with orchestra and the names of any major pieces included in broadcast programmes.
>
> I want this information before the end of this week in connection with the arrangements being made with the Royal College of Music.

David replied promptly the following day. His letter was uninhibited and engaging and certainly not written by an 'introverted' young man. As Sir Frank says: 'I would regard him as having been somewhat extroverted and excitable but not introverted.' Neither does the letter give any indication that he was in any way 'impractical'. Answering from 460 Beaufort Street, Highgate, on 7 December 1965, David wrote:

> Dear Professor Callaway,
>
> I have just received your letter; and am attempting to frame a reply which I hope will be sufficiently adequate (in connection with the arrangements being made with the Royal College of Music).
>
> I passed my A. Mus with 184 marks and was awarded the J. B. Vincent Memorial Prize.
>
> The L. Mus I passed but not too well with 171 marks. (Disgraceful!) I

have entered the Concerto Competitions 6 times, reached the State finals 5 times; won the State finals 4 times and represented WA at the grand finals 3 times. (I might enter again this year; though it looks like I'll never win!) I have played with orchestra the Piano Concerto in G major by Ravel; the First Piano Concerto of Franz Liszt; a movement from the Rachmanninof Third Concerto also a movement from Chaikovsky First (most recent); and the two movements from the Mozart C minor (No. 24).

I have played major pieces in other recitals: 'Gaspard de la Nuit' of Ravel; 'Dante Sonata' and 'Mephisto Waltz' of Liszt; 'Waldstein' Sonata (unsuccessful!!); Debussy's 'L'Ile Joyeuse'; Beethoven's Sonata No. 24 in F sharp major.

It's rather difficult to give you the names of any major pieces included in broadcast programs for the simple reason that the time I was allotted (often only 8 mins) was too scanty to allow selection of 'major' pieces, and I had to content myself with minor trifles. Still I did play Islamey (Oriental Phantasy by Mily Balakirev), the Mephisto Waltz (unsuccessfully!!), but practically everything else I did was inconsequential and relatively unimportant, e.g. Chopin Etudes; Toccata of Khatchaturian; Etudes of Liszt; Rhapsodies of Liszt, etc.

When I was approximately 11 or 12 I represented WA in the ABC Talent Quest which covered the Continent (and naturally got nowhere!) In this competition I performed Malaguena by Lecuonia; and in the Grand Finals La Campanella by Liszt.

When I was between 9 and 10, I performed Chopin Polonaise in A flat (unexpurgated!!) at a Country Music Festival and as a result didn't win the particular section but was awarded a 'special prize' (I suppose for courage!)

In theory I obtained 85% for sixth grade, and have 5th grade Musical Perception.

I think this just about covers my musical accomplishments to date. I might have left out something, but I don't think that could be very important. I must say however that most of my musical development is intimately connected with the Concerto Competition; this gave me a great deal of opportunities which otherwise I would have missed.

I'm sorry for bothering you with this long letter, Professor Callaway,

*but just a few more words. I am also interested in Composition (as well as
Poetry) but haven't achieved anything worth noting in this field.*

*I hope when I go to London I'll have the chance to study these sorts of
things also.*

*At the moment I'm busy preparing a recital for recording as you
requested; and I hope to be able to contact you within a few weeks with
everything 'ship shape' and polished.*

*I look forward to seeing you again, Professor; and please don't hesitate
to write to me if there is anything more you want to know; or if anything is
unsatisfactory (Heaven forbid!) Well I must close now; but best regards to
you and your family and I hope you are all enjoying the best of health.
Au revoir till the Recording.*

After receiving David's reply, Professor Callaway wrote to Mr
Keith Falkner (later Sir Keith), director of the Royal College of
Music, on 9 December 1965:

Dear Mr Falkner,

*You will recollect our conversation when I visited you in September about
a West Australian student whom we would like to see enrolled at the
RCM. He is eighteen-year-old David Helfgott, a recent recipient of a
bursary for overseas study by the Music Council of Western Australia, an
organisation representing most of the major musical groups in this State.*

*I note from your prospectus that you customarily accept students in
September and that applications close early in February. Would your
office please send me (airmail) the necessary application forms.*

*As it will not be possible for Helfgott to attend the entrance examination
in April, I am sending the following summary of his development to date
and, if you would like it, I could arrange for a tape of his playing to be sent
to you.*

The letter then outlined in detail David's repertoire and his
achievements, which were as David had listed them, with one
exception. David neglected to mention that he had been the top

candidate in the Licentiate Diploma examination and that as such he had been awarded the Kylie Club Prize. Perhaps this omission calls into question both his sisters' contention that David was an arrogant young man.

The letter continued: 'You did suggest Mr Cyril Smith as a possible teacher for Helfgott were he accepted at the RCM and I hope that this can be arranged.' The letter also covered other points such as David's need for London accommodation and the fact that the bursary was insufficient to support him completely during a three-year period in London.

Mr J. R. Stainer, registrar at the Royal College of Music, answered Professor Callaway's letter on behalf of Mr Falkner, who was ill and unable to attend to his own correspondence, on 15 December 1965:

We are sending separately by airmail the current prospectus and application form. We will certainly accept David Helfgott on your recommendation and I will correspond with him direct when the application form comes back. There is no need for a tape to be sent. It should be possible for us to allocate him to Mr Cyril Smith.

Mr Stainer noted that unless David were to be in the country in the week beginning 18 April 1966, he would be ineligible to compete for scholarships until 1967.

In January 1966 Professor Callaway wrote what appears to be a memo to Professor Fred Alexander in the Department of History at the University of Western Australia (and President of the Music Council of Western Australia) to bring him up to date on the 'Helfgott situation'.

Helfgott has now filled out the official RCM Entrance Application Form which needs to be in London by February 1. You will see from the copy of the attached letter from the RCM that Helfgott will be accepted on our recommendation and that it is likely that he will study with Mr Cyril Smith.

I think it important for us to discover if and how the balance of the money needed for the boy's subsistence in London is to be obtained. To this end I suggest you and I might meet with him and his father. In my last talk with David he revealed that there is a chance of an Eastern States relative being able to assist and that he would be able to clarify this shortly.

All the Helfgott children have talked about a shocking fight which took place the night when David made it clear that he was determined to go to study in London. When I first asked David about that night, when Professors Callaway and Alexander met with himself and Peter, he avoided answering, saying, 'Mustn't talk about the bad times. Got to be positive, is that the idea? . . . Got to be positive.' However, at a later date he had indeed become 'positive'. 'They tried to scare Dad. He said nothing. He was silent, he said nothing. They forced him to accept . . . it was incestuous.' I asked David if he knew what incestuous meant and he said he did. This was a somewhat dismaying development and had all the hallmarks of one of David's *double entendre* responses. I later questioned Sir Frank about this and he described the meeting with Peter Helfgott. 'I remember us explaining to Peter that the planned R.C.M. training would be to David's advancement, but more than that . . . no.'

Obviously something or someone convinced Peter that David should go to the college. Among the application forms for entry to the college the DECLARATION BY PARENT OR GUARDIAN IN RESPECT OF APPLICANTS UNDER 21 form is signed E. P. Helfgott and dated 22 December 1965. But the clause 'and will be responsible for the payment of College fees' is crossed out.

Referring to the scene of this argument in the film *Shine*, which is inspired by David's life, David says, 'They put it all together, all the fights . . . That's what they do, don't they . . . Do you know why, Bev?' I told him I did, that it was a matter of conveying an overall picture of events within a reduced time frame. This was something I suspect he knew all along. Because he measures time by the length of various pieces of music and concertos, he said: 'You can't play Rach Three in ten minutes, can you? The fight was that other night, not that night, the first time, the first night.'

Because the family had only mentioned one terrible occasion when Peter and David had fought, I asked him to be more specific.

'I was in the bath when he slammed the door . . . I knew it was going to storm. The family was running scared, beyond belief, beyond belief! Daddy gave me a back-hander and I wrestled with him around the house . . . I played the Liszt E-flat at the Capitol that night after the fight. Daddy was going to lock the door so I couldn't play . . . but Santa Margarita [Margaret] said she would get the police if he did. Santa Margarita saved me . . . Daddy shouted at me, "You won't win!" But I did, I did win, I did win the competition . . . I did win!'

The first time I spoke to Lady Callaway she urged me to believe whatever David might tell me because he is 'so innocent and so naive he simply doesn't know how to lie. It's not in his nature to lie. If he wants to tell you something you listen to him, and you believe him.' I agree that David doesn't lie. He may appear to be 'muddled', as Margaret says, and '[make] no sense at all', but it should be remembered that David is more intelligent than most and that most people who know him are charmed by this beguiling childlike man who commands their affection. Once caught in this trap, one becomes vulnerable to accepting as truth everything he says — or at any rate in danger of interpreting his clever one-liners and disjointed statements to support him. True, David doesn't lie, he tells it like it is, or was, rarely qualifying what he says. But the truth is found not in what he says but rather in what is left unsaid. On some occasions, David seems happy to allow his listeners — myself included — to misinterpret his meaning.

After having threaded my way though this minefield many times and drawn some conclusions which have since proven wrong, I quizzed him several times about the accuracy of his memory, but he remained adamant that this fight had taken place before he played in the 1962 state final of the Concerto and Vocal Competition.

This time it was evident that David had been subjected to horrendous pressure by Peter at a time when he was coping with the pressure to perform. Once again it was obvious that David, far from being 'emotionally fragile', was, as a teenager, able to produce a strength which many adults, under the same pressure, would find themselves unable to bring forth.

Margaret's version of the second fight, which occurred on the night after Professors Callaway and Alexander met with David and Peter, does not mention how, according to David, Peter, shouting and screaming in blind rage, pursued David through the house, chasing him from room to room, wildly swinging at him with a chair, trying to knock him down. Instead she recounts what appears to have been purely a bout of volatile verbal fisticuffs: 'My father said, "If you want to go overseas leave it to me. I have contacts and I will be able to arrange it for you and it will be done in the proper way and in a correct way." But David didn't want to listen to Dad. He was all sold on the idea of going abroad. I remember there was a terrible fight between David and my father, and my father shouting, and David insisting that he would go overseas and my father shouting, "If you want to go overseas I'll arrange it, you don't have to go to others, we'll do it within the family and it will be done in a proper manner." David was not interested and left home under this awful cloud of a terrible row and went to live with other people in Perth until eventually he went to London.'

When questioned about that night, David said, 'Daddy was cruel. Daddy was jealous.'

Because David was becoming anxious, I suggested that he calm down and talk about something else but he took no notice, saying, 'Mustn't get agitato, mustn't get agitato,' and repeating, 'Daddy was cruel, Daddy was jealous.' Seeing that he didn't intend to move to another subject, I asked him what Peter had done which he believed to be cruel and what he meant when he said Peter was jealous.

'Daddy was cruel. Daddy never stopped screaming. Got to concentrate . . . got to concentrate. Daddy never stopped screaming. I've told you before, Daddy was jealous . . . You're going in circles.' I agreed with him that each of us was going around in circles, adding that each of us had 'got to concentrate' — one of his constantly repeated expressions, along with 'got to survive, got to survive', and 'got to be positive, be positive, is that the idea?'

By this time I was becoming a bit 'agitato' myself but I decided to try once again and asked him just why he had said that Peter was jealous of him.

'Daddy was jealous and money, and money.' I assumed that David was saying he meant Peter was jealous of both his musical ability and his opportunity to go to London, and because any fame and money which might sensibly be expected to ultimately come David's way would be David's alone if Peter were not with him. However, I had misunderstood him.

'Daddy was funny with relatives. Johnno was a lovely man. They were very supportive. They despised Dad.'

Thinking we were now pursuing another line, I asked him why his relatives despised his father. 'Because Daddy was Janus, two-faced. They were rich. Some Jews are rich, some are not. Daddy was jealous.'

Knowing that 'Johnno' was Rachel's half-brother and David's uncle, and that he was a successful Melbourne businessman, I asked if 'Johnno' had contributed some money which he needed to support himself in London.

'Of course he did! And his father,' he answered, almost in relief. The implication was that I had been particularly thick not to have guessed before that Peter was jealous because Rachel's family were 'rich' and was furious with David because he had gone to them for money. Which, on reflection, explained Margaret's account of what Peter had said during that fight.

Because I wanted to be sure I had understood what David was trying to communicate to me, I repeated to him Margaret's account of what Peter had said to him that night. Hearing Margaret's words clearly shocked and stung him like a whiplash. Suddenly he snapped up, straight and tall, an unusual stance for David to take. For the first time I had a fleeting glimpse of another man, an indignant, angry man, a man I didn't know and one I never suspected existed.

'Daddy didn't have any contacts, he didn't have any friends overseas, he didn't have any money, he never had any money! But,' he said in a tone of almost vindictive triumph, 'I've got money!' For a few short seconds he maintained that confrontationist attitude, challenging anyone to contest the truth of his statement.

David says that when he left the house that night Peter screamed after him: 'Leave this house and you will be punished for the rest of your life and you will end up in the gutter.'

David was just eighteen, still an adolescent. Until that time he had employed not one but all the adolescent survival techniques, leaving him nothing else with which to defend himself from this searing, anxiety-provoking threat — it was 1962 all over again, only worse. In his highly charged, emotional state, Peter's words must have bitten into his soul like a curse, a curse hurled at him by a father who was supposed to love him.

Given that the defences David had employed to protect himself in the past and which had become strongly entrenched within his personality were now useless, and given his emotional immaturity, the confusion caused by Peter's violent attack would have generated even greater anxiety. He had no other choice than to submerge the memory of Peter's rejection by pursuing his own objective.

If Peter believed that he had convinced David of his inability to care for himself, and that David was totally dependent on him, he made an error of judgment by attempting to emotionally blackmail him to stay. For David defied him, leaving the house to live with Mr and Mrs Luber-Smith, two of his so-called patrons, for a period of approximately six months before his departure for London.

When David defied Peter by taking the opportunity to continue his advanced musical studies at the Royal College of Music, he too made an error of judgment. Although he had been given the financial means to be independent of Peter, he didn't understand himself well enough to know that financial independence and emotional emancipation are not one and the same.

12

'...And Then it is True'

David's elderly uncle Johnny Granek, a Polish Jew also born under the Russian flag, is a survivor of the Holocaust. Rachel's half brother Johnny came to Australia with his mother, Bronia, on the first migrant ship to arrive in Melbourne in April 1946, after World War II.

Johnny, who knew Peter for seven years before he took Rachel and the family to Perth, rounds out some of the family history from the Granek point of view: 'The first time we heard anything about the family after they went to live in Perth was when Isaac Stern said David should go to study in America. The next time was when Peter and David came to Melbourne for David to play in the ABC competition.'

While Johnny claims Peter and David stayed with him and his wife Helen during this visit, Rachel and her sister-in-law, Gertie Granek, verify that Peter and David in fact stayed with Rachel's brother Maurice (Morry) and his wife Gertrude (Gertie) when they visited Melbourne.

Johnny tells the story of how David was not allowed to put on his own shoes or to tie his own shoelaces, and enlarges upon it to include a report that David was not allowed to cut bread or butter it himself, nor pour himself a drink because he might hurt his hands. Whether Johnny heard all this from Gertie or Morry matters little. Johnny comments: 'At ten, eleven, twelve, thirteen, fourteen, David was a very capable pianist. He was not slow; he was made to be slow in those things. If you keep telling a child that he cannot do something, before long he believes it, and then it is true.' These comments do confirm that David, for whatever reason, was still having his shoelaces tied by Peter when he was fourteen. Did David learn to manage to master such mundane tasks before he went to London, where certainly he had to do these things for himself? Or did he simply drop his pretence of inability?

Accepting that there is an element of truth in Johnny's statement, one is tempted to wonder if perhaps, in David's case, the opposite could be equally true. Perhaps music lessons every night, over a two-year period, were akin to telling David he could play the piano until he believed it.

It seems possible that in his obsessive concentration on David's creative musical ability Peter did not insist that his son learn those simple skills which were essential for his self-sufficiency. I suspect that David was content with his unnatural dependency on Peter and his family and that this gave rise to his sisters' belief that David was 'slow'. Which would confirm Leslie's conviction that there 'was nothing wrong with David'.

Although Johnny was only eleven when the Granek family was split in 1938, he recalled that when Rachel left Poland at eighteen she was a 'very beautiful, lovely, charming, happy girl'. However, when next he saw her in Melbourne in 1946, three years after her marriage to Peter, 'She had changed, she was completely different. She was fearful of everything.' When compared with the atrocities that Johnny and Bronia had witnessed and suffered at the hands of the Nazis, what seemed to them to be Rachel's fear and Peter's overprotectiveness or excessive possessiveness, or both, were bewildering. 'We were shocked. We couldn't understand why this should be.'

In an effort to explain why it was impossible for himself and Bronia to comprehend Rachel's fear, Johnny tells their own harrowing story with overwhelming simplicity.

'In 1938 my father had to make a terrible decision: to leave Poland at any cost before the Nazi invasion. He left Poland with his two children Rachel and Maurice, because they were old enough to work, and left my mother and my two little sisters and myself. We were caught by the Nazis.

'When the Nazis came into Czestochowa they herded the people into the ghetto and separated them into two groups; the older people on one side, the young ones on the other. My mother and the elder of my two little sisters were with the older people. My mother was looking for the youngest, for Henya. My sister ran to the other side to bring Henya to my mother. That was the last time my mother saw either of them. They were murdered in Auschwitz.'

After the passing of some fifty-six years, Johnny blames no-one, philosophically blaming the hand of fate for what happened to his sisters.

'My mother was sent to Bergen-Belsen and I was sent to Buchenwald. In 1945, when the Nazis knew that capitulation was unavoidable, they took two thousand people from Buchenwald and sent them on what the Germans called a *Todesmarsch* [which means, in German, "death march"]. I was one of those people. We marched for three months. At the end of three months there were only 500 of us left. At the end of July 1945 they started us to walk again. We had been walking three, four days and nights non-stop. I was so exhausted, I started to walk backwards. I kept walking backwards. When I came to a soldier I said, "Kill me, please kill me." But the soldier refused.

He said, "You are young, you can run." He let me go and I ran into a forest and woke up four days later in an American field hospital.

'Just after the German capitulation, when I was able to leave the hospital, I went to Czestochowa to see if anyone was alive. As I walked there a man said to me, "What are you doing here? Your mother is alive in Bergen-Belsen!" I couldn't believe it!

'I hurried there and found her in that horrible place, lying in rotten, stinking straw with other people who had typhoid. They had been left by the Swedish Red Cross to die after they had taken to Sweden those they thought would survive. I took her out of there into the fresh air and looked after her and when she was better we came to Australia. It was like coming from hell to heaven.'

The immutable bond forged between Bronia and Johnny from that point in time was as the union between sun and Earth. Johnny faltered only twice while telling his story. Once was when he began to describe the stench and appalling conditions at Bergen-Belsen when he found Bronia. The second time was when, almost overcome with emotion, he said, 'Not once, not ever, have I ever been called a bloody Jew in this country.'

The reunion which took place between his father Mordecai, Rachel and Maurice, and Bronia and himself was strained and difficult. The eight years which had passed were as divisive as 800 or 8000 years. Neither group could understand the other. Although each had survived, only two of the four Mordecai had left in Poland had experienced, endured and survived the terror of the Holocaust.

Johnny and Bronia couldn't believe what had happened to Rachel; for them it was beyond comprehension that someone who had never experienced the horrors of war should be anything other than happy in this Land of Milk and Honey.

Johnny says that the relationship between Bronia, himself and Peter was cool right from the time they arrived in Melbourne. 'Peter rejected us. He refused to allow Rae [Rachel] to see her mother, although she wasn't really her mother. Bronia married Mordecai when she was seventeen after Rae's mother died. She looked after Rae from the time she was two years old. While Bronia was Rae's aunt, she really was like her own mother. Anyway Peter hardly joined us, he didn't want to know us. To the best of my knowledge we never sat down and talked. We were condemned by him.'

Peter's friend Ivan Rostkier first met Peter in 1937 and knew Mordecai, Rachel and Morry from the time they arrived in Melbourne in 1938. He gave me his account of the relationship between Peter Helfgott and Rachel's family and the events which led to the break between the two families. When I asked him if he had any idea why Johnny believed that Peter had 'rejected' him and Bronia after they arrived in Melbourne in 1946 his response was harsh and dismissive: 'What would Johnny Granek know, I'm asking you? He was only a boy of nineteen or twenty when he got here; he hadn't seen his father or Rachel or Morry for many years, not since he was a little boy! All Johnny would know was what they told him and that wouldn't have been much!'

As Ivan was 'asking' me what Johnny knew, or thought he knew, it seemed reasonable to tell him. At the same time I reminded him that since it was Johnny and Bronia who couldn't understand why Peter and Rachel seemed to 'reject' them, and since — as he had observed — a protracted period had passed during which much may have happened for which they could not reasonably be expected to take responsibility, he was perhaps being dismissive of Johnny without good reason.

'When the family came to Melbourne in 1938 Peter advised

them how to invest — they brought money with them, you know — they got rich. Anyway, Peter had a clothing factory, he started a company — Original Suits. Well, they were all in it and when it really took off they did him out of it!

'I knew Peter Helfgott and he was a good man,' Rostkier continued. 'He was a very clever man who could do anything; he made other people rich and he stayed poor. Peter helped to establish clothing factories, knitting mills and invented machines but his partners used him up. People made fun of Peter because he was so trusting but only after they'd got all they could out of him.'

Rostkier was unstoppable. 'I knew Rachel before she married Peter. She was a simple, honest girl but she had no self-confidence. She had her father and her brother — they were her bosses and she worked very hard for them — too hard. When Peter married her he took care of her but the family disowned her after she married him because he wasn't rich. And who made him poor, I'm asking you?' Before I could answer he was off again. 'Peter had a coffee shop and he used to sing and dance and play his music all the time. He was a happy man but his partner cheated him and Peter lost that too!'

By about this time I had heard enough to convince me that Peter had every reason to become disillusioned with the entire human race. When I got the chance I asked Ivan if he thought it might be possible that Johnny and Bronia, who had come on the scene after Peter and Rachel had broken with Mordecai and Morry, and after his marriage to Rachel, were only given a version of the truth which suited the circumstances.

He paused before he answered: 'It's possible, anything is possible when it comes to money.'

Ivan Rostkier's and Johnny's accounts of what happened do appear to have certain similarities. Johnny's account, which must have come from Mordecai, is this. When Peter married Rachel, he too had a clothing factory like the Graneks but above everything else he wanted to be an inventor. According to Johnny, Peter's driving urge to invent something which 'would make him very rich' led, through neglect, to the loss of his business. Following the loss Mordecai is alleged to have employed Peter because he was 'family', but Peter, still determined to be an inventor, spent most of his working hours doing very little work, in the belief that, as the son-in-law, he should be supported by the family while he pursued his dreams.

Mordecai, however, who is supposed to have been torn between attempting to support Peter and Rachel and his desperate need to save every penny to pay for his family's passages to Australia, is said to have reluctantly reached the decision that he could no longer continue to employ Peter. Johnny says Mordecai discharged Peter with a clear conscience, knowing that owing to the war and the resulting lack of manpower he would have no trouble finding alternative employment. Clearly, as Johnny and Bronia were not in Australia during the period referred to, this story must have been told to them by Mordecai.

Johnny's account, when aligned with Rostkier's, does seem to confirm that Johnny and Bronia were given only information designed to keep Peter and themselves apart and that Peter was probably a victim of guilty consciences. Rostkier's scenario answers a number of questions, in particular why Rachel didn't see Bronia and Johnny when they arrived and why she was so exhausted and in such poor health when she and Peter married. It also raises one or two other questions. Why did Mordecai leave half the family in Poland if he had enough money to bring with him to Australia to invest? And why did he and Morry work Rachel so hard if they were already 'rich', as Rostkier claims? Obviously there are no true answers to be had. However, it is not difficult to understand how Rachel became dependent on Peter.

While the Granek family believed then and still state that Peter was a wonderful father, Johnny questions what he calls his 'overprotectiveness'. It is Johnny's contention that Peter's strict control robbed his children of their childhood.

Ivan Rostkier lived close to Peter, and saw and spoke with him every day as the pair travelled to and from work. He says, 'Peter worked very hard and struggled to support his family but luck was not with him. Peter finally went to Perth to try to change his luck. 'Moving doesn't change your luck,' he observed, 'only you can do that, and Peter still found it hard in Perth. Peter was an exceptionally clever man, he changed his luck by hard work, he went to night school and got his electrical licence, not bad for a man with no real schooling who left home at fourteen!'

Perth might just as well have been on the dark side of the moon. The Graneks had no further contact with Rachel and the Helfgott children until David and Peter visited Melbourne for the Commonwealth finals of the ABC Concerto and Vocal Competition in 1962.

13

Privileges and Pianos

David maintains that from 1961, when Peter refused to allow him to further his studies in America, he and Peter barely spoke to each other. Both David and Margaret confirm that Peter's refusal was the basis of David's simmering resentment towards his father. It was this bitterness which fuelled his determination not to be diverted from his goal, breaking free of the family and Peter's dominance.

Margaret says that the relationship between David and Peter from 1961 was far from cordial and that David himself determined to take the opportunity when it arose to pursue his studies in London. Like Leslie, Margaret steadfastly maintains that all would have been well with David had he not been encouraged with 'outside interference' from people such as Sir Frank Callaway and certain members of the Perth Jewish community, like the Luber-Smiths. But it was, after all, David who was determined to make the break.

Margaret recalls, 'I remember there was a concert to raise money for David . . . and that was how he eventually went to London. At that time, David didn't want to have much to do with our family at all.'

A few years before Mordecai's death in January 1966, Johnny

took his father to Perth because the elderly gentleman was determined to see Rachel and his grandchildren before he died. The Helfgotts were living in Beaufort Street, Highgate. It was yet another stressful and uncomfortable reunion, a reunion made more disturbing for Mordecai who, according to Johnny, couldn't believe that his family was living in what to him were such dismal, substandard conditions. Louise confirms that the house in Beaufort Street 'was very dilapidated and I think it was at one stage condemned as unfit for human habitation'.

David also claims that he recalls Mordecai giving Peter money, which Peter took without hesitation, 'smiling all the while' and then 'stabbing the relatives in the back for giving him charity. The poor things had such a bad time. Daddy should have been nicer,' he says. Assuming Ivan Rostkier's account to be correct, David's assumption that Peter '[stabbed] the relatives in the back' was perhaps based on Peter's understandable response that he was being given much less than he was due — in fact charity!

It was necessary for David to call not only on Perth's Jewish organisations but also upon his grandfather, Mordecai, the 'eastern states relative', to raise funds.

Johnny is unable to confirm the details but he says he does have a vague memory of his father sending money to a Jewish society in Perth to contribute either to David's support or to his fare to London. He adds that the money was paid through the society so that Peter could not trace it directly to Mordecai, whose involvement would upset him.

Mrs Luber-Smith, together with two other women from the National Council of Jewish Women, called on Peter 'to inform him that the Council of Jewish Women would like to honour David with a concert; the father flatly refused, saying they would not accept charity and that he was opposed to David going to

London and would not give his consent.' It was only a few days later, Mrs Luber-Smith writes, that David 'phoned me from a phone box . . . and said his father had thrown him out of home! He was not allowed to go back; I advised him to come to our home at First Avenue, Mt Lawley. I then phoned a few friends to ask if they would put him up, but no-one consented. So David arrived with his suitcase. I told David my husband Philip and I had agreed he should stay with us until he went to London.'

I asked Mrs Luber-Smith if David couldn't tie his shoelaces when he came to stay with her and her husband. She laughed. 'Well, I can tell you I didn't tie them for him while he lived with us! My husband might have but he never mentioned it, I'm sure he would have if that had been the case. He was not a tidy boy and he had no etiquette nor any table manners but he was a very fast learner, it didn't take long to teach him. He wanted to eat with his fingers at the piano — he never left the piano if he could help it — I told him he had to use a knife and fork and sit at the table with us for meals. David told us he couldn't use a knife and fork because his family didn't have knives and forks, they just used their fingers! I couldn't believe they were that primitive! Anyway, when it came to it, David could use a knife and fork without any trouble at all. I just think he didn't want to leave the piano, or stop playing, using cutlery would have stopped that.'

The concert went ahead. The Jewish journal *The Maccabean* of May 1966 carried an article publicising David's forthcoming farewell recital, to be held in the Government House Ballroom on 17 May in the presence of His Excellency the Governor, Sir Douglas Kendrew, Lady Kendrew, and other distinguished guests.

When I asked Sir Frank Callaway about David's well-being before he went to England, he offered an opinion that at that time David was not mentally unbalanced but was highly excitable. He felt that there were problems with David's social behaviour, that he experienced difficulty in decision-making and that he could be quite unpredictable. There was nothing, however, to suggest that he, or the Trust, had any reason to feel disquiet about sending David to London alone. In a further discussion with Sir Frank I raised the possibility that David's lack of decision-making skills and his awkward social behaviour were the result of a childhood devoid of training, or experience, in these areas. He agreed, saying, 'It would seem that these idiosyncrasies would most likely be the product of his environment.'

The recital organised by the National Council of Jewish Women included the celebrated soprano Mollie McGurk and her accompanist, Stephen Dornan, David's former music teacher. The ballroom was packed to capacity and David was presented with £400. In addition Mrs Luber-Smith approached the Phineas Seeligson Trust, an organisation in the Jewish community that gives help to needy students. The trust provided David with all the clothes he would require, '. . . a tailored suit, sportswear, overcoat, shoes, underclothes, etc., befitting a gentleman'. Mrs Luber-Smith says, 'when David left for London he acted and looked like a gentleman'.

When I asked David if his family had attended the concert he emphatically answered, 'not likely! But my lovely KSP [the writer Katharine Susannah Prichard] did, and she never left Greenmount!' 'Greenmount' was the name of Prichard's home in the Darling Ranges, about twenty kilometres out of Perth, where she settled after her marriage to Captain Hugo Throssell. Today, Prichard's home is used as a writer's centre.

The same article in *The Maccabean* lists the many visiting musical celebrities before whom David had played: 'Abby

Simon, Isaac Stern, Daniel Barenboim, Julius Katchen, Tamas Vasary and Louis Kentner, all gave him encouragement and predicted for him a brilliant future.' It concluded: 'David has given generously of his talent to assist all communal causes and deserves recognition because of his devotion to hard work and determination to be a success.'

James Penberthy covered the sparkling evening and, as usual, was lavish in his praise of David. However, he criticised the ABC for not lending David its Steinway for the concert, noting that 'The piano, though the best available and generously donated, had bathtub tonal qualities.'

The *West Australian*'s music critic, Sally Trethowan, also covering the evening's recital, wrote:

> Mr Helfgott's farewell recital, given at Government House Ballroom last night, demonstrated that he deserves all the support that this music community can give him.

> He can already cope with bravura work of the most demanding nature, and indeed there was a touch of bravado in last night's choice of programme. Few experienced pianists would in one evening play Beethoven's 'Appassionata' Sonata, the Liszt 'Dante', a bracket of Chopin's Studies, and the Mussorgsky 'Pictures at an Exhibition'. Prudence would normally limit the choice to two of the above, with less demanding music to fill up the recital.

Ms Trethowan also was unimpressed by the offending piano:

> It is unfortunate that the piano used last night was a recalcitrant instrument of hard, dull tone. Mr Helfgott nonetheless coerced much exciting playing from it as he assaulted and demolished the technical obstacles liberally scattered through his chosen works.

> The coming years in London should do much to plane the rough-grained surface of Mr Helfgott's present impressive technique. Also his interpretive powers should be stimulated by a growing awareness and

understanding of what a composer is about when he organises patterns of sound into logical structure.

It would appear that Ms Trethowan and Leslie Helfgott shared the opinion that David needed the rough edges smoothed, although, had they met, they would have disagreed over his need to go to London for the final polishing.

Three months would pass after David gave his farewell recital before he was able to leave Australia for the United Kingdom. In June 1966 Mr E. Walton, secretary of the Music Council of Western Australia, wrote to Mr J. Stainer, registrar at the Royal College of Music, in answer to Stainer's letter to Professor Alexander requesting confirmation that David was intending to enrol at the college when the September 1966 term began.

> *I regret the delay in writing to you but it was not until last week that we were able to secure a firm booking for David Helfgott on the Himalaya, <u>scheduled</u> to leave Fremantle on 14th August. The underlining is made necessary by the seamen's strike and we may yet have to arrange for him to travel by air.*
>
> *In any event we expect to get him away in time for him to commence his studies with you in September.*

The seamen must have returned to work before 14 August, as a photograph titled 'David in Egypt', dated 11 September 1966, mounted on a family album page titled 'And so . . . Goodbye to Perth . . . (for the time being)', shows David, wearing a fez and a face-busting grin, standing with a group of people making the pilgrimage 'home'. They too are wearing the obligatory fez for the tourist's photo. Two ladies are shown perched somewhat uncertainly on camels, while another reclines on the noseless Sphinx overlooking the group and the ruins.

David says that none of his family farewelled him when he

sailed from Perth but he recalls that once again Katharine Susannah Prichard left Greenmount, this time to say goodbye and wish him well in London. Mr and Mrs Luber-Smith, who felt that David's three-month stay with them had transformed him, were also there to see him off.

David's departure brought about some significant changes in the Helfgott family. Margaret says, 'When David went abroad, suddenly I felt I could breathe again and it was okay for me to practise again. I went on to do my Associate in music in piano performing, and in fact began to blossom.'

Nine months after David left Perth, Margaret reached the state finals of the ABC Concerto and Vocal Competition playing a Liszt work with the West Australian Symphony Orchestra, conducted by Sir Bernard Heinze. She reminisces, 'I remember how excited I was because we were given a free trip [to Melbourne], of course, and we stayed at the Menzies Hotel. There were practice rooms and it was a big thrill for me.'

James Penberthy briefly waxed lyrical over yet another Helfgott pianist: 'The concerto finals judges of the ABC said that Margaret Helfgott's performance of Liszt's Hungarian Fantasy was magnificent by any standards; but didn't give her first place.' After the first paragraph, Penberthy devoted the rest of the article to David and referred to a photograph of the Helfgott family grouped around the piano: 'Mr Peter Helfgott, violin and Leslie 15, violin' and Rachel stand at the back of the picture, while 'Margaret, 22, piano', sitting on the piano stool, looks fondly at 'Suzie, 14, piano and soprano, [and] Louise, 7, mouth organ and piano'. (See illustrations.)

In the same article Penberthy made pointed mention once again of the $10 000, although this time he does not refer to the money as a fund, but as an offer: 'David is now in London on a scholarship given by the Perth people, but he could have gone years ago after publicity in the *Sunday Times* had resulted in an offer of $10 000 for his overseas study.' There seems to be a little confusion here, caused by the change to decimal currency. Whether the 10 000, pounds or dollars, was an 'offer' which Peter refused or whether the money resulted from a fund-raising campaign mounted by the *Sunday Times* will probably never be clear.

After David left Australia Margaret started to participate in the Guild of Young Artists of Perth programmes. Suzie says, 'Margaret was a brilliant pianist. It was terrible that Dad set her aside for David, only David. He wanted us all to play music and insisted that we did. However it was only David who was to have the career in his eyes.' In the absence of David, who had defied him, Peter switched his full attention to Margaret, concentrating on her music, fussing over her at every public appearance, now doing his utmost to propel her towards a musical career.

The following year, 1968, Margaret again competed in the state finals of what had now become known as the ABC Instrumental and Vocal Competitions. After winning, she was again flown to Melbourne to contest the Commonwealth final, in July 1968. She played the Rimsky-Korsakof Concerto in C-sharp Minor, with the Melbourne Symphony Orchestra conducted by Willem van Otterloo.

In November 1969, the National Gallery Society of Victoria presented a recital by Margaret Helfgott in the gallery's Great Hall. The programme included three pieces by Bartók, one Brahms, one Schubert, two studies by Chopin, one Liszt, two Prokofief. At that time Margaret was living in Melbourne and studying music under Ada Coder, later to be Mrs Ada Freeman M.B.E., teacher of the famous Australian pianist Nancy Weir. So it was that another of Peter Helfgott's children was to receive critical acclaim and to be recognised as a very talented pianist.

Margaret says that she left home sometime in 1969 and lived in Melbourne until the later months of 1971, only returning to Perth to spend the Christmas holidays at home. She doesn't say what caused her to leave. The fact that she made the break at a time when she was reaching her potential indicates that she wanted to be free to make her own choices and establish her own identity; or perhaps she realised that if she didn't take control of her life at that time it would become impossible for her to escape living out Peter's dream, a role which David had discarded.

Suzie says, 'We all broke with Dad. He wasn't interested in me at all. Margaret broke with him at sixteen, but then she came back when she was about nineteen and made her peace with him.' No-one speaks about what had happened between Margaret and Peter to create the schism. It is only obliquely referred to by Suzie, who says: 'Margaret is like Mum. She only wants to believe that everything was good. She won't admit, even to herself, that there were bad times, or what Dad did wasn't always wonderful.'

Johnny recalls that Margaret had a flat in Melbourne for a time and that he saw her often because 'she wanted to know more about her past.' He also says that living in Melbourne was good for Margaret, who found for the first time that there was an 'outside world'. It was a new experience for her, for until that time she had lived under Peter's restrictive rule. Peter's family was expected to accept his canon, 'The world is here inside my four walls.'

When David and I talked about Margaret he became quite intense, saying, 'Poor David and Margaret. The others were too young. Poor David and Margaret.

'For Margaret it was heaven and hell. Poor Margaret was very muddled. Daddy was a tyrant. I reckon Daddy was a tyrant.

Daddy gave privileges, pianos and privileges, but you pay a price for privileges, don't you? Always pay a price.'

'*Always pay a price.*' His last words hung in the air. Then, brightening, he said, 'You pay for privileges, don't you? But I'm very privileged. You and Gillian and Jocular John love me. I don't have to pay, do I?'

14

London

Mrs Luber-Smith arranged for David to be met at the ship by a member of the Hillel Foundation, a Jewish organisation which helps students. She says she was told that David didn't wait at the organisation's headquarters to be taken to the accommodation found for him. He was to stay at the home of Mrs Strauss, a widow who lived at 14 Rowdon St, Willesden. 'He was very independent, he jumped in a taxi and went straight to the address.' Rowdon Street runs along the top of a hill and at night would have had quite a nice view to the north of London. It is located on what might be called the better side of High Street. The house was set back from the road, had a bay front and a balcony, and was built of dark-brown brick.

In November 1966 David wrote to Professor Callaway. The letter contained profuse apologies and possible explanations as to how a letter which had apparently been sent to David by the University Music Council might have gone astray. After assuring Callaway that he would immediately fully reply to any questions asked when he received the missing letter, he went on to outline his current activities:

I like the College, Professor; and I feel that now I understand better the
implication of a concert pianist's career; and am more than ever

*determined to achieve it. I'm sorry I haven't written to you Professor, after
all you've done for me; but I am so engrossed; and I have an exam this
Friday in the History of Music; I am singing in the Bach B minor Mass this
Tuesday at the President's Concert; for Mr Smith I am preparing the C
sharp minor Prelude and Gigue (Bach) and Beethoven Sonata in C, and
there also will be grading tests to ascertain which grade you belong to.*

*Anyhow Professor, as soon as I receive the urgent correspondence, I
assure you I will answer immediately.*

Thanking you again for everything.

Regards, David

Professor Callaway answered David on 30 November, assuring
him that the missing letter concerned 'payment of the money
due' to him 'as the holder of the Board's Scholarship', and
making it clear that 'This money is in addition to that which you
receive through the Music Council.' The letter closed with a
request for David to give Mr Cyril Smith his best regards.

On 7 December 1966 David answered Professor Callaway,
relieved that the missing letter had not jeopardised his financial
support:

*Thank you very much for your letter; it took a load off my mind, because
Mrs Smith's [Mrs Luber-Smith] letter seemed to imply that all support for
me would cease, through no fault of my own. Mr Smith is a marvellous
teacher, but he's terribly strict, every note has to be perfect!! He's always
hammering away at the idea, 'discipline', which I am sadly lacking in.*

Smith, like Sergei Rachmaninof, who was a great friend of his,
lived by Rachmaninof's credo: 'Work, work, work.' The balance
of David's letter contains a list of the music which Smith had set
for him to work on over the Christmas holidays. Obviously
Smith was not one to allow his students time to think of
anything other than music; the fact that David had only been in

the country a few weeks clearly was not a consideration.

In his autobiography *Duet for Three Hands*, Smith writes: 'Drawing from my own experience I have always tried to impress upon them [students] these essentials; patience, will-power, an awareness of the possibilities of achievement and a colossal capacity for hard work.' These were what he considered the basic necessities for a pianist who would aspire to the concert platform. He was a concert pianist of note himself. Rachmaninof stated that he thought Smith gave the best rendition by an Englishman of his Third Concerto. Smith required much, much more than simply 'patience, will-power, an awareness of the possibilities of achievement and a colossal capacity for hard work'.

As evidence of his workload and his involvement in the college, David wrote:

Over the holidays I am to work at a Bach Prelude and Fugue, Beethoven's C minor Sonata (Op. 111) and Liszt's 'La Campanella', plus all the works we have done (or attempted) so far, i.e. Chopin's Scherzo No. 1 (E minor), Beethoven's Sonatas Op. 2 No. 3 (C major) and Op. 109 (E major), Liszt Sonata etc. etc. And I am doing exercises to strengthen my shoulders, arms etc., which is vital for a pianist. I like the college very much, tomorrow morning is the final rehearsal of the Bach B minor Mass, and in the evening is the performance. I sing the tenor, and enjoy it very much. I think the Mass is incredibly beautiful, 'Crucifixus', 'Sanctus' etc. My composition is still up in the air, but I hope it will come down to earth soon, I'm still on Counterpoint!!

Well, anyhow Professor, thank you very much for your letter.

Bye for now,

Best and warmest regards, David

Christmas 1966 came and went with no indication of how David spent it, except in the Christmas card he sent to Professor Callaway:

I'm on holidays now; and I'm really working hard. I'm really trying to achieve something worthwhile. Of course the piano doesn't give up its secrets very easily; it's a long and arduous road it seems.

Indeed, struggling to master the piano, a percussive instrument with notes which diminish as soon as they are struck, is a long and arduous road', but the boy from Western Australia had already traversed much of its distance for, as soon as he arrived at the college, he was immediately placed in grade 4B, 5 being the highest.

At the end of December, David wrote to Professor Callaway:

I am just writing to tell you that I sung the complete B minor Mass on Wednesday (today is Saturday) and I was pouring with sweat by the time it was over!! It was absolutely colossal, I've never enjoyed anything musical more, and I can imagine what it must be like for you; when you're conducting some magnificent choral work, what fantastic pleasure you must get from it!!

After mention of 'foolishly' attending a party he continued:

At the moment I am engaged in a complete overhaul of my piano playing, endeavouring to discipline myself to play in the correct way!! I hope never to play another note which hasn't been thought about.

Apart from his own music David was just beginning to discover the joy of attending London concerts and hearing great musicians perform, then impossible dreams for most Australians and little better now. 'Tomorrow night I'm going to hear Igor Oistrakh play the Beethoven and Shostakovich violin concertos, I think London is marvellous, so many things going on.'

In closing he became, once again, profuse in his gratitude to the professor for all his assistance. Despite the fact that he had written some four letters to Callaway between late November and the end of December 1966, he closes his letter with a curious statement. It seems to indicate that he had either forgotten he had written the earlier letters, or that someone other than Callaway had berated him for not sending more letters to the professor.

Perhaps this letter reflected his anxiety about continued financial support. For David, although he was 25 000 km away from family and friends in Australia, the pressure to perform was just as intense as it had ever been, perhaps more so. It seems that, possibly because of a remark by Mrs Luber-Smith, he was ever aware that he was at the college by the grace of the university, the Music Council and the Jewish community, and that he should gratefully acknowledge such support regularly, otherwise it might cease.

Professor Callaway's letter of reply to the young musician was kindly and encouraging:

5 January 1967

I was especially interested to know that you had sung in the B minor Mass, which must have been a great event in your life. It was a milestone in mine when I first encountered this remarkable work and I never fail to wonder at Bach's genius.

Keep working hard for Mr Smith and at all your paperwork and other things, for you have a fine opportunity to lay the foundations of a worthwhile career in music and we all know that you will achieve it.

Please give Mr Smith my warmest greetings.

It is disturbing to read David's early letters to Professor

Callaway, which are crammed with repeated avowals of almost abject gratitude and affirmations of his continuing efforts to improve, and his disappointments when his higher grade precludes his participation in scholarship examinations which would have supplemented his income. David's letters may suggest that Professor Callaway had for a time replaced Peter as David's father figure and become the symbol of all those whom David was obliged to please.

Going to London had changed very little for David. He was still under pressure to achieve but now, superimposed upon all his personal frailties and emotional intensity, the isolation of being in a strange land and his financial uncertainty, came the ultimate demand — he must totally embrace in all its nerve-shattering intensity a discipline which is primarily concerned with the emotions.

From the moment he played the Polonaise at the age of eight, David's life had been one long upward curve of unrelenting stress and anxiety related to perfecting his talent. It is surprising that those mentors who knew of his background failed to recognise his emotional vulnerability. If they did, then it is incomprehensible that he wasn't provided with some form of counselling, or at the very least given the opportunity to take an extended break from music, before he was catapulted into intensified study.

Focused as they were on the attainment of perfection of his so-called 'gift' or 'natural flair', which Cyril Smith said is never 'heaven-sent' but a matter of ability and effort, and then more effort and intensive, ceaseless work, these well-intending benefactors saw only the brilliant pianist and not the nineteen-year-old boy suffering from battle fatigue.

Although David gave the impression of being strong and happy, when he joined the college he had to make even greater and more unrealistic demands on his nearly exhausted nervous system than he had done in the past. Bolstered by his driving desire to be a concert pianist and by his passion for music, David forced himself to acquire the ever more constricting self-discipline Cyril Smith demanded from his students.

Smith, however, was not merely a disciplinarian, he was a teacher who gave much more to his students than mere technical knowledge. The intensity of his passion for music embraced intellectual and spiritual elements which he revealed in *Duet for Three Hands*, written after he suffered a devastating stroke which paralysed his left arm and to some extent his left leg, ending his own impressive career as an internationally acclaimed soloist virtuoso. For Smith it was the union between the brain, the soul and the hands, closely allied with the pianist's emotional life, which allowed the music, 'sometimes beautiful, sometimes utterly devastating', to flow from the pianist's subconscious through his fingers. This concept he attempted to impart to his students.

He insisted that they acquire enormous craftsmanship, which would allow their playing to become so automatic that their spirits would be free to interpret with integrity music written by composers two or three hundred years before, and to play it as originally intended.

Smith, as he reveals in his memoirs, was critical of concert-goers who thought that playing the piano was something of a pleasurable pastime from which the indulged pianist was fortunate to make a living. These people would never understand that the mind-bending, soul-tearing, continual seeking after infinitely subtle nuances and the sheer physical effort involved are not just facets of the concert pianist's life but almost his or her entire life. Neither would they understand that no matter how great he or she is, the concert pianist practises for hours every day; and sometimes, every now and again, the result of all this effort will be music which touches the soul of perhaps just one listener.

To have the audience respond to his playing is magic to the pianist. For David his greatest delight seems to come when his music makes someone cry. Tears, to David, are greater accolades than a thousand voices shouting 'bravo', for then he knows he has interpreted the composer's music in truth. Of course David enjoys having a good cry himself. He says it makes him happy, a statement which could perhaps be attributed to his 'emotional fragility'. This would be nonsense. When David cries he is responding to the pure emotion of the music and the magic of the moment.

As David plays he listens closely to the music he creates and he chats to himself, saying *sotto voce*, 'Must concentrate, must concentrate, think about every note, got to feel every note, every note is important, is that the idea?' Or on the occasions when he has executed a passage which he is pleased with, he says, 'That's nice, that's nice, darling, that's worth repeating.' As he murmurs these phrases and instructions, it isn't hard to imagine that he might have heard these very words long ago from his teacher Cyril Smith. Sometimes the odd classical music buff, or critic such as James Penberthy, will detect a passage repeated in a recital. Penberthy says he believes that David the 'genius' isn't concerned about what people think of his performance: 'genius and a general disregard for the impression eccentric behaviour makes on observers often go hand in hand. I believe that David is phenomenally gifted and exceptionally intelligent. I also believe that David found at a very early age that being eccentric, if you like, or different, worked well for him, it got him the attention he craves and left him free to do exactly as he liked.'

When David entered the Royal College of Music he crossed

the border into the world of the serious pianist. Surrounded by other gifted students, he found himself in an extraordinarily complex place where he had to learn to operate almost independently of any reasoning process and where he was required to master the technical aspects of his craft so thoroughly they become almost automatic. From that point Smith expected him to live in a world virtually ruled by intuition and intense concentration on every facet of music, simultaneously, at every level.

To quote Smith's memoirs: 'His [the pianist's] life is bound up with judging the quality of the sound, and sound is never pure, not even from the piano. The man sitting at the keyboard hears the hammer hit the string a fraction of a second before he hears the sound of the note, and this constant percussive sound is a tremendous strain on the nervous system. After several hours of practice I have often got up from the piano with my head ringing, unable to bear any more noise of any sort.'

In short, the concert pianist's world is for the psychologically and physically strong. David was physically strong when he enrolled at the college but psychologically he was on shaky ground. As usual it was difficult to get a straight answer from David when I asked him how he felt when he first attended the college. He gave what he sometimes refers to as 'stock answers'. The stock answers signify that not only is David not in the mood to play questions and answers, he doesn't intend to give the question a great deal of thought, or he has no intention of answering it.

Trying a more direct approach, I asked, 'Were you excited or were you apprehensive the first time you entered the college?'

'I really can't say, darling.' Then he muttered under his breath, 'Apprehensive, pensive! Is that the answer, darling? Apprehensive, pensive. Is that the answer?'

'I heard that, David. You were apprehensive and a little pensive? Is that the answer, darling?'

'You're playing games with me, Bev!' He laughed his peculiar laugh as he threw his arms around me, at the same time snuggling up in his most childish and endearing manner, laying his head on my shoulder for a second before diving up again, saying, 'Give us a kiss, you gorgeous creature!' (also one of his favourite requests). He planted a number of rapid, misdirected kisses on my cheek and forehead. When David manages to place a kiss in what he feels to be a satisfactory position he congratulates himself, laughing and saying, 'That was a good one!'

Almost everything David does is a contradiction. He is so sure-fingered and well coordinated when he plays difficult works which require great manual dexterity, yet he cannot manage to plant a simple kiss where he wants it to land. Constant personal contact is most important to David. While kissing, patting and hugging may be regarded as an expression of a tactile personality, David's unrestrained displays of affection towards everyone spring not only from a need to touch but from his deep-seated need to keep reassuring himself that he still has your attention and affection.

After I took a break from questioning to return his hug and his erratic, frenetic kisses David's mood changed and he seemed happy to go on.

'Apprehensive and pensive!' I said. 'Don't tell me that you were quiet, David. I don't believe that! Not you, David, you don't know how to be quiet!'

'Excited, I was excited! Is that it? Smith wasn't excited. Smith just said, "Concentrate and practise, and practise. Concentrate and practise and listen." Got to listen. Got to listen to every note and concentrate and practise, is that the idea?'

Clearly David was recalling his first months at the college. A letter which he wrote in February 1967 to Callaway confirms his memories:

Mr Smith has been pleased with the Beethoven Sonata in D minor; he says (did I tell you?) that my playing of it is 'excellent'; 'very fine' (this week's lesson) and 'superb' (last week's!!) Of course I've got a long way to go yet; but I think I've solved the problem, practising!! It makes me feel awful when I think of all those wasted years mucking around at the piano!! But what's past is past; and I am very happy with my present style of practising; which is mainly great concentration and intense listening, apparently everything depends on the brain!! If you're thinking clearly you can't go wrong.

If you're thinking clearly you can't go wrong: shades of Cyril Smith, who declared that 'all serious playing is a triumph of mind over matter.'

David goes on to write that he was going to a concert to hear Wilhelm Kempff play the Mozart Concerto in C Minor, 'which I have fond memories of'. And then, for the second time in the same letter, he declares his gratitude to Professor Callaway: 'I will always be grateful to you for this wonderful opportunity; and I'm doing my best to make the most of it. I look forward to that distant day when I can show you some concrete results!!'

Then he closes with: 'I went to see the Student Councillor last week; and he said I look in glowing health; and much better than in the 1st Term. I feel much better too!!' Until this point his letters held no indication that his health had not been good. This remark establishes the fact that the college had a student counsellor whom David had visited.

As his autobiography shows, Professor Smith was a practical, no-nonsense but highly sensitive man. Smith tells with touching honesty of the desolating depression he endured in the months following the stroke he suffered in Moscow in 1956. While

David was not showing overt signs of stress in the opening months of 1967, one has to wonder why, at a later date, Smith, himself no stranger to depression, did not accept David's assessment of his own deteriorating emotional condition, especially when David voiced his wish to consult a psychiatrist. Nor, it seems, did Smith suggest that he seek help from the college counsellor.

David's letter to Callaway of 9 March 1967 included the usual report on his work progress and the fact that he was going to as many concerts as his finances would allow. He wrote: 'I will have to miss some, because there are 150 being held this month alone!! 150 imagine!!' It also contained his second mention of his landlady, Mrs Strauss, and the fact that she was about to go away on holidays.

> I'm not terribly happy staying at Mrs Strauss's; I've been about 6 months here; and it's getting a bit wearing, but next month Mrs Strauss is off on her holidays; and I'll find a room (there's plenty about). However I hope to find a room; where if I install a cheap piano people won't mind!! But I believe this is almost impossible, so what can you do?!!!

Despite claims that David was unstable, there is not one shred of evidence in his letters to Professor Callaway to support this. His hand, if a little spidery, is perfectly legible; his spelling is excellent and his vocabulary is excellent; he crosses out nothing. Obviously by 24 March, with the prospect of moving to a new address and leaving Mrs Strauss, he was in good spirits:

> Dear Professor,
> How are you? I am well, and working hard. Mrs Strauss is leaving shortly; and this has necessitated finding a room which I have done; and I will be moving in after Easter. I will be able to install a piano there; and practise to my heart's content in the daytime and what's more the rent is

substantially reduced from what I have been paying (only £2/10/- as against £8!!) Actually Professor, I think I ought to tell you my frank opinion, I think moving in with Mrs Strauss was a mistake! It was wrong to prearrange an address with a family atmosphere (of which I'd had too much already back home!!) I am happiest when I am on my own; and have my privacy to work undisturbed; and with full concentration, in any case, how else can we hope to progress!! For me it is essential to escape from the Jewish Family Atmosphere?? (don't tell this to Mrs Smith!!) which I personally find repugnant. My experience at home conditions me this way; and now I am glad I have found such a suitable place (with a wonderful landlady!) I must buy myself a piano within the next few days (I have saved a little!) and get really to work.

In this letter David clearly expresses his desire to escape 'the Jewish Family Atmosphere', as he calls it. This strong rejection of his past conflicts sharply with statements later made by David and Suzie to the Australian press when he was struggling out of obscurity in 1983. At that time, 'missing his family' was offered as one of the possible reasons for his 'breakdown'. In 1985, when David had achieved a measure of balance and lucidity, he would give journalists a number of reasons for the breakdown, 'missing the family' not being among them.

In 1967, however, almost twenty years old, he was not simply turning his back on his family and his cultural heritage but making a bid for ultimate freedom from all the ties which had bound him. David Helfgott, the private person, preferring his own company, craving privacy, happiest when alone, was establishing his independence.

15

Hot with Chutzpah

In March 1967, David moved to 169 Chapter Road, Willesden, London. He wrote to Professor Callaway with the news that he had indeed bought a piano and was able to practise all day until about six o'clock, when the landlady's baby was put to bed for the night.

'That piano cost five pounds ten shillings and they carried it all over London just for me,' David told me. 'Imagine that . . . five pounds ten shillings to carry a piano all over London, that dreadful old piano cost me nothing! Nothing! But I prepared my triumph on that old piano, it was triumph, a triumph!'

'Your triumph? You mean the Rach Three?'

'It was triumph, a triumph.'

I assumed he was referring to Rachmaninof's Third Piano Concerto, which he was to play in 1970 with the Royal Amateur Orchestral Society and which by all accounts was indeed a triumph.

David was delighted with his new landlady, Colleen, whom he still refers to by the simple name 'Irish'. The Kilburn/Willesden area had at that time, and still has, a strong Irish population. Chapter Road is a congested, built-up, narrow street with house upon house quite close to the railway line. The house itself, probably Victorian or slightly later, is just like every other house in the street, narrow, with two rooms upstairs and two rooms downstairs overlooking a tiny front garden. It could very fairly be called 'on the wrong side of town', but to David it was a haven.

'I was alright with Irish,' he says somewhat wistfully, recalling his time in Willesden. As memory carries him beyond those 'good times', he continues: 'Mustn't talk about the bad times.'

Obviously his move away from the Strauss home put David in good spirits, as he wrote to Callaway:

I feel tremendously better physically and mentally since I left Mrs Strauss's; It was stifling there; the food was poor; mainly cake and rubbish like that; and 'You are what you eat' as all the dietitians tell us! Now I look after myself; and drink milk and yoghurt, eat fruit etc., do exercise every day and so on! And besides I have privacy here; which is essential to anyone; and especially to me and to any student attempting to achieve something! So to sum it up in a nutshell I think I've found the perfect lodgings!

He was attending as many concerts as he could afford:

Whenever I go to a concert, which is rather often; I usually buy the scores of some of the works being performed; I have accumulated over 20 miniature scores; quite a collection ranging from Respighi's Pines of Rome 'Pini di Roma' to Beethoven's 'Eroica' (I love this work!!); all Chaykovski's symphonies including Manfred. I adore the 1st movt. of the 3rd 'Polish' Symphony especially; I think the bouncing melody etc. etc. wonderful! [Here David has drawn five bars of music and notes to illustrate the melody which took his fancy.] Another work I love is the Suite No. 3 in G major; and especially the final polacca! I can't describe what I feel when I hear this! I have been to two Barenboim recitals (all Beethoven sonatas). What a pianist; and what a personality he's got! But he plays superbly!!

He is enjoying a vogue in London at the present moment; all the critics are ecstatic about him; all the seats are sold out at all his concerts (he conducts as well!); and he's only 24!! I wonder if when I'm 24 I'll be in such a lucrative position, I doubt it!! I learnt a great deal from watching him (and listening); even if he does thump the pedal in climaxes!! Arrau will soon be here; I'll have to buy myself a ticket for that!! By the way, Professor; another bad thing about Mrs Strauss's was that tea was always late; it was only ready round about 7.30; and if a concert starts at 7.30 or 7.45 or even 8 you will be late for it!! It was so inconvenient you see, why I missed some wonderful concerts; because I stayed in for tea. Two of them were a cello recital by Edmond Wurstz; (I had a ticket too!!) and Vladimir Ashkenazy in Brahms' 2nd Concerto; which was acclaimed!! I really was upset about missing that concert!! Well, bye for now, Professor; I am working hard for the summer term; and my grading exams etc. I hope I can win a scholarship!!

Yours with all my affection and regards,
David

This letter explodes the myth that David was 'completely helpless in practical matters'. The fact that he was able to find for himself suitable lodgings at a far cheaper rent where he could have the piano which he had bought with money he had saved does not speak of a person who was unable to cope with the real world. While it may have been true that, as a boy of fourteen, he had needed to be 'looked after, cooked for and cared for' (a necessity for most fourteen-year-olds), it was not true of him by the time he reached nineteen. As the letter shows, his attitude towards his nutrition was sensible and responsible.

There is little on record to indicate what David did between April and his next letter to Professor Callaway, postmarked 11 October 1967, except the official Royal College of Music report on his progress covering the 1966–67 year.

THE ROYAL COLLEGE OF MUSIC

REPORT ON STUDIES, ACADEMIC YEAR 1966–67

Mr David Helfgott.

Subject Piano. Professor Mr Cyril Smith: 'He has bursts of brilliant playing, but needs a steadier application to sound work and more attention to basic rhythmic problems.' C. S.

Composition/Analysis. Mr Kelly: 'A rather muddled year, a keen pupil but emotion dominates over mind and the results are hectic.' Bryan Kelly.

General Comments (where necessary): Nil (signed) Sir Keith Falkner, Director.

As there were no general comments, it would appear that Professors Smith and Kelly did not find anything particularly untoward in David's behaviour. Margaret, however, feels the subject comments made by Smith and Kelly, 'objective observers', clearly indicate David's 'emotional and mental instability'.

After a break of six months since his April letter David wrote to Callaway:

Dear Professor,
How are you? Gosh! I am so ashamed of myself, not writing for so long;
what you must think of me! But I always think about you a lot, Professor;
and hope someday to make it up to you for everything you have done and
continue to do for me. I can't put it into words, but I'm sure you
understand what I mean! I'm on tenterhooks now; as I have to play
Islamey next week at college (it's an evening chamber concert), I have
been putting in preparation for this; I do hope it goes off alright, as it's a
great opportunity to show what I can do (or can't do) as the case may be!!
Islamey is a difficult piece. (It's the first time it's been performed at college,
Mr Smith says.) Composition is coming along alright, Professor. I write
when I feel in the mood (i.e. when I have 'ideas', if you can call them that!!
and I don't write when I haven't any ideas!! (which is most of the time!)

*Today I played for a teacher (who was standing in for my regular teacher)
a piece which I thought wasn't too horrible and un-original etc., He had
very little criticism to offer. He advised me to extend it; and orchestrate it;
he thought it quite modern of all things!! I was quite stupefied to find
myself classed with the moderns, seeing as I have such a penchant for
imitating Rachmaninof, Tchaikovsky etc!! I started off with a discord, you
see, Professor [here David drew a bar of music, scored mostly above and
below the treble stave] and this [referring to the music he had notated] put
him on the wrong scent!*

*Professor, I have been down to Halstead to see Jack Lindsay the writer
(author of Early Life in Roman Egypt, Turner etc.) I had an introduction
from back home. They're wonderful people, the Lindsays, and they've
invited me down again. Naturally I feel very thrilled about it; last time I
was there, we talked about every imaginable subject, though music
cropped up large naturally.*

Well bye for now Professor; again my apologies for not writing sooner.

All of my most affectionate regards, David

Artist Norman Lindsay's son, Jack, poet and author of twenty-
five books, arrived in England in 1926. He was accompanied by
Jack Kirtley, the publisher of his first book, *Fauns and Ladies*.
The two had come to London, with Norman Lindsay's blessing
plus some backing, to establish a publishing venture, the
Fanfrolico Press. They planned as their first publication a folio
of Norman's private erotic writings and illustrations. The writer,
political activist and Rhodes scholar P. R. Stephensen, better
known as 'Inky' (subject of Craig Munro's biography *Wild Man
of Letters*), soon became involved in the press, deposing Kirtley.
Stephensen and Lindsay were responsible for some controversial
publications during the period in which they formed the
Mandrake Press, and were thought to be involved in
revolutionary (communist) groups, as they had been in earlier
days at the University of Queensland.

Apart from their bias toward communist philosophy, Jack Lindsay and David Helfgott shared one or two things in common. Jack had arrived in London carrying letters of introduction from his father, letters which did not open doors as he had hoped but left him standing in the long shadow cast by Norman Lindsay's fame. The letter of introduction which David carried from Katharine Susannah Prichard, however, obviously unlocked the door of the Lindsay home, where he was warmly welcomed. Both David and Jack, although for different reasons, experienced the psychological stress created by dominant fathers. Jack, who was in his mid-sixties when he met David, had by then forged his own creative identity. David was still searching not only for his creative identity but for an identity divorced from Peter.

Then on 26 November 1967:

Islamey went off very well; I've had a lot of favourable comment on it from my fellow students and in spite of a few wrong notes etc. it was alright because I wasn't a bit nervous on stage; one friend told me he'd never heard me play better! (But I said there were quite a few faults!)

There are two big BBC piano competitions coming up next year, Professor! Mr Smith says I may enter both; but I'll have to really work hard! One's a Mozart competition, first prize is £500 + concert appearances; and you have to play a Mozart Concerto (I think I'll do the C minor) and a Mozart Rondo, some modern music etc. at the different stages of the competition. The other competition is wider in scope; I'll get the programme from the BBC and see exactly what you have to do. This could be my opportunity if I really work! Of course I don't think I have a chance; but there's no harm in trying! Professor, Thank you very much for continuing to support me in the coming year, I'll do my best to really get some results; I had a good piano lesson this week; on Brahms, B flat concerto. Mr Smith says it is hanging together very well; and he was generally very pleased! I love this concerto! It's magnificent from beginning to end; one tremendous outpouring, it reminds me of the ocean! Well I must close now Professor, or else I shall be late for college.

P.S. I heard Louis Kentner's recital at the Queen Elizabeth Hall last week! He is terribly good. Islamey was magnificent; his Mozart C minor Fantasy was glorious and the Schumann (Op. 17 Fantasy) was great!

In May 1968 David played two works in the final competition of the Royal Overseas League Music Festival: Balakiref's *Islamey*, a very fast, very complex, difficult and vivid oriental fantasia, based on exotic strands of melodies, rhythms, and harmonies of Russian folk music; and Mozart's Rondo in A Minor, which, like the Adagio in B Minor and the Fugue in G Major for piano, is an harmonically audacious work consisting of one main theme or tune alternating with other themes or sections. Mily Balakiref was the leader, and the only thoroughly trained musician, of a group which became known as the Russian Five, or the 'mighty five'. The other members were Borodin (a brilliant chemist), César Cui, Mussorgsky and Rimsky-Korsakof. The five invented a specific harmonic style and type of orchestration in a successful bid to establish the principles of what they felt to be truly Russian music, colourful enough to portray the vivid scenes they had in mind.

Although David didn't win the competition he was delighted that he had reached a level of expertise which Smith agreed was sufficient to allow him to enter. David and Smith had been working hard at bringing *Islamey* to something like competition standard for over a year. The previous year, on 9 March, David had written to Professor Callaway reporting on his progress with the elusive piece:

I had a lesson with Mr Smith this morning on Islamey. I 'murdered' it because I went to bed too late the night before; but Mr Smith said there wasn't another pianist in England who could play it like that (I think he meant that it was so bad!!) and then he modified his remark saying very

few pianists in England. But I didn't finger it thoroughly; and Mr Smith
had a few words to say about that!! From now on I am going to finger
every note I play!! I am determined to!! I have to struggle against all the
bad habits accumulated over the years in Islamey, but I know what's
wrong, and that's the main thing. Mr Smith said either I'll do 'miserably'
or I'll carry all before me (in the forthcoming exams), depending on how
hard I work!! I hope it's the latter!!!

Then, because David thought he should qualify his earlier statement: 'He [Smith] didn't use the word "miserably" but something like "not very well!" '

In August 1968, Professor Callaway wrote to Mrs Muriel Fels, thanking her for allowing him to see a letter written to her by the renowned Australian pianist Eileen Joyce:

As you know, I have been pretty close to the various projects that have
helped David Helfgott and in fact laid the way for his going to the RCM
and Cyril Smith in particular. Last month I saw David in London and
talked about him with Sir Keith Falkner (Director of the RCM).

Miss Joyce's interest in David could well be just what the boy needs at
this time. There appears to be genuine keyboard talent there but it is not
yet sufficiently backed by poise as a person. This lack is probably the
result of his early background and we all hope that he will now quickly
mature in the non-musical attributes so necessary for the eventual success
on the musical side.

If Miss Joyce is able to encourage David she would not only be helping
him personally but also the musical development of her own home state of
Western Australia. It would also be splendid if we could give Miss Joyce
the names of other young West Australians who go abroad from time to
time.

Eileen Joyce had been 'discovered' by the Australian-born, American-naturalised, composer and pianist Percy Grainger. She enjoyed the great good fortune of being sent to Germany, where she studied under the eminent German pianist and teacher Robert Teichmüller, who spent forty-two years on the staff of Leipzig Conservatory. Later she studied in London under Tobias Matthay, a man of formidable talent who closely observed the physical and psychological aspects of piano playing, developing a scientific and artistic system of piano teaching. Eventually he wrote several books on his theories. Joyce also studied under Artur Schnabel, a man with many and varied musical accomplishments, who had edited and recorded all of Beethoven's sonatas.

Given that Eileen Joyce had herself benefited so much from Grainger's initial patronage, it seems that Professor Callaway may have been hoping that she might take an interest in David, even if that interest only consisted of encouragement. However, her interest in David did not go beyond listening to him play and then only because 'Smith insisted.'

I asked David what Eileen Joyce's reaction had been to his playing. David indulged himself in his reply. 'It costs a fortune, I reckon it costs a fortune. You've got to be grateful, it costs a fortune. You know raggedy Eileen said, "You've got to control it, David. It will be marvellous if you can control it." '

Then, in an aside to himself: 'If you can control it, David, I reckon it will be marvellous. Concentrate. Got to concentrate. It costs a fortune. You've got be grateful. You've got to be grateful. You're too exuberant, David. Too much chutzpah. I was full of chutzpah then. Jumping up the stairs three at a time! Full of chutzpah!'

The year closed with his report:

THE ROYAL COLLEGE OF MUSIC

REPORT ON STUDIES, ACADEMIC YEAR 1967–68

Mr David Helfgott.

Subject Piano. Professor Cyril Smith: 'He has extraordinary pianistic talent, but his work is ill-organised and spasmodic.' C.S.

Composition/Analysis. Mr Bryan Kelly: 'Enthusiastic, but convinced that emotion is more important than mind.'

General Comments (where necessary): Nil (signed) Sir Keith Falkner, Director.

'Ill-organised and spasmodic', 'enthusiastic, but convinced that emotion is more important than mind': these comments didn't faze David Helfgott, the exuberant boy from Western Australia with 'extraordinary pianistic talent'. He was hot with chutzpah.

16

Medals

In 1968 David had played Beethoven's D Minor 'Tempest' Sonata, Chopin's Etude Op. 25 No. 11 'Winter Wind' and Balakiref's *Islamey* in competition for the Marmaduke Barton and Hopkinson Silver Medal Award. But it was not until 6 July 1969 that he received a letter from the Royal Amateur Orchestral Society notifying him that he had won.

> *Royal Amateur Orchestral Society*
> *Founded 1872*
> *Patron: Her Majesty The Queen*
> *Dear Mr Helfgott,*
> *Silver Medal Award*
> *On behalf of the Royal Amateur Orchestral Society, I am very pleased to confirm that you are the winner of our Silver Medal Award for 1968.*
> *You are invited to appear as soloist at one of the Society's concerts next season and I will contact you in due course.*
> *With my sincere congratulations on winning this competition and every best wish for your success in the future.*
> *Yours sincerely,*
> *Ann C. Kelynack*
> *Honorary Awards Secretary*

On the back of this most cordial letter can be seen the first of David's extant doodlings. These are odd assorted shapes and images of wavering circles, jagged triangles and squares, an elongated bed-like structure with jagged triangles rising above as in a bed-head, and something which looks as if it could be an axe. There is also an attempt to draw an elevated view of a car and truck on a road which winds before what seems to be a large building with small windows. Perhaps these doodlings may hold the key to David's abiding passion for talking about 'the cars in Trafalgar [Square, London]' and in other major cities such as Chicago and Paris.

In the first scrapbook which David kept there is a photograph (probably taken some time after receipt of the letter) clipped from the *West Australian* newspaper of himself, head bowed, suitably demure, receiving his Silver Medal from the Queen Mother. The caption reads:

> *Young West Australian pianist David Helfgott receives from the Queen Mother the Marmaduke Barton Prize and the Hopkinson Silver Medal at the Royal College of Music, London. Next to the Queen Mother is Sir Keith Falkner, director of the Royal College of Music. A bursary from the W.A. Music Council helped Mr Helfgott to study at the college and this will be his last year there.*

On 18 July, the day following his first public performance in England of Rachmaninof's Third Concerto in D Minor, he received a letter from J. R. Stainer, registrar at the Royal College of Music:

> *Dear David,*
> *Congratulations once more on your performance last night and I am glad to tell you that you have been awarded the Dannreuther Prize for the best performance of a piano concerto during the year. I enclose a cheque for £13.*

I have some more good news for you: you have been awarded a
Leverhulme Scholarship which is tenable for the coming academic year.
The value of the scholarship is £500. In other words it provides free tuition
and £245 towards your living expenses. I am writing to Mrs Luber-Smith
to give her this news.

On the same day Mr Stainer wrote to Mrs Luber-Smith in Ireland, where she and her husband were staying:

Dear Mrs Luber-Smith,
I am very glad to tell you that the Director has approved the award of our
Leverhulme Scholarship to David Helfgott. It is normally tenable for one
year but might conceivably be renewed for a second. In other words it
provides a year's free tuition plus £245 towards living expenses.
I wish you could have been here last night. David had a wonderful
success with his concert and I have not heard a bigger ovation since I have
been at the college. This performance has earned him the Dannreuther
Prize for the best performance of a piano concerto during the year. The
value of the prize is £13.
Thank you for the interest you take in David. I wonder if you would
kindly let me have your address in Australia.

Shortly before the 1969 Christmas term began, Mr Stainer also wrote to Mr Walton, secretary of the Music Council of Western Australia, the one person, aside from Professor Callaway, he conceivably should have first contacted concerning David's progress:

5th September 1969
Dear Mr Walton,
David Helfgott
David Helfgott has done excellent work during the last year and we have
been very pleased with his progress. It is certainly essential for him to
continue his studies here for a further year and I am glad to tell you that

Above: David's mother, Rachel, on her wedding day, Melbourne, 1944.
Below: Rachel and Peter Helfgott with baby Margaret. On the left is Rachel's father, Mordecai Granek.

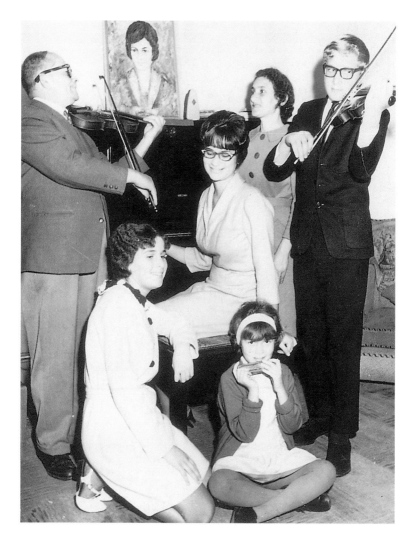

Above: The Helfgotts in 1967, about nine months after David's departure for London. *L-R* Peter, Rachel, Leslie, Margaret seated at piano, Suzie and Louise.
Left top: Leslie, Peter and Suzie Helfgott outside Highgate State School, Perth, 1961.
Left centre: L-R David, Rachel holding Louise, Margaret, Leslie and Suzie.
Left bottom: David being tutored by Peter at the time of Isaac Stern's visit to Australia in 1961.

Left: The Royal College of Music, London, where David studied from 1966 to 1970.

Above: The Queen Mother presents David with the Marmaduke Barton Prize and the Hopkinson Silver Medal at the college in 1969. At the rear are Sir Keith Falkner (Director, RCM) and Mr J. R. Stainer (Registrar, RCM).

Above: David practises with his long term friend and teacher Alice Carrard (then 84), in 1985.
Below: With the music critic James Penberthy ('Lord Jim').

David plays the classics at Riccardo's, Perth, 1984.

Above L-R: David, Gillian, Rachel, Leslie and his wife, Marie, and child, Mel (Louise's husband), Louise, Suzie and her husband Bill.
Below: With his wife Gillian (right), and the author, Beverley Eley in 1994.

Above: With Kirsty Cockburn at a Leuwin Estate Music Festival.
Below: At home in the Promised Land.

we have been able to award him a Leverhulme Scholarship here, which is
the to value of £500. This will cover his fees and the balance, which will be
available towards maintenance, is £245. It is very desirable that your
Trust should provide the additional amount to bring up the maintenance
to what it has been before. I hope you will be able to do this.

David gave a splendid performance of the Rachmaninof Piano Concerto
No. 3 at the end of last term and received a standing ovation for this.

Yours sincerely

J. R. Stainer

Registrar

Both of Stainer's letters, which are so positive in praise for David
and his progress over the 1968–69 college year, are surprising in
that the report from his music masters for the corresponding
period does not imply such satisfaction. Judging from the
somewhat confused tone of Smith's remarks on David's report,
he may well have been questioning his decision to accept David
as his pupil. Bryan Kelly, his composition master, had obviously
reached the end of his patience:

THE ROYAL COLLEGE OF MUSIC

REPORT ON STUDIES, ACADEMIC YEAR 1968–69

Mr David Helfgott.

Subject Piano. Mr Smith: In many ways he is, even now, scarcely
reliable, never having his feet placed quite squarely on the ground, but
there have been moments and even minutes of near genius.' C.S.

Composition. Mr Kelly: 'Mr Helfgott is, without question, the most
frustrating student I have ever tried to work with. Being totally
undisciplined, incredibly sloppy, and oblivious to suggestion, he has
produced no single, complete, meaningful piece of music. Behind his
incomprehensible (but often delightful) exterior, there seems to be
considerable talent but it is thoroughly confounded by his approach to
things.' Lloyd (last name illegible).

General Comments (where necessary): Nil (signed) Keith Falkner, Director.

Despite, or because of, all the exciting events taking place in his life David did not find time to write a letter to Professor Callaway until 12 December 1969:

Dear Professor,

Sorry I haven't written to you for such a long time; and I do hope you will forgive me! I attempted the Brahms 2nd Concerto last week, and it could have gone much better, unfortunately. I was in a very bad mood (what shall we call it, end-of-term malaise!!), but still I think generally speaking I had the right approach. I may get a concert yet! (doing it with an orchestra, that is). And I have to do Ravel's Toccata and miscellaneous other pieces at Luton soon, These will go well I'm sure. I've been accompanying some violinists lately, it's great fun, very enjoyable, one violinist in particular is exceptionally brilliant, just tosses off Moto Perpetuo like a 1st grade exercise! We'll be doing concerts together next term, I hope! Rubinstein has been surpassing himself lately, imagine doing 3 Beethoven concerti (3, 4 & 5) in one night at the age of 82!! Well he did it, and superbly, If only I could have heard him play before I did the Brahms, I'm sure I would have played better! He's full of beans, the master of the keyboard, I shook hands with him afterwards, Professor; and told him I would never forget that memorable evening! Professor, how's the weather over there? Here it has been rather icy lately, snow, plenty of snow, rain etc. All in all it's distinctly unpleasant! How have you been keeping? And your wife and family? Anyhow, I take this opportunity, Professor, to wish you and your family a lovely and happy Xmas; and a prosperous New Year!

Yours affectionately,

David

P.S. I have been writing all my 'compositions'?? in full score lately, as I think it's much better than a mere piano score! It's more impressive: 22 staves as against 2! Not that I use 22 staves all the time; 5 or 6 is more the general rule!!

What do you think I ought to do during the holidays, Professor?

Practising and composing is naturally what I intend chiefly to do, this should occupy me fully!

Bye again!

David

Margaret also corresponded with David in this period. 'During the initial years when David was in Britain we received letters from him which told us of his difficulties abroad. He was always cold in the winter because he was unable to budget properly and frequently he had no money because he spent his last five pounds on a front-row ticket for a Rubinstein concert rather than look after himself, buy food or pay the rent, and his letters in fact revealed much confusion and distress and unhappiness.'

This is rather curious, as in his letters to Professor Callaway, not once over three years is there a word or any indication of 'much confusion and distress and unhappiness'. In fact, as David says himself, he was 'full of spirit, full of chutzpah'.

David says that he didn't often write to the family, certainly not in the early days, and that when he did he really only wrote to Margaret. Margaret, however, says he also wrote to Peter from London. I asked him if he complained, 'kvetched', in those letters to Margaret about the cold and a lack of sufficient funds to buy food and pay the rent. In short, did he ever write telling her that he was unhappy? He was surprised that Margaret had taken this impression from letters which he termed 'chatty'. Unfortunately these letters have been either destroyed or lost with the passing of time.

Later, because I was unable to sight the letters from David to Margaret, I put the question directly to Sir Frank Callaway, asking him whether David might be capable of writing to him only what he believed Sir Frank would want to read. At the same time perhaps he was writing Margaret totally different letters which could have led her to believe that David was confused, distressed and unhappy. Sir Frank chuckled his quiet, warm chuckle and replied, 'No, not David, he couldn't, he wouldn't know how!'

It does appear, then, that a certain confusion, or misinterpretation, exists about David's emotional condition at that time. The following letter from Mrs Luber-Smith to Mr Scott Hicks, the director of the film *Shine*, would support this. Mrs Luber-Smith is a highly respected and accomplished member of the community, having served on many boards for many good causes. Age, and the twenty-six years which have passed between the time she and her husband were involved in David's affairs and March 1995, when she wrote to Hicks, are reason enough for any inaccuracies which appear to exist in her recollections.

In reference to the six months during which David lodged with Mrs Strauss, Mrs Luber-Smith writes:

> *David lived there for about three and a half years when his landlady asked him to find other accommodation as she was going abroad on a holiday for a short time. Although David could have been helped by the Hillel Foundation, he found himself some appalling dilapidated dirty accommodation and had no piano!*

> *David wrote that his final year was coming to an end and did I think he could have an extension of a further 12 months. My husband and I then decided we would go to London to see David & look into his affairs. After a few days in London, I had an appointment for an interview with the Bursar at the Royal Academy & at the conclusion of this interview, the Bursar informed me that they never grant a scholarship beyond 3 years, but they would see what they could do. After a few days, the Bursar phoned me to advise me that the Board had given consideration to David's request and agreed to extend his scholarship for an additional 12 months. I then asked the Bursar if it*

would be possible to give accommodation to David at the College; this the Academy agreed upon & we had the satisfaction of leaving London with David living in a good environment & the desired extended scholarship.

There was already evidence that Stainer wanted to support David's continued studies at the College. There was his letter to David notifying him that he had won the Dannreuther prize and the Leverhulme Scholarship; his letter to Mr Walton of the Music Council of Western Australia which stated, among other things, 'It is certainly essential for him to continue his studies here for a further year'; and his letter to Mrs Luber-Smith, which says, in reference to the Leverhulme Scholarship, 'It is normally tenable for one year but might conceivably be renewed for a second.' Through Mrs Luber-Smith's intervention, David obtained not just an extended scholarship of one year but a possible two years in excess of the standard three-year scholarship at the Royal College of Music.

By the end of 1969 he appeared to be heading for what promised to be a spectacular career.

17

Triumph and Trauma

At the age of twenty-two, David performed Rachmaninof's Third Concerto in D Minor at the Royal College of Music with the Royal College Orchestra, on the evening of 17 July 1969. It was a triumphant performance which began a traumatic twelve months, a period which saw him slide from the heights of elation into depression and frustration. The twelve months ended with a disturbed and disappointed David coming home to Perth in August 1970 to a father who he claims initially rebuffed him and a mother who couldn't help him.

How could such a brilliant beginning to his fourth year at the Royal College of Music end so badly? What went wrong?

The only way to come close to some understanding of what took place between the end of 1969 and July 1970 is to trace the known events which occurred during that period. And to do this we must go back to the memorable night when David performed Rachmaninof's Third Piano Concerto.

Trying to talk to David about this period was extraordinarily difficult. Such conversation was made more torturous by the fact that previously, when a disturbing memory visibly upset him, I had told him that if something was too painful to discuss he didn't have to talk about it. Subsequently many topics, for a variety of reasons, suddenly became 'too painful'.

On a number of occasions when I tried to get David to talk about the events of that last year, he responded that it was 'too painful'. Having consistently failed to break through by using tactful means, I decided it was time to employ a direct approach:

'Okay, David, it's gloves-off time,' I said with a confidence I didn't feel. 'Stop playing around and tell me what happened. If you don't tell me, someone else will and it probably won't be the right story.'

'It's all too painful, too painful,' he said, pulling a miserable face as he turned to walk away, protecting himself with a storm of unconnected, indecipherable, scatter-shot chatter. I realised that if I couldn't come up with a softer appeal our conversation would either end or turn into a conflict of wills, a competition which I knew I couldn't win.

'You know, David, you could help a lot of young people by telling your story. You have survived your tragedy and triumphed. It takes courage to do that. You've always been courageous but some people need to know about other people's troubles before they can find their courage.' If David had identified what I had said as 'preach speech', I would have deserved it, but he didn't.

'If I can have a glass of lemonade I will cooperate.'

This wasn't the answer I had anticipated. Sugar and caffeine have a 'hyper' effect on David: too much, and he plays very badly and becomes even more erratic and incomprehensible. The Helfgott house is the only place I know where the sugar, tea and coffee are kept in a briefcase with a combination lock. Nothing with sugar in it escapes David's notice. If he is searching for a 'lift' he will drink an entire bottle of concentrated cordial when he finds one left unguarded. Each morning he is allowed three tea bags, 'monsters' as he calls them. Managing

David's moods is a difficult act. Too much caffeine or sugar and he is uncontrollable; too much medication and he is far too sluggish to play, not enough and he becomes rebellious.

I have witnessed the disturbance created in David by sugar and caffeine and know that to grant his requests for these substances can be irresponsible, especially if he is already in hyperactive mode. Yet I cannot avoid feeling that refusing is unfair treatment of an adult. Saying 'no' to David, who can be most appealing, on those social occasions when everyone else is drinking and eating whatever they wish is extremely hard. I found myself in this difficult position when he asked for the lemonade. I deliberated on my need to know and tried to assess his mood. As he appeared calm, I decided it was worth taking a chance with a glass of low-calorie tonic water. He agreed this would be a suitable substitute for lemonade. Then he spied the coffee plunger. Coffee being his first and greatest addiction, he said, 'If I could have a plunger, darling, I'll tell you.'

Feigning outrage, I told David, 'That's bribery and corruption! Are you asking me to bribe you with coffee?'

'Yes!' he answered, laughing his peculiar laugh, hugging me furiously. The coffee went down in double time. I asked him once again what had happened to cause such a rapid decline.

'It all got to be too much, just too much,' he answered simply. 'It was a tragedy, Beverley, an historic tragedy. It's too painful. But I reckon we have to cherish these times together . . . it's a privilege, it's a privilege. It costs a lot . . . very expensive . . . very expensive. Got to be grateful, got to be grateful.'

Once again David was going around and around in his private circle of language: 'it's too painful', 'it costs a lot, it's very expensive', 'got to be grateful', and 'it's a privilege'. He was using all his key words, including, 'I reckon you've got to be aware', which he has phases of repeating several times a day.

As usual, to understand what David was saying it was necessary to associate his seemingly unconnected phrases not with questions concerning the unknown but with what was known. To do this successfully is like cracking an especially complex code. Sometimes making this connection is impossible but when one does achieve it, it is a rewarding experience.

Although he repeated several times that it 'was too painful', he did not deny that he had slowly slipped into depression or that his behaviour had consistently become more and more unbalanced from mid-1969 through 1970. Each time David said it was 'too painful', he repeated it in conjunction with, 'I reckon you've got to be aware; got to be grateful; it's a privilege. I reckon you've got to be aware . . . Is that the idea? It costs a lot, it's very expensive . . . very costly.'

It was then that the full implication emerged of what David was saying and what he had been saying ever since I have known him. He seemed be telling me that being constantly aware that he had to be grateful for the costly privilege of studying at the college and living up the expectations of those who made his study possible had become all too much for him to cope with.

Attempting to establish if David thought his depression was the result of loneliness and absence of family, I asked him if he had had friends at the college. He answered in his usual repetitive fashion: 'Of course I did! Of course I did! They said I should have gone to America, it was paradise, a paradise of music, I knew that! But Daddy wouldn't let me go to paradise!' When I asked if there had been a girl, or girls, in David's life then, the answer came back much the same. This time he recalled an association with a young student who, although he didn't really remember her name, he did recall played violin. Then he volunteered an assessment of himself: 'I was a loner, a bit nervous, a bit nervous sometimes, but a bit of a loner really I suppose.'

If David had been identified as 'a loner', as he describes himself, by those busy people who knew him for the years leading up to his breakdown in 1970, then the changes to his personality signalling emotional problems most likely would have been virtually undetectable.

Despite his growing tension, David scaled his Everest. Because of mental turmoil and his inability to reach out and communicate his need for sympathetic assistance from those around him, it was inevitable that a wild toboggan ride down the other side was waiting. Little wonder that, aside from the other very personal emotional dynamics creating turmoil in his life at that same time, the entire episode was 'too painful' for him to talk about.

If you tell David now how superbly he has played, he will usually say, 'Well, I reckon it was very nice.' Then he will immediately rattle off his key phrases, which I believe is his way of saying: 'I was aware, I was grateful, I know it was costly and I didn't let anyone down!' These are the times when understanding this gentle, sensitive, lovable man, who lives for his music, who believes he should be forever 'grateful' for 'privileges' he didn't demand, makes it difficult for a listener to remain objective.

Cyril Smith in *Duet for Three Hands* writes of Rachmaninof's Third Concerto:

> The most difficult of all his piano music is the third concerto, which I have recorded and played to audiences many times. Learning it was as big a challenge as the Brahms B flat had been. For just as the Brahms is the greatest classical concerto, so this is thought to be the greatest virtuoso concerto. It is the most technically exhausting, the most physically strenuous of all. It has more notes per second than any other concerto, a lot of the music being terribly fast and full of great fat chords. Many performances are marred because soloists simply cannot

carry on, and Rachmaninof, himself, after playing it one night at the Queen's Hall, came off the platform shaking his hands up and down and muttering, 'Why have I written so difficult a work?'

Smith also writes of the intense physical effort required to play the Rachmaninof Third:

Clifford Curzon once calculated that since every note of the piano weighs about 2 oz, playing an ordinary concerto is as physically arduous as moving a ton of coal. Rachmaninof's third concerto is like moving ten tons of coal.

Rachmaninof and Smith each had a span of twelve notes. David has a span of nine but has no difficulty in playing Rachmaninof's Third Concerto. As he proudly points out, he can play C, E, G, C and top E with the right hand, starting with the second finger, with the left thumb underneath the right hand.

Smith also records:

The two opening bars of orchestral music are rarely played fast enough. Rachmaninof, playing at the Queen's Hall, was waiting for his cue, when to his intense disapproval, the orchestra started slowly. He put his head down, ignored the lot of them and entered at his own speed, which was about forty per cent faster than theirs.

Depending on the interpretation, Rachmaninof's Third Concerto is approximately forty-one minutes and forty seconds of unbelievable melodic beauty charged with escalating, palpable tension. For the listener this tension becomes almost unbearable when the work is performed by a gifted pianist who intuitively identifies with the composer. It is a work which should not be played by the pianistic athlete just because it is a challenge, for without true empathy the magic of Rachmaninof's poetry is destroyed. Clearly Rachmaninof's Third Concerto is not to be attempted by the faint-hearted, the physically puny or the mentally unstable.

David was just twenty-two when he was awarded the Dannreuther Prize for the best performance of a piano concerto at the Royal College of Music for the year of 1969. The piano concerto was Rachmaninof's Third. At the same time he was awarded the Leverhulme Scholarship. Roberta Dodds, who was the college's lady superintendent at the time, recalled that she was in the audience: 'I was present at the college when he played so magnificently and he is one of the few performers who have received a standing ovation in my time.'

Mr J. R. Stainer, registrar of the college, who was also present, wrote: 'David had a wonderful success with his concerto and I have not heard a bigger ovation since I have been at the college.'

When David talks about that performance he does so with a mixture of excitement and nostalgia, but more with excitement.

'The hall was packed with all the professors and the students. Smith said it promised much, so the hall was packed, the word had got around. They were all there expecting an historic performance. It was inspired, inspired. Well, it all clicked together. Well, it was historic. Historic tragedy.'

There was no need to decipher what David was telling me about that night. His success is engraved in his memory.

'They shouted and cheered and stood up and stamped and banged their chairs on the floor. Sellick [Mr Smith's wife, Phyllis Sellick, who was also a concert pianist of great ability] said it was compelling, unprecedented, scarcely credible and unique. Not to be repeated. It was the highlight of highlights.

'Smith said I was near genius. Smith gave me a ride in his car,

*Angelinski, yes he did. And Sir Keith Falkner was very proud of me ...
I won him over for all eternity when I played the Rach Three. Sir
Keith said my potential was limitless. I was celebrated after I played
the Rach. Historic performance. The greatest performance ever.'*

Then he paused, talking to himself:

*'Just once in your life you should be happy with the most wonderful
performance in all the world, shouldn't you? Smith said he was proud.
Smith had the best practice room and the best piano. He had three
pianos, all Steinways. His left side was paralysed, you know, he used
to push me aside with his left side . . . shove me along the piano stool
when he wanted to show me something. He brought out all the voices
I'd never heard and made me find my own interpretive solutions.
Lessons were wonderful with Smith. It all worked out that night.
Stayed on the right track. I'd do anything to improve, anything.
Sellick was impressed. She called me "that genius" when I played the
toccata. Sellick was impressed because I was so fast, played it twice as
fast, and it was three times as good!'*

Then his excitement passed and he became thoughtful. 'It
worked while I was there. I reckon it worked, for a while; 1966
was a vintage year, 1966, 1967, 1968 and a bit in 1969.' Then he
said wistfully, 'I played so wonderfully then. All this,' waving his
arms towards the garden and the lagoon in the Promised Land,
'is a reward because I lost America.' David never refers to
America as 'the states' and will correct anyone who does so.
'America', another of David's key words, is for him synonymous
with El Dorado and frustration.

On two known occasions David had experienced prolonged
periods of intense frustration both of which had promised him
much but which had produced nothing more than extreme
anxiety. The first of these occurred between the ages of six and
eight when he desperately wanted to learn to play the piano and

was being pushed by Peter to do so; and the second was in 1961, when Peter refused to allow him to go to study in America.

His reference to America, coming unexpectedly as it did and tied, as it was, to what he believes to have been his crowning performance, seemed somewhat incongruous. However, that performance, which Cyril Smith said 'promised much' and which David also refers to as an 'historic tragedy', once again, for the third time, led only to an exhausting frustration.

David says that he should never have stayed at the college to complete a fourth year of study. That year 1969–70 he was left almost alone, receiving very little direction from Cyril Smith. David says he felt he should have had more lessons. For whatever reason, it would seem he didn't clearly understand that the previous years dedicated purely to study were past. The time had come for him to make the transition from student to performing student; he would receive diminishing direction during this period, in which he was expected to establish his career.

However, while Smith recognised David as a genius or 'near genius', he didn't realise that David and he were at cross purposes. He probably also had no way of knowing that David lacked practical experience in organising mundane matters such as arranging bookings and scheduling engagements. Even the simple act of keeping a diary and regularly referring to it, basic managerial clerical work needed to establish and advance a career, would have been difficult for David, simply because his entire being was centred on music alone.

Two classical musicians, one a harpist and classical guitarist, the other a pianist, both confirmed to me how difficult, if not impossible, it is for a performing artist to prepare for a recital without someone to take care of their schedule and the routine running of their day-to-day life. Preparation for a recital requires at least eight hours of practice a day of the one piece for perhaps months, depending on the magnitude of the work. Both these musicians were stunned to hear that David had been virtually cast adrift and expected to maintain and progress his career alone; and both understood, without knowledge of his background, why he had collapsed under the pressure.

For Cyril Smith the end of any performance released him to work on his next. Smith claimed never to have looked back on past performances, good or bad, only forward in anticipation that the next would be the best he had ever done. Perhaps if Smith had been able to impart this attitude to David following his 'triumph', when he was so emotionally fired with his success, it might have helped him to focus more on the future.

One can only conjecture as to what might or might not have happened if David had received instruction on how to manage his professional life during that fourth year. Perhaps practical guidance was all he required and, once a routine had been set in place which embraced more than practice, he might well have eased himself into the professional world.

Perhaps he also needed counselling from an expert who understood the potential for psychological distress that any young artist who receives sudden, overwhelming acclaim may suffer when he finds, just as suddenly, that fame is fleeting. Possibly neither counselling nor practical assistance would have proved adequate unless the anxieties persisting from David's childhood were also addressed. There are no simple answers, but we do know that David for whatever reason, experienced crippling frustration, which destroyed his confidence and undermined his potential.

Some time during this desolate period, following his magnificent performance of Rachmaninof's Third at the college, while wandering aimlessly in Hyde Park in search of the warmth of human companionship, he found a substitute for care and understanding in a brief homosexual encounter, from which he contracted gonorrhoea.

For David this episode is definitely 'too painful' to discuss. Unfortunately, while some degree of homosexual experience is common to many young men, and thousands of creative people are proud to be known as practising homosexuals, David still has a problem accepting this episode. Sadly, he felt compelled to write to both Professor Callaway and his brother Leslie to assure them that he was not involved in any homosexual activity. Perhaps his letters were written in an attempt to forestall any questions which might arise when, or if, Callaway and Leslie discovered that he had been admitted to hospital for treatment of his gonorrhoea. Because David was reluctant to talk about this incident in any detail, he refused to name the hospital he attended, saying only that it was close to the college. I assume it to have been Royal Brompton Hospital.

Emotional trauma followed emotional trauma. While David was in hospital he received a parcel. When he opened the parcel he found it contained all his letters and other objects which he had given to Katharine Susannah Prichard over the years and the news that she had died on 2 October 1969. His 'lovely KSP', the intelligent, educated, motherly woman who had opened her home and her heart to him and encouraged him to believe in himself and to further his studies, was no longer there to come home to. The news of Katharine's death, coming as it did at a time when he was stressed and confused, almost destroyed the excruciatingly sensitive David.

The already shaking foundations of his world began to crumble, but even so, despite this extreme emotional pressure he was able to take some control of his life after his discharge from hospital. The only constant in life is change. Scarcely had he returned to his lodgings to take up the strands of his life when he had to move from 169 Chapter Road, Willesden. This move was made necessary by the imminent birth of Colleen's second child and as a consequence Irish's need for David's room.

On or around 17 December 1969 David took a room at the Royal College of Music's Robert Mayer Hostel, in Evelyn Gardens. Notes taken from one of the entries in the David Helfgott file kept at the college library, author unknown, show: '17.xii.69. Told him he could enter Robert Mayer Hostel at once. To ring Dr Carabine before 9.10 on Friday morning to make arrangements. Single room £63 p. term.'

The loss of the continuing security of permanent lodging, where he had been happy in an undemanding family environment for over three years, contributed heavily to David's growing, empty feeling of isolation and loneliness. His sense of desolation was exacerbated by the Christmas season, an emotional time for anyone but made worse by the fact that he felt he was somehow an outcast, cut off from rest of the world at a time when he most needed companionship and compassion. Despite the fact that David is Jewish, albeit not 'observant', he enjoys Christmas, which offers an excuse for him to partake in what he calls a 'festiva'. Taking part in festivals, religious, birthdays or otherwise, gave him a sense of being embraced by society. However, Christmas 1969 was quite different, for he found himself in the cheerless atmosphere of the almost deserted Robert Mayer Hostel. The majority of boarders had gone home to their families for the Christmas holidays and as his letter dated 17 December 1969 to Professor Callaway shows, he was at a loose end, with no plans for the Christmas holiday period other than to practise and compose.

And practise he did, for six hours and more each day, not only over the holiday period but for the balance of his time at the college. According to Roberta Dodds, 'He practised for hours at the Robert Mayer Hall and rather "hogged" the practising room.'

On 1 March 1970 David wrote to J. R Stainer:

Dear Mr Stainer,

Firstly I hope you and your wife are in fine health and enjoying life as I am. And, To be quite frank; I can't thank you enough for all you've done for me!!

Secondly, I would be very much honoured if you and your wife could come to the Duke's Hall on the 24th of March at 8 p.m.; and on the 24th of April. (7.30). It would be a real thrill for me; and a great honour.

Yours sincerely,

David

David played Rachmaninof's Third once again on the evening of 24 March at Duke's Hall, Royal Academy of Music, with the orchestra of the Royal Amateur Orchestral Society. Founded in 1872 by the Duke of Edinburgh, who became its first president, the society is the oldest of its kind in England. There is no record of whether Mr and Mrs Stainer attended the concert. However, Roberta Dodds commented on David's performance that night:

I was also present at his performance with the RAOS at the Duke's Hall, Royal Academy. Like others, I was embarrassed by his performance, which was so histrionic that I could not concentrate on the music. It was not a balanced effort.

There are no other comments available except David's, who says, 'I did not play very well that night.' This confirms that his playing was not of the same standard as his performance the previous year at the college.

Cyril Smith believed that a pianist was subject to many variables which dictated the quality of his or her performance. Among these he included biological factors, emotional disturbances and intellectual input. Given this he believed that every performance is the best that a pianist is capable of at any given time. In view of David's growing tension and frustration, his 'histrionic' performance is not surprising.

However, on 24 April he performed Liszt's Piano Concerto No. 1 in E-flat with the Essex Youth Orchestra to a full house of 8000 at the Royal Albert Hall. This was the first time that all the members of the orchestra, in addition to the conductor and soloists, had given their services to raise funds for the Christian Medical College and Hospital in Vellore, South India. The proceeds brought a record £2000. Her Royal Highness Princess Alice, Countess of Athlone, dignified the occasion with her presence.

David Chesterman of the Buckinghamshire *Examiner*, under the heading 'Albert Hall sold out for Vellore concert', wrote of David's performance:

> The concert ended with a sensational performance of Liszt's extremely difficult First Piano Concerto by the young Australian pianist David Helfgott. He completely identified himself with this romantic music, his fabulous technique in the louder passages being equalled by the exquisite poetry of the more lyrical places. I am not in the least surprised that he has been recently awarded the Silver Medal of the Royal Amateur Orchestral Society.
>
> The Australian Government certainly acted wisely when they sent him here to develop his rare talent under the guidance of some of our best professors of the piano.

The year before, David Chesterman had attended David's first performance to raise funds for the Amersham branch of the Friends of Vellore. On that occasion he had played at Germains, hosted by Mr and Mrs Biro, and Chesterman wrote:

> David Helfgott is a man who, once seated at a piano, moves straight into the world of music, oblivious of everything else. Certainly the

highlight of the evening was his performance of Mussorgsky's 'Pictures at an Exhibition'. His technique cannot be faulted, though his interpretive ability does not yet match it; for instance, when in an art gallery, one does not thunder from one picture to another. But Cyril Smith, Helfgott's teacher, will soon put this right. 'The Great Gate of Kiev' was absolutely thrilling in its intensity, and though during the final climax Mr Biro may have feared that his fine Bechstein would disintegrate, we safely reached the resounding E flat major chords which terminate this wonderful piece of programme music.

Clearly, if Chesterman's assessment of his expertise is to be accepted as professional, then David's technique and his interpretive ability had acquired its final lustre between his first Vellore concert at Germains some time in 1969 and his second at the Royal Albert Hall on 24 April 1970.

The 'histrionic' performance mentioned by Ms Dodds must have been an aberration, for his superb performance of the Liszt No. 1 in E-flat at the Royal Albert Hall brought him an invitation from the League to perform at Terling Place. This was the home of Lady Rayleigh, David was advised, 'You will be the guest of Lord and Lady Rayleigh for the night. Lady Rayleigh will arrange for you to come back to London on Monday morning either by car or train.' That night, Sunday 14 June 1970, David played Beethoven's 'Appassionata' Sonata and 'Feux Follets' from Liszt's Etudes d'exécution transcendante.

Ms Dodds, who drew up a report on David early in October 1974, writes:

I knew him quite well and he came to see me from time to time. He was in the Robert Mayer Hall for a while, but went there as a senior student and just dashed in and out so that the Warden (Dr Carabine) could not know him well at all.

I liked him very much but there was no doubt that he was unbalanced emotionally.

One of the things I advised him about was food. When he was at the Robert Mayer Hall, he existed on muesli and milk because he could not cook. I pointed out that as a concert pianist he must build up his strength and eat a balanced diet. He then started to have college lunches as well as proper meals and said he felt much better. He told me all about his father and obviously had a complex about it all. He was being treated by a psychiatrist and was taking sedatives under his guidance, but was very vague about this. Obviously he considered it was his own affair. He was not treated by the doctor at the Imperial College Health Centre, I have checked on this. The centre has no record of his name.

I spoke with Miss Phyllis Sellick this week, wife of his professor, the late Mr Cyril Smith. She tells me that her husband was against him seeking psychiatric help. Although David was most undisciplined, Mr Smith's insistence on self-discipline had a marked effect. This resulted in his splendid performance in college. Afterwards he went to a psychiatrist, and developed this father complex. Although Mr Smith told him to forget it and put it behind him, Miss Sellick feels that the psychiatrist dug up this history most unnecessarily, so that David went downhill and lost the ground he had gained. Finally he had to leave college, as you know.

I have been unable to trace his doctor or psychiatrist and know only that he went to group therapy classes.

Ms Dodds' statement that 'there was no doubt that he was unbalanced emotionally' is perhaps valid and consistent with his behaviour. However, it does not reflect on his mental stability. Mentally dysfunctional people are rarely, if ever, aware of the need for psychiatric treatment, and are most unlikely to seek help of their own accord, as Ms Dodds reports David did.

A number of misconceptions concerning the state of David's

mental health while at the college need, for his sake, to be corrected. It was David himself who sought and obtained psychiatric help, not the college, as myth would have it. Neither did he suffer a 'nervous breakdown'. Although David expressed a desire to seek psychiatric counselling when he first entered the college, he was not supported in his decision to do so by Cyril Smith. In fact Smith, who was opposed to his seeking psychiatric assistance, was instrumental in delaying what might have otherwise proved to be successful treatment until it became necessary, as Ms Dodds' report shows, to treat David with sedatives.

Now we arrive at the biggest single problem in David's last year at the Royal College of Music: the use of sedatives. Here, I believe, is the reason for his appalling performance of Rachmaninof's Third on 24 March. David, now sailing on his own, in an attempt to deal with the tension that had built up in his life from many and varied sources, sought help from sedatives which instead visited upon him his greatest affliction.

Anyone attempting to function under the influence of sedatives, medications which, almost thirty years ago, were not as sophisticated as those available today, cannot be expected to be reliable or organised. In David's case, it would have been impossible to perform demanding musical works without experiencing enormous frustration and the distress which comes from knowing that under such circumstances he had performed badly. Sedatives by their nature slow down physical, mental and even emotional responses, all of which are crucial to the musician's art.

It is difficult to discuss with David his use of sedatives during this period. When I asked him if he could remember the names of the drugs and whether he took more than one type, he replied, 'I don't know, lots and lots, I don't remember.' And then he said reflectively, 'Cold water wakes you up. Lots of cold water. Lots of water.' From this I can only conclude that he must have tried to counteract the effect of the sedatives by dousing himself with cold water.

It isn't surprising that he doesn't remember; perhaps he has simply shut out the memory. In view of his stress and confusion then and in many of the intervening years, and his evident distress when asked these questions, to have pressed him for further information about that shadowy, dark time would have been brutally insensitive.

By July 1970, as David said, 'it all got to be too much.' From the age of six he had continuously coped with continuous pressure, much of it from himself. In 1961, aged fourteen, he experienced great frustration when Peter, who had to that time given him everything, refused him permission to go to the Curtis Institute. Peter's reason was that David was 'impractical and unable to care for himself'. In so many ways, David clearly was not these things. But if they formed part of a persona he had adopted, then could he be said to have become victim to his own persona? In 1964, when David thought he had achieved his goal to study overseas, Peter refused him permission yet again. This time Peter's refusal had been violent and verbally cruel. It is possible that at this time an important part of David's great ambition became gaining supremacy over his powerful father, against whom he may have felt much anger. Once again David managed to hold fast to his ambition — leaving home against Peter's wishes, he pursued his goal and won. However it was a pyrrhic victory.

After the applause died David found he had no goal left to achieve and worse — he had not secured his place in the sun, he had to practice and work hard to establish his career, alone. The world was not clamouring to receive him as he had expected —

he still had to work to achieve the acclaim he thought would naturally be his after his 'triumph'. In London he was only one of many talented students. Once again David was frustrated and angry, only this time with no goal to achieve. Fighting the sedatives which killed his ability to sensitively interpret his beloved music, his slide into depression was inevitable.

It was not a lesser soul who cabled Professor Callaway: 'I WANT TO COME HOME NOW, PLEASE.' It was a battle-exhausted young man, crippled by his own expectations and the expectations of those around him.

18

I Want to Come
Home Now, Please

THE ROYAL COLLEGE OF MUSIC

REPORT ON STUDIES, ACADEMIC YEAR 1969–70

Mr David Helfgott.

Subject Piano. Professor C. Smith: 'His life has been so disordered and chaotic that pianistic progress has only been allowed sporadic opportunity. Nevertheless, such fantastic hands have sometimes produced almost unbelievably brilliant passages.' C.S.

Composition/Analysis. Mr Kelly: 'A calmer approach wanted in work, a very hectic year.'

General Comments (where necessary): 'Best wishes for a successful career. You have had many ups and downs, some brilliant and some less so. I hope you will have great success and be able to stabilise your life and work. Keep in touch.' Keith Falkner, Director.

This was David's last report. It seems 'general comments' only came at 'graduation'. Three days after receiving it, on 9 July 1970, David wrote to Professor Callaway:

Dear Professor,
I am writing to find out if I can come back to Australia as soon as possible.
I can't survive out here.
 All my best regards and affection,
 David
 P.S. Could you convey my best regards to Prof. Alexander.
 P.P.S. I am starving; I have no money; no job; nor any accommodation
after next week.

This was followed on 13 July 1970 by a sad cable received in Professor Callaway's office: I WANT TO COME HOME NOW PLEASE, DAVID HELFGOTT. Lorna C. Trist, Callaway's secretary, answered:

Dear David,
Your cable message to Professor Callaway was phoned through to this
office this morning. You are probably not aware that Professor Callaway
is overseas at this moment in Moscow. He will not be visiting England at
all this brief trip so your message will not reach him until he arrives back
at the office next weekend.
 In his absence I took it upon myself to pass your message on to Mr
Walton, the Secretary of the Music Council, who informed me that he had
just sent off a draft of money to you. Will this affect your attitude about
remaining in England? Perhaps you could send a note to Professor
Callaway to reach him when he arrives home next week.
 Yours sincerely,
 Lorna C. Trist

David wrote to Callaway, again in Perth, on 18 July:

Dear Professor,
I am writing to ask if I could come home as soon as possible. I feel at the
present moment this is the best thing to do.
 I hope you and your family are well and thriving.

Looking forward to hearing from you,
All the best,
David

Professor Callaway answered David's letter on 6 August 1970:

Dear David,

I am sorry I have not written before this but, as you are aware, I have been overseas. Unfortunately I did not get to London this time, so missed seeing you. I am aware that you are now keen to come home and I expect that Mr Walton of the Music Council will be making the necessary arrangements. You will appreciate that the financial aspect of things is not my concern but rather that of the Music Council. When your plans are made and you know when you will be arriving in Perth do let me know, as I will be keen to do anything I can to help get you established in Australia. There will be difficulties, of course, but all artists have to face up to such problems and I only hope that appropriate opportunities will be forthcoming in your home country.

I was very pleased to hear of all your successes at the Royal College of Music and I know how proud Mr Cyril Smith and Sir Keith Falkner have been of all your achievements.

With best wishes,
Yours sincerely,
Frank Callaway

While these letters and cables were flying between London and Perth, Mrs Luber-Smith wrote to Johnny Granek, David's uncle in Melbourne, on 16 July.

Well, it seems that David's career has reached a climax. I am enclosing copies of letters received from our Perth rabbi, Dr S. Coleman, David's teacher, Mr Cyril Smith, and a letter I received from David himself, which seems to confirm that David is psychologically unstable and unless something can be done to overcome this mental frustration, he will never attain the desired success of his talent.

One of the copies Mrs Luber-Smith enclosed was of a letter written by Rabbi Shalom Coleman to Alex Breckler, the businessman who David says Peter believed had wished to 'steal' his family when they first arrived in Perth from Melbourne. Why the rabbi wrote to Breckler at this time and not to Mrs Luber-Smith or any one of a number of other people who had been directly concerned with David's career is unclear.

It is David's belief, however, that when he showed his independence by breaking with Peter to go to London, Breckler renewed his interest in his career. He also says that Breckler had tried to provide the money for him to go America to study in 1961. I asked David if it had been Breckler who had offered to donate the mysterious, now somewhat mythical, $10 000. All David would say was that Breckler was 'as concerned and anguished' about his welfare, and the welfare of the other Helfgott children, then as he had been in the early days. Because he refused to give me a direct answer, I raised the question with him again a few days later.

'I told you!' His response was sharp and short, quite uncharacteristic.

'I don't recall exactly what you said, would you like to tell me again?' Even before I finished speaking I felt ashamed of myself for treating him like a child. At the same time I realised that David not only forgets nothing, he also knows when a mind game is afoot almost before it starts.

'Yes, you do! You wrote it down! You know you wrote it down!'

I was embarrassed. I knew it was useless to press him for a yes or no to my question about Breckler. At that time I had been talking with David and questioning him about his past for some months. Throughout this period he had never recanted or given me a version of any incident which varied from his first or second account, even though I had often confronted him with another person's interpretation of the same event. Given his honesty and his consistency, and now his indirect avoidance of a simple yes or no answer to this question, I can only conclude that, as he said, he had 'told' me. Perhaps he even regretted inadvertently letting the truth slip but, having done so, he was not prepared to be direct because he had sworn never to reveal Breckler as the source of the $10 000.

There is no evidence to support the following conjecture but, judging from the rabbi's letter below, it appears that Breckler could have had some influence or contact with the Music Council of Western Australia and the Bursary Trust members. If not, the trust he mentions may well have been the Phineas Seeligson Trust, the Jewish community aid organisation. Perhaps Breckler also contributed financially to the 'trust', thereby indirectly and silently supporting David.

Northumberland Avenue,
London WC2
6th July 1970
My Dear Mr Breckler,
I do hope you and & Hannah are well, and in particular that Hannah is feeling very much better.

I am enclosing a letter from Cyril Smith regarding David Helfgott. I have had a long talk to him and he feels that David may be served best now if he returns to Australia, and the ABC should be informed of his talents and perhaps arrange several concerts for him. Perhaps you would speak to Brig. Masel.

Strictly between us, and in confidence for the Trust members only, David is apparently still not yet 'grown up'. He is unreliable at times, forgetful of his rehearsals, and while being a lovable person he often irritates Cyril Smith and others such as the conductors because he forgets to 'turn up' on occasion, and they have to chase him. Of course they respect his playing, but cannot recommend him to teach because of his unreliability and this means he is not earning. On the other hand this may be engendered by the fact that he has relied solely on the support of the Trust and therefore his mind is not geared to responsible undertakings leading to independence. Cyril Smith therefore feels that once on his own in Australia, where he will have to concentrate on his commitments, he may grow into fuller maturity, since neither he nor his colleagues can spare the time always to remind him of his commitments here. Cyril Smith assures me he is now quite capable of leaving him to practise on his own and at times shows that touch of genius which of course may be the reason for reflecting eccentricity also (my comments).

Please put your enquiries into motion and when I return we shall communicate our ideas to Mr Smith. I have not yet seen David. He does not ring me back. I shall try again.

God bless you all,
Shalom Coleman

The rabbi, known for his wisdom, seems to have assessed David as being an 'eccentric' rather than 'psychologically unstable'. However, despite the facts that in his letter the rabbi, like James Penberthy, aligns genius with eccentricity, and that at the time of writing David had not suffered his mental collapse and therefore was not readily identifiable as suffering mental illness, the Helfgott family reject his comment. They point out, 'It is obvious to anyone who meets David that he is psychologically unstable. Comments by laymen re such a condition do not hold professional expertise. Only a psychologist or psychiatrist is qualified to comment on David's condition.'

The rabbi's statement, 'Cyril Smith assures me that he is now quite capable of leaving him to practise on his own' may seem to imply that David was a naughty child on whom Smith had to work hard to reach the point of being able to leave him to work alone. This is not as it seems. The standard period of study at the Royal College of Music is three years. To be given an additional year, as David was, is a great privilege extended only to the very few, who are themselves rare and exceptionally talented individuals. This extra year, the fourth year, is one in which the musician is expected to become totally self-motivated and to attain, with very little supervision, the finish which will make him a sought-after performer.

Rabbi Coleman had called on Cyril Smith while visiting London. After the rabbi's visit Smith wrote to him on 3 July 1970. Obviously Smith realised the rabbi had not clearly understood his verbal assessment of David's phenomenal artistry and felt the need to send a letter of explanation, a copy of which Mrs Luber-Smith also sent to Johnny:

Dear Dr Coleman,

I was very glad to have the opportunity of meeting you earlier this week, and I feel I would like you to have my written view of David Helfgott. He does not cover the whole range of the piano repertoire with equal felicity but in the romantic and virtuoso works such as Liszt and Rachmaninof, his talent amounts almost to genius. I would describe his Liszt Sonata and Feux Follets, as well as the 1st Concerto of Liszt and the 1st and 3rd of Rachmaninof as being temperamentally and technically in the Horowitz class.

The passion and feeling which generate these performances is almost equally noticeable in the more dramatic sonatas of Beethoven and in the virtuoso concert works of Ravel.

I hope this note will serve to clarify my opinion of this young man's truly exceptional talents.

Yours sincerely,

Cyril Smith.

Scarcely a letter which confirms psychological instability! It suggests that David has brilliance, that yes, he is a passionate interpreter of the great romantic composers, if, perhaps, depending on musical preference, a little too focused on the romantics. But there is no implication from Smith, David's mentor and closest associate, that David was unstable in any way. Smith, however, must have been aware of David's confusion and disturbed mental state at the time he wrote to Coleman, for David did not conceal his distress from Smith. Perhaps Smith chose only to address David's talent, deliberately avoiding putting in writing any comment on his student's mental state, knowing that if he were to do so any hint at instability might become graven in stone. Alternatively, Smith may well have believed that David's problem was of no great moment, that he was purely a little eccentric and, given time, 'once he was on his own in Australia', he would recover and achieve maturity and balance.

The third letter Mrs Luber-Smith enclosed, written by David on 5 July 1970, is unhappily the one which caused her to label David 'psychologically unstable':

Dear Mrs Smith,

I was glad to get your letter dated 27th June, and glad to hear you are having such a good time in Queensland. When I said I wasn't well, of course I was referring to the 'psycho-trouble', it's a terrible thing, you know, and it's really not my fault.

The rehearsal with Dr Cripps is on the 10th of this month; I do have a lesson this Wednesday at 10 a.m. so that's a great help. My chances for the moment anyhow, at the Overseas League and at Australia House, have been affected by this illness; what an awful thing it is.

I do have a new passport. The recording for the ABC wasn't good but that's done. It's nice of you to be concerned about the future; well I'll have to get a job just like anyone else (who isn't rich); or at least try to get one. And keep music for a hobby for a while; when I'm really healthy I could

always go over to New York or Philadelphia etc. I've always done my best,
you know, but when you're unwell one's best simply isn't good enough for
the very high standards which prevail today. You say if definitely
returning, what are the arrangements? Well, nothing yet, and there's
nothing much I can do; it's up to the Music Council to help me out here. I
dare say Mr Smith will write to you and tell you what he thinks.

Cheerio for now, all my love always.

David

P.S. I may have to leave Robert Mayer Hall soon and a winter in
London without a roof over my head doesn't appeal to me, I must come
back to Aust.

David's fellow students at the college were shocked to hear
about his collapse after his return to Perth. No-one recalls that
he showed any indication of psychological instability. He is
remembered as being 'good fun' and even better fun at a party.
Almost to a man, everyone who knew David then and during
the time he was studying at the college, when told of what
happened, says, 'It's a tragedy what happened to that boy, it's a
tragedy.' Even David says regularly, 'It's a tragedy,' or 'It's tragic,
it's tragic.' 'Tragic' is one of his favourite words. David does not
clarify exactly what he means by 'tragedy' in talking about this
period. In my opinion his greatest tragedy was being labelled by
laymen as 'psychologically unstable' even before he came home.

As Johnny Granek said, 'If you keep telling a child that he
cannot do something, before long he believes it, and then it is
true'; and 'Being made as nothing, you become nothing.' Now
David was being told he was 'psychologically unstable'.

Mrs Luber-Smith's letter to Granek continued:

It is really tragic that he is so brilliant, and yet cannot adjust his life to
meet the demands of his profession. It is all so sad, yet what can we do? He
has had four years in London. He has had the average financial

assistance, if not more than the majority of students, but I am afraid he has just not grown up and proved incapable of budgeting, or organising himself in any way whatsoever.

On top of every other shortcoming David was now being accused of never having grown up. If only the rabbi had not mentioned that David 'had never grown up' to Alex Breckler, if Breckler had kept that to himself as the rabbi had asked, if all the well-meaning people involved in David's life had given him a little more leeway, he might have survived. But instead they kept labelling him, bemoaning his lack of maturity.

For some, maturity comes with the years as easily as breathing. For others it is hard-won, but most have parents who guide them through the maze of youth, helping them through the rough times. Today's teenagers attend courses during their high school days which cover survival skills, offering rudimentary lessons in budgeting, banking, paying for services such as gas and electricity, renting and sharing accommodation with friends or strangers; they are also given dietary education. David appears not have been allowed to butter his own bread, boil a kettle, light the gas, or 'tie his own shoelaces'; he wasn't permitted to handle his own money, much less pay accounts.

Margaret insists that Peter, 'given David's genius and passion for the piano, did everything he could to help David to lead a normal life. David himself elected to devote himself solely to the piano. Everything else was unimportant to David, except of course, reading and chess.' She says: 'David was encouraged to "boil a kettle and tie his shoelaces" but he was unable to. Certainly as child. I remember this distinctly. He may have learned since.' Accepting Margaret's memory and knowing David's determination, I believe that what she says confirms that in David's case it was not a matter of *couldn't* do those simple things but of *wouldn't*. Why should he, when his family pandered to his every need?

Margaret does not address the fact that he was not permitted to handle his own money. In David's mind, money and trauma were synonymous. Asking his father for two pounds from his own prize money to buy music had resulted in the first terrifying confrontation between them which had earned him a 'backhander'. It was a request that ended up bringing the entire Helfgott family to the point where they were 'running scared, beyond belief' and Margaret was threatening to go for the police.

Bearing in mind that David was no ordinary young man, it is true that everyone, apart from Peter, had been fascinated by the prodigy, the genius, not the boy or the man. It was unrealistic, perhaps even unfair, to have expected him, unskilled as he was in the most basic elements of day-to-day living, to suddenly become proficient in those practical aspects of his life while, at the same time, fulfilling his ambitions.

As evidence of his irresponsibility, Mrs Luber-Smith wrote:

Professor Alexander, who was formerly President of the Music Council of WA, also saw David in London very recently, made it his special business to see David on several occasions. He got him to make out a list of his expenditure and he said some of the items were ridiculous. Approx. £5 a week for dry-cleaning, extravagant spending on the best seats for concerts, when concession seats were available at the college, taxis, etc. Music, when he could get all he required from the college library. Prof. Alexander is of the opinion that David should return to Australia.

Professor Alexander's findings do not exactly represent flagrant examples of outrageous or excessive expenditure. However, they were enough for him to recommend banishment back to the colony. Who knows what the recommended sentence might have been had Alexander found David knee-deep in cigarettes, whisky and exotic women, rather than getting in and out of taxis, immaculately dressed in spotless, dry-cleaned clothes, clutching new sheets of music, and sitting in front-row seats at concerts (which he took because, as a student musician, he wanted to see the hands of master musicians and watch their technique)?

It is worth noting that inclement and unreliable English weather makes dry cleaning the only suitable and efficient laundering method. In addition David, as a 'performing student', was required to dress appropriately, frequently in tails, when he played in public or at private functions. For instance, at the last concert David performed in at the Royal Albert Hall, when he played the Lizst Piano Concerto No. 1 in E-flat, he was advised that 'There will be a dressing room for you, so bring your tails and you can change between the rehearsal and the concert.'

As for extravagance with taxis, one only has to consider the London weather and the fact that David could not, under any circumstances, arrive at a recital or concert bedraggled, wet and bothered. Then there are the schedules he was required to maintain and the amount of time at his disposal. Against the criticism of him buying his sheet music instead of borrowing it from the college library, one must take into consideration that David's first and last love is, and was, music. Music was his life-blood — the only thing he lived for then, and the only thing he lives for now. If David, even today, was presented with a choice of whether to eat or play the piano the choice would unquestioningly be music. To leave him bereft of his precious sheet music by making him return it to the college library would be like casting him adrift in a boat without a rudder or oar.

Rather than being subjected to such picky and destructive observations, David should have been congratulated for doing as well as he did.

Apart from his alleged 'extravagant spending', he had perhaps offended Mrs Luber-Smith by not becoming involved with Johnny Granek's London relatives or her own friends:

I cannot understand David not contacting the relatives you mention in London. This is what he has missed so badly. Some family to look after him and guide him. This your relatives may have been pleased to do. He has mentioned so many times he has missed not having any home. My friends in London have been wonderful and tried to act as parents. Made their home available to him on all occasions, but he resented any guidance or advice they offered him and adopted the attitude that they did not like him. Unfortunately he always says, yes, yes, to everything, and goes away and does just what he feels like doing, irrespective of it being right or wrong.

Perhaps David should have told Mrs Luber-Smith, instead of Professor Callaway, that he was not committed to Jewish family life.

I suspect that Mrs Luber-Smith had unwittingly stumbled on the key to David's behaviour when she wrote: 'he always says, yes, yes, to everything . . . and does just what he feels like doing, irrespective of it being right or wrong.'

The purpose of Mrs Luber-Smith's letter to Granek was to solicit his assistance in providing accommodation for David in Melbourne, where the opportunities for him to follow his career were greater than in Perth.

What he will do for a living when he returns to Perth I haven't a clue. There is little in the musical field here. Maybe in Melbourne or Sydney he could find some scope. I am wondering if you would care to foster David for a while and see what influence you and the rest of the family would have on him. If his passage was booked through to Melbourne, the extra cost is very small. He could break his journey in Perth, stay here for a few

weeks and then go to Melbourne. I am doubtful if he could ever live at
home with his parents and I am not prepared to have him living with us,
as I am afraid it would become a permanent responsibility, which I do not
feel like accepting.

Granek doesn't recall his response to Mrs Luber-Smith. In fact
no response from him would have changed the events which
preceded David's final letter to Professor Callaway:

Dear Professor,
Thank you for the great letter you wrote to me.
I am back home now, with my parents; and I hope I get well soon. I shall
certainly try to keep up the music as I do love it.

I'm very grateful for the years of study in London; it certainly was
wonderful and I do hope the Music Council and Mr Walton realise how
much I appreciate what they did for me.

Cheerio for now, Professor; and I hope you & your family are in the
best of health.

Yours,
David

19

Shut Out

Margaret records that David was 'shipped home, ignominiously'. In fact he returned to Perth as he had left: of his own volition. His return was not accompanied by dishonour, disgrace or public contempt. Memory, a fickle and unreliable source of information in many instances, gives rise to differing accounts of what happened at that time.

Mrs Luber-Smith writes of David's return to Perth:

> When he arrived back in Perth he came directly from the airport to our home where we once more cared for him; he came with a suitcase but no clothes, only what he was wearing. In his case were odd socks, a little music on scraps of paper. Once again the Seeligson Trust gave me money to buy clothes. However eventually those kind people in London sent his clothes to Perth. He stayed with us for a time.

It is also possible that his luggage was mislaid by the airline and sent on later, which, as any traveller knows, is not inconceivable.

The Phineas Seeligson Trust had written to Mrs Luber-Smith on 7 August 1970, nine days before David arrived in Perth, confirming that they were 'prepared to pay the $30 involved in buying a ticket through to Melbourne', and were 'also prepared to subsidise Mr Helfgott for a maximum period of 13 weeks after his return at the rate of $25 per week'. The trustees were hopeful that David would 'be able to settle down and that the community at large will benefit from his near genius'.

At around that time Johnny Granek must have responded in the affirmative to Mrs Luber-Smith's request that he help David when he came home. Otherwise there would have been no reason for Alex Breckler to visit Granek in Melbourne as he did, or for the Seeligson Trust to advance the $30 for David's fare to Melbourne. It also appears that Mrs Luber-Smith's original proposal must have been agreed to: that David should break his journey in Perth, stay there for a few weeks and go on to Melbourne and the Granek family.

Records show that David arrived in Perth on 16 August. He recalls that he was in a very distressed state and that after waiting there for five hours he telephoned Mrs Luber-Smith from the airport, subsequently taking a taxi to her home, for which he says she paid the fare, as he didn't have the money himself.

Although David claims that Peter sometimes wrote to him while he was in London, perhaps indicating that tensions had eased, he chose not to go to this family home but to the home of Mrs Luber-Smith. Margaret says that in the days following his return, many people in Perth took David under their wing, the family was shunted aside and they were not taken into consideration at all. David, however, recalls that he was unsure how Peter would receive him, which was why he went straight to Mrs Luber-Smith's. He says he also recalls that he did not stay long with the Luber-Smiths and that Rabbi Shalom Coleman drove him home for a visit. It appears, however, that it was Rabbi Ruben Zacks who informed the family of David's return and brought him home.

Louise remembers that day clearly. 'We did know David was

coming home. Dad had me put a piece of cardboard in the front window, one to let him know if David was in the house and the second piece to let him know when David was out of the house. Dad kept walking around the block waiting for David to leave before he came inside, because he didn't want to see him. Les was there but he doesn't remember. I don't know how it happened, I didn't change the signal or I got them mixed up, anyway Dad came in while David was there. It was an emotional meeting. David was emotionally upset, they were both upset. Someone had brought David over. But Dad did know in advance that David was coming.' Since this discussion, Louise has said that she did not mix up the signal, as she previously stated, nor change it and that Peter chose to come home. Both David and Louise describe the encounter as 'emotional'.

It appears that David didn't return to the Luber-Smith home then, but stayed with the family for about ten days. During this period he visited Alice Carrard, his old music teacher. Frightened by his deepening depression, Alice took him to a psychiatrist, who admitted him to the psychiatric wing of Perth's Charles Gairdner Hospital.

Alice, who is ninety-nine, cannot remember or will not discuss that incident in detail. 'Speak up, dear,' she told me. 'Shout at me. There's nothing wrong with me except my ears.' Alice does not seem to have any difficulty with her memory, which is phenomenal. However, she does have one blind spot: she is adamant that David was twelve, rather than sixteen, when she first took him as a pupil. She says that it was Peter who brought David to her to continue his studies and that both she and Peter were opposed to David's going to London, of course for different reasons.

Alice will not be drawn to offer an opinion as to whether or not Peter pushed David too hard as a child. In fact she steadfastly refused to comment on the way Peter handled David, always referring to him as 'the father'.

She is scathing in her criticism of Cyril Smith, who, she says, 'taught David nothing, nothing at all. He only continued to teach him the music I had already taught him, nothing new.' However, one must not discount a little professional jealousy on Alice's behalf. She brushed aside my reference to David's performance of Rachmaninof's Third Concerto at the Royal College. 'He could play all Rachmaninof's concertos, One, Two, Three and Four, before he left. I taught him to play all of them and he never forgot a note! One of my best friends who was an adjudicator, you know, when he played the Rachmaninof Third in Melbourne, said he was faultless, and she knew, she knew he should have won.

'David is brilliant. He isn't just a pianist, he can play all the orchestral parts as well, you know. He could play them equally as well before he went to London as he does now.' When I mentioned that I knew he played the *tutti*, she said: 'Yes, the *tutti*, have you heard him play the Brahms D Minor? Well, his performance of that is world-class. It always was. He didn't need to go to London. It was because of Professor Callaway and those interfering women that he went to London, more those women; they thought they knew best, but they didn't.'

Then Alice dropped her bomb: 'When he was in Charles Gairdner, they gave him that electric treatment, you know.' This came as a surprise, for until now it has generally been accepted that David did not receive ECT until he was a patient at Graylands Psychiatric Hospital.

'It didn't affect his music though,' Alice continued. 'Nothing affected his music. It did make him better for while. It's a mystery what happened, a mystery. He wasn't always like that. The brain is strange. No-one really knows about the brain, do they? Do you know his wife, Gillian? She's a wonderful woman. David is better with her. He will get better, you know. The brain is a strange thing but he will get better.'

When I told her David had said that if he had any sense he would have married *her*, she responded, quite seriously, 'If I had been younger I would have married him! He used to come to my house a lot. He was always welcome. It was like home to him.'

At the close of the conversation she suddenly said, 'You did say you were writing David's biography, didn't you? I am glad someone is telling it all. You know the film doesn't. You know they don't even mention me once, not once!' Her name does, however, appear in the credits.

The psychiatric wing of the Charles Gairdner Hospital is much the same as those attached to all major hospitals where people suffering from depression and other conditions such as anorexia nervosa receive treatment. It is not, of course, the same as an institution where patients with severe and debilitating mental health problems receive long-term treatment.

David recalls that the entire Helfgott family visited him once during the five months he spent at Charles Gairdner. He also recalls that Leslie visited him quite often. Leslie remembers being shocked by David's appearance. 'David was very thin and almost unable to stand up.'

Because David is emotionally unwilling to seek information which is available only to him and his doctor, we have only Alice Carrard's statement to support the contention that he received ECT at Charles Gairdner. If he was suffering from depression, a painful but common condition experienced at some time by one in seven Australians, that does not necessarily indicate that David had any other mental illness or difficulties. In fact there is no general agreement among psychologists as to what exactly defines mental illness. Some even argue that there is no such thing. If David was suffering from depression, he was in the company of any number of intellectual and artistic giants who have been victims of what Winston Churchill called 'the black dog'. Among them, regardless of what name they gave to their depression, are Abraham Lincoln, Ernest Hemingway, Vincent Van Gogh, Patrick White, Sylvia Plath and Marilyn Monroe.

Depression can strike anyone, at any age, without warning. It has long been recognised that creative people and high achievers are more prone than most to depression. David is readily identifiable with these creative depressives. His long-term anxiety, sustained frustration and continual striving for perfection of his art are classic examples of the pressures experienced by exacting and hypersensitive personalities, people who demand much from themselves.

Lina Safro, a doctor and filmmaker whose documentary *Brainstorm* examines the consequences of depression, says the condition builds up slowly and gradually until some event in the sufferer's life precipitates a continuous state of severe depression. It is probable that David's apprehension concerning his forthcoming meeting with his father, particularly in view of their last, highly stressful encounter, may have provided the catalyst which finally pitched him into extreme and debilitating depression. What is surprising is the enormous personal strength and courage which had carried him through all the traumatic years before his first collapse in the closing months of 1970.

David was discharged from Charles Gairdner on 16 January 1971. He says that after he left the hospital he did not go home but returned to stay with the Luber-Smiths. During this time Mr Clifford Harris, then president of the now defunct Music

Council of Western Australia, became interested in David and his welfare. David moved from the Luber-Smith's to live for a short time with Mr and Mrs Harris in South Perth. There David had full use of their grand piano and gradually regained his confidence until he was able to move to a flat overlooking the Swan River which Cliff Harris and his wife Rae generously rented for him.

Now he was able to resume control of his life and care for himself in his own peaceful environment. His association with the Harrises proved a pleasant and productive one. David would go to the Harris home, which was close to his flat, to practise each day and have dinner with them. Before long he was giving recitals there for their friends and music associates. As Alice Carrard said, 'Nothing affected his music.'

20

A Wedding for David

Cliff Harris became totally committed to David. So concerned was he for David's continuing peace of mind that he called for donations to establish a trust fund to ensure his personal security. When invested, the contributions were enough to ensure a return which would allow David to build his career at a leisurely pace over at least three years.

At twenty-four, David, for the first time in his life, was able to set his own pace and enjoy a measure of peace without pressure. In fact, all looked set for him to build a career and continue to enjoy a stable and productive working life. However his respite was short-lived.

Mrs Luber-Smith writes:

David then met a woman. I was shocked when he phoned me one day and told me he was going to get married. I asked him to come and see me, he came that evening with the woman and I pointed out the foolishness of such a wedding. The woman had several children, a son around the same age as David; however my advice was of no avail and they were married within a few weeks. The woman cleared everything from the flat at South Perth and Mr and Mrs Harris were very shocked and disappointed that their good intentions and plans had come to a sudden end. The woman demanded that the trust money be handed over, but Mr Harris was not

prepared to do this and all the money collected was returned to the
generous donors.

As Mr and Mrs Harris are both deceased, there is no way of confirming the information contained in this letter to me, titled 'The Authentic Story of David Helfgott', from Mrs Luber-Smith.

David married Clara (or the anglicised 'Clare', as she is called by Margaret), a divorcee of Hungarian Jewish origins, on 9 July 1971, a mere five months after his discharge from Charles Gairdner.

Mr and Mrs Harris were not the only people shocked by David's marriage. The Helfgotts were also taken by surprise. Margaret says, 'We knew nothing of the marriage and no-one from our family had been invited to the wedding.'

As the first Mrs Helfgott is not prepared to be interviewed, and because any questions put to David about this period upset him, I have had to rely on indirect information from other sources. One person claims that Alice Carrard introduced Clara to David. When I asked Alice if she remembered this meeting, she couldn't recall the name, much less introducing them. Mrs Luber-Smith states that David and Clara had been introduced by a friend of Clara's, a doctor, who was treating David at the time.

In her letter, she writes: 'Only a short time elapsed after the marriage before David phoned me that he wanted a divorce, however I did not feel disposed to become involved in any marital dispute and advised David to get legal advice!' She adds: 'I had nothing to do with David after that. I was so upset that he had left the Harrises after all they had done for him I just couldn't get involved any further.'

David's marriage lasted two years and two months. Gillian Helfgott says that during this period his dignity was destroyed by his public and private humiliation. She says David has told her that he remembers, in the days before Clara had him admitted to Graylands Psychiatric Hospital, lying in bed and dribbling for hours: a condition which, by his account, approached a catatonic state. She also says David was not permitted to share his meals with Clara's family, being made to eat alone in his room. However, Margaret says: 'Clare informed me that David did not wish to eat with her family, but insisted his meals be brought to him at the piano, whereby he could eat and play at the same time.'

It is true that David seems to prefer to play rather than eat. I have often been at dinner with the Helfgotts when David has asked, mid-meal, to be allowed to leave the table to 'serenado'. What he really likes is to stay at the piano playing, leaving it only when he is tired or coerced by friendly persuasion to stop and eat; then, he usually takes his meal with him to the bedroom, where he eats while listening to the ABC Classic FM 'rados', as he calls it. There must be music at all times in David's world.

There is little or no evidence available as to David's reason for wishing to divorce Clara. On the one hand he is said to have been so appalled when he discovered she had demanded the money from the trust Cliff Harris had established that he refused to go back to living with her after his discharge from Graylands and sought Peter's help to obtain a divorce. On the other hand, Margaret says: 'David was also extremely upset with Clare because she put him back into the hospital again. This may have precipitated his desire to divorce her.'

Margaret, who visited Clara, adds: 'I have no reason to believe that Clare would have humiliated David in any way. He was quite ill when they married and she was very concerned about his health and tried her utmost to help him. As Clare had four children of her own at the time living at home, it became increasingly difficult for her to manage David's illness, as well as look after her own children, and it eventually became necessary for David to re-enter hospital.'

On 8 February 1974 Clara admitted David to Graylands Psychiatric Hospital. This is described by Gillian Helfgott as an expedient solution to the problem of Clare's own impending hospitalisation for a kidney ailment. However, in view of David's own appraisal of his mental state at that time, it would have been impossible for Clara to have left him unsupervised.

On 28 August Clara wrote a letter to Sir Keith Falkner, who was at that time still the Director of the Royal College of Music. She could not have known that David had written from Graylands to Sir Keith three weeks earlier, on 1 August.

> Dear Sir Keith,
> I am writing to you after a considerable silence, because I want to keep in touch with you. I am well and working at music. The piece is Tschaikovsky's 1st piano concerto; if you could send me some hints and ideas about this piece I would be grateful.
> I did a tape for the ABC recently, and wrote for a competition. Cheerio for now.
> All best regards,
> David Helfgott

In light of this letter one would imagine that when Sir Keith received Clara's letter he would have found the contents a little confusing. After introducing herself as David's wife of over three years, Clara began by saying that she would like to tell Sir Keith about David. She observed that when David had returned from London he had had to contend with a large number of obstacles. Referring to Mrs Luber-Smith and David's family, Clara claimed that none of them wanted to have anything to do with him. She implied that, as David had nowhere to go, he had been admitted to hospital for months of psychiatric treatment and that, following his release, as he was unable to find work he had applied for unemployment benefits. Clara added that he had worked unpaid for the Western Australian Opera Company. She recounted how doctors who were concerned about David's future had decided that his only hope of security lay in marriage, which might stabilise his life, and offered this as the reason for her marriage to him.

Clara told Sir Keith that she had been able to give David some degree of stability but, although she had found some work for him, his employment was short-lived and he had later regressed to the point where he had had to be admitted to a mental hospital. She noted that at the time of writing David's condition had seriously deteriorated. She also mentioned that the state director of mental health, at her request, had placed her husband in the care of a doctor of wide-ranging experience. As David's trouble had originated in childhood, she said, his was an extremely complex and demanding case.

The chief purpose of Clara's letter was to obtain medical information, perhaps held at the college, which might provide David's latest doctor with further insight into his medical background. To this end she asked for information about any drugs which he might have taken and inquired about David's London lifestyle, urging Sir Keith not to withhold anything which he might consider would upset her.

We cannot know why Clara's version of what had taken place after David returned home differs so significantly from other accounts on issues such as the assistance the Luber-Smiths gave to David; why she does not acknowledge that David had lived successfully by himself in the flat; and why she claims that the Western Australian Opera Company did not pay David when he worked as a *répétiteur*, accompanying the opera singers during rehearsals, and, he says, was most definitely paid. 'Of course I was!' he splutters. And further, there is no way of knowing why Clara did not mention that David did have support, and the security of the trust fund established by the Harris family.

Sir Keith asked Roberta Dodds for a report on David which might throw some light on the treatment he had perhaps received while at the college and on where he might have received it. She was unable to provide any definite information; neither could she find any evidence of David's ever having been hospitalised for psychiatric treatment or otherwise:

He was not treated by the doctor at the Imperial College Health Centre, I have checked on this. The centre has no record of his name.

I have been unable to trace his doctor or psychiatrist and know only that he went to group therapy classes. It is possible that these classes were held at the Tavistock Centre, but when I telephoned the clinic the receptionist told me that she could not tell me whether or not he had been a patient there, as the information was confidential. I can only suggest that David's doctor in Australia writes to the Tavistock Centre to see whether or not they know anything about him.

I think it ought to be pointed out to Mrs Helfgott that, however well-intentioned her letter, the information she asks for is confidential and in this country is normally only passed from doctor to doctor. I, or any other such contact, would never be told clinical information about a patient. If by chance a student told me clinical information in confidence, I would not pass it on except to a doctor, so that even if I thought I knew what drugs David was taking, I would not comment, as this would be dangerous and my information could be inaccurate.

Roberta Dodds,
Lady Superintendent
3rd October 1974

There is no documented evidence that David's doctor wrote to the Tavistock Centre.

A little over a month after writing his first letter, David again wrote to Sir Keith from Graylands.

5th September 1974
Dear Sir Keith,
I am writing to keep in touch; as I have been out of touch for quite a while. I am working at music and at trying to relax, and unravel; I hope you will write to me.
Yours sincerely,
David Helfgott

Until the end of 1974 David's contact with his family had been virtually nonexistent. Margaret says, 'It was only at a later stage when David was hospitalised in Graylands that my father started visiting him on a regular basis.' She continues: 'History seemed to be repeating itself with regard to first Hannah, my auntie, being ill and then my brother. In fact, while researching my father's family tree, I discovered that my great auntie had a sister in Poland who was also not quite normal. So having Hannah become ill and then his own son, David, was truly a huge blow to my father and an end to all his dreams for David.'

Louise says that Rachel remembered Hannah's being worried about her appearance. 'She refused to socialise, she wouldn't dance or go out at all. She was very clever and everyone tormented and made fun of her because she wasn't like them.'

Ivan Rostkier, who had known Hannah from the time she arrived in Melbourne from Poland in 1938, is able to round out the story a little. He has fond and sad memories of Peter's sister: 'Hannah was a very tiny, knowledgeable woman who read a lot; she was like Peter, you could discuss anything with her, she was very clever, very intelligent. But she married a very big man who lived all his life with his fists. He used to hit Hannah around the head with his closed fists. He hit her if his dinner wasn't on the table when he came home, he'd hit her that way for any reason at all. That's why she gave up after Joe [Hannah's son] was born. She just gave up and let herself go. Poor Hannah, she just wanted to forget everything.'

It appears that Hannah had much to forget, for, according to Rostkier, she had also been raped by two soldiers in Poland, a violation which left a legacy of fear and unresolved distress. When the German invasion of Poland was clearly imminent, her family's concern for Hannah grew and they decided that she should leave Europe and join Peter.

The Helfgott family confirm the story that Peter had sent money to Poland before the war to pay his brothers' passages to Australia. They do not refute the claim that he was upset when Hannah was sent in their place. Peter had hoped that once his brothers arrived they would be able to 'work side by side' with him to help save the money to save their family from imminent death at the hands of the Nazis.

As Rabbi Brasch points out in *The Unknown Sanctuary*, 'Jews throughout the world are for ever in Australia's debt regarding two dramatic episodes in modern Jewish history'. The first of these was in 1938, when Australia was one of the few countries to offer free entry and the chance to live, to 15,000 Jews. Unfortunately the advent of war meant that only 3000 could make the journey. Later, Australia provided the lead in the United Nations General Assembly vote on the creation of the State of Israel, voting positively.

At the time when Peter was struggling to bring out his family, it was necessary in some cases for migrants or their sponsors to hold an amount of landing money. It took more than money to immigrate to Australia. One had first to secure a landing permit. The number of landing permits available was minimal and the immigration waiting lists were long, as was the time it took for approval to immigrate. It could take up to five months to obtain approval for entry from the department of the Interior. After that it was necessary to wait until the department issued and forwarded the permit certificate. Only then was it possible to book a passage to Australia. It is not surprising that, despite Australia's commitment to providing a safe haven, many refugees waiting for entry approval took a cynical view of Australia's immigration policy.

Ivan Rostkier says that after much perseverance and trouble Peter managed to obtain a landing permit, not for his brothers but for Hannah. When one bears in mind that at that time only 600 permits were available for Jewish immigrants with family guarantors, and that these were allocated to be used over a three-year period, Hannah's permit to land would have been hard come by or simply a matter of sheer luck. Perhaps the issue of who came to Australia, Peter's brothers or Hannah, was resolved by the fact that Peter was able to secure only one landing permit. Rostkier says he sent the permit to Poland and the family paid the fifty-five pounds sterling needed to book Hannah's passage to Australia. If Peter had not obtained the permit, Hannah would have died in the Holocaust with her family.

Hannah's reprieve lasted only until her marriage in 1949: eleven years. Five years later Hannah was committed to Mount Park, then a Melbourne mental institution. Her son Joe was about two years old. Here she was confined for thirty years until Mount Park was closed by the Victorian government. Following the closure, she and other inmates were moved to a government hostel for the mentally disabled, where she stayed until her death in 1994.

Despite the fact that his father was alive, Joe was placed in a

Jewish orphanage. Although he never really knew his mother, when he did visit her he found her to be 'off in her own world'. Joe was unsure whether Hannah had lost her memory: 'You couldn't tell, she couldn't or maybe wouldn't carry a conversation. Perhaps everything was still there, all in her head, how would you know? It was all a bit frightening for me as a kid to go there. When you went there they unlocked the door to let you in and then locked the door behind you. Those were the bad old days. It was cruel to keep her there.'

Louise Helfgott, who visited her aunt at the hostel, says Hannah had gentle eyes which were 'very sweet and childlike' and that, when she gave her a box of chocolates, Hannah received the gift with childish delight.

It seems that life mercilessly forced Hannah to take refuge in the exclusive sanctuary of her own world. No-one but she had to live with her memories, and at the same time cope with a young baby and violent domestic brutality. She was probably also tortured with visions of the horrible deaths suffered by her family at the hands of the Germans, made worse by the knowledge that *she* had survived, and for what? Perhaps Hannah believed she was being punished because she had survived; who can tell what torment she suffered?

In view of Hannah's experiences, which might well have pushed others less strong to suicide, it seems very subjective to describe her as 'mentally fragile'. Hannah could well have suffered from amnesia, either self-induced in the desire to escape her memories, or the result of brain damage caused by blows to the head. Given her escape into isolation and Peter's knowledge that his aunt was regarded as 'not quite normal', it is possible to understand how Peter viewed her difficulties as an inherited mental weakness.

The influence of heredity versus environment in mental

issues is a subject of continuing debate, and it would be foolhardy to attempt to put forward any sweeping generalisation about the psychological processes involved. James A. Whittaker, however, in his *Introduction to Psychology*, writes that it is a common misconception that people who have a blood relative suffering from mental illness are more likely to develop mental illness themselves. Whittaker writes that such fears have little basis in fact, and adds that many cases of mental illness striking more than one member of a family may be the product not of inherited characteristics but of environmental ones.

Sadly, Peter didn't know that his fear that David had inherited what he believed to be his family's tendency to mental instability was probably unfounded. He was haunted by the belief he had passed this affliction to the son he loved so dearly and for whom he had held such high hopes.

Louise recalls that she grew up hearing Peter say all his children would let him down, that it was 'the Granek blood coming out in them'. Louise believed that he said this so often because 'Dad was so disappointed by [the Graneks].'

While Peter may have had reason to be disillusioned with the Graneks, he had no reason to suppose that his children, who were all high achievers like himself, would not succeed, unless he feared mental instability was lurking in their genes, waiting to overtake them.

Hannah's son, Joe, says that Peter was a great 'ideas' man, who invented many things other than his press, but he was not a practical businessman. Many of Peter's inventions were apparently stolen from him by people he trusted in the belief that they were friends. Joe says: 'He was always being ripped off but there's nothing new about that.'

David says that when Peter took the family from Melbourne to Perth he sold his press patent for £1000. David, who was obviously too young to remember this, cannot name the source of this information other than to say, when questioned, 'I know he did.' I can only assume he has heard it said by someone in the family. That was big money then, especially when one considers that, at that time, £2000 bought a house.

Perhaps Peter was simply desperate to try to change his luck in a new environment free of the ever-present influence of Rachel's family. Perhaps there were other anxieties which contributed to his decision to leave, concerns he didn't communicate to Rachel. The Helfgott family insist that it was evident from a very early age that David had been born with a mental disease or disorder. They cite the fact that he has been forced to spend so many years in hospital as confirmation of this.

Perhaps Peter thought he recognised in David's extremely sensitive and introverted nature the same tendencies he saw in Hannah (who was admitted to Mount Park in about 1953, the year the Helfgotts moved to Perth). If so, perhaps he also saw in the move to Perth the added benefit of a new environment for David and the children.

Once in Perth, when David showed such an overwhelming interest in music and the piano, Peter, through nurturing his son's ability, may have tried to comfort himself that mental instability did not exist in his children. When David seemed not to be able to recognise or remember a note during those two years between the ages of six and eight, his fixation on the boy seems to have become obsessive.

Perhaps the reason Peter did not pay as much attention to Margaret's musical progress was simple: it was unnecessary. Margaret was a well-balanced, exceptionally musically gifted child. Neither did he find it essential to focus on the other children: they too were clever and outgoing in their own right.

Peter was surely obsessed by his desire for all his children to share his passion for music. But at same time he must have seen David's nervous introversion, his 'difference', as a possible sign of instability and to counteract it, perhaps, resolved to focus his attention on his son's musical potential.

The fact that David was a high achiever both musically and academically wasn't enough to convince Peter that he also had the potential to be a normal, if reserved, child. David either allowed himself to be, or was, totally dependent on Peter and the family for all his physical care. This, combined with what Peter believed to be David's 'genius', led him to believe that David really was 'different'. Under these circumstances it would have been impossible for Peter to even consider Isaac Stern's proposal for his son to study in America. This would also explain Peter's absolute opposition to David's studying alone in London.

David says, 'Daddy was a tyrant, I reckon he was tyrant. Daddy was always screaming, Concentrate, you've got to concentrate. Daddy was a great hater. He hated everyone . . . The only good German is a dead German, Daddy said that . . . He said that all Americans are criminals, he always said that . . . He didn't like the Jews either. I was ashamed to be Jewish. Poor little Mamushka, she just followed orders.'

Taken independently or collectively such statements are understandable, coming as they did from a man who had a reason to hate the Germans, a reason to make his son dislike the Americans, and a fanatical desire to force on David the importance of concentrating. The 'self-hating' tendencies in David's comments reveal a dark and self-destructive attitude towards the family's Jewish ancestry. Sadly, this is a not uncommon response among people who have experienced persecution because of their religious and cultural backgrounds.

Clearly at some point Peter lost sight of reality, becoming

embittered, hating and fearing everyone, and at the same time attempting to extend his control to embrace not only David but his entire family.

Margaret and Suzie fought back by leaving home and making their own way. After her return from Melbourne, Margaret lived in Perth for approximately two years before going abroad for a holiday in July 1973: 'It was a "Sea-Jet" affair which was popular during that time. I sailed on the *Eastern Queen* to Singapore and then flew to London, where I had a short holiday, and then flew to Israel, arriving in August 1973. I stayed in Israel until March 1974, and then flew home to Perth. The Yom Kippur War broke out in Israel on 6 October 1973, just over a month after I arrived, which turned the whole country into chaos and depression. Israel lost around 3000 young men at the time which was, for a small country like Israel, a national tragedy. In all I was away from Perth for eight months.'

Eventually Leslie left home at nineteen to work as an electrician, a 'sparkie' as he says, on the $257 million development of the Robe River, an iron ore project, which included a mine to extract limonite deposits. These deposits were estimated to contain 3000 million tons of 55 per cent iron around Mount Enid, near where the Robe River comes out of the western end of the Hamersley Ranges in north-western Australia, very hot country. There, Leslie worked twelve-hour shifts. The pay was good and when he eventually returned home he bought the first home his family had ever owned, a home where Rachel still lives. Louise, being the youngest and still at school, steadfastly pursued her own goals.

It was David who bore the full weight of what had become Peter's patriarchal and authoritarian rule. Leslie says his father was 'arrogant and domineering', but denies that he was a dictator. To David, however, Peter was a fearsome, arrogant, domineering tyrant, who appears to have gradually eroded David's self-confidence until he was sufficiently disturbed to know when he arrived in London that he needed psychiatric help.

All Peter's worst fears had been realised by the time David was admitted to Graylands. According to Margaret it was only after this that Peter started visiting him on a regular basis. 'I remember I would drive my father there and we would visit David. My father couldn't wait to see David. He loved David very much and to see him in such a condition tore his heart apart. I remember every weekend he would say to me, "When are we going to see David? Get the car out and let's go to see David." And off we would go and see David in hospital. It was very, very sad to see David in such a condition. Of course a lot of it, I guess, was due to drugs because he was heavily sedated with psychiatric medication.'

David cannot remember these visits. In fact he questions whether they took place at all. However, heavy sedation may well have interfered with his memory of that period.

In January 1975 he wrote to Sir Keith Falkner to thank him for a letter he had received from him:

16th 1st 75
Dear Sir Keith,
Thank you for your letter which thrilled me no end. Please keep writing to me.

Is it nice countryside at Bungay? I would love to come back, and see you and your family again. I am keeping up the music, and working hard. Am in a marvellous hospital in a therapeutic situation, I'm sure that it's doing me good, and I hope to justify your faith in me.

Yours very sincerely,
David

In April he wrote once again to Sir Keith:

8-IV-75
Dear Sir Keith and Christabel,
Thank you for your card, which I appreciated very much. I am still in
hospital, but your cards act like tonics; and I'm sure I shall be out soon.
You are right, I do get much joy from the piano and I'm sure will continue
to do so. Once again thanks very much.
  Yours affectionately
  David

Where David had been only five months in the psychiatric section of Charles Gairdner Hospital, in Graylands he was hospitalised for fifteen months. He was discharged on 10 June 1975. Despite objections from the family, who felt that they couldn't cope with David, he went home to them after refusing to return to his wife, Clara.

On 5 August Peter wrote to Margaret, who had by that time migrated to Israel, where she still lives with her husband, Dr Allen Fisher:

I presume you know all about David. He's been home nearly 3 months,
not a symptom left of his sickness. He's good as gold but he has not learned
his lesson yet. I could write a book about this subject. One day when I feel
in the mood, I will let you know all there is to know. One thing, he is not
going back to his wife, he wants to divorce her.

For many reasons, David wanted a divorce. However, before this was to happen he was to endure a number of destructive encounters with Peter, who had opposed to the marriage in the first place.

Despite Peter's protestations of his boundless love for David, he once again re-asserted his control over him. Four years before, when David had left home, he had done so with a curse ringing in his ears. Then Peter had screamed at him: 'Leave this house and you'll be punished for the rest of your life and you will end up in the gutter!'

This time, when David returned home, Peter's invective was brutally destructive. His words, like Cyril Smith's words of praise for his performance of the Rachmaninof Third Concerto, are burned into David's memory: 'You thought you would go from concert platform to concert platform, but you'll go from one psychiatric institution to another psychiatric institution for the rest of your life.' At one stroke Peter destroyed David's faltering self-confidence. In so doing, he fractured any of the good results that may have been achieved at Graylands.

'The fog' descended once again and the '*dommage*', David's term for deep depression, rolled over his mind yet again. When David speaks about the '*dommage*', he uses the French word to embrace and express his perception of himself as 'damaged', both physically and mentally, a perception which, today, is rapidly diminishing.

Speaking of this occasion, he held his fingers to his temples to indicate that his psychological distress, 'the fog', was the result of the '*dommage*'. 'Daddy didn't know about the *dommage*,' he said recently. 'Daddy wasn't very wise.' Then, after a reflective pause, he said sharply, 'Yes he did, he did know!'

Today, David's progress along the road to restoring his sense of self and self-worth and repairing the '*dommage*' is a matter of three giant steps forward and two small steps back. It is not a simple matter and it is impossible to anticipate his complete recovery. However, it seems that David does believe Peter caused the '*dommage*', in particular 'the fog', which he says began in 1961 and destroyed him for a second time in 1975.

It appears that apart from his encounter with Peter no other emotionally disturbing circumstance occurred during that period which could be held responsible for his need to again seek psychiatric care.

Once again David was under Peter's control and influence.

21

To Be as a Child

When Peter's prodigal son returned home after a nine-year absence to resume his position on Peter's right hand, new problems arose in the Helfgott home. Apart from the fact that David had become an enormous responsibility which his siblings had no desire to cope with, his needs were once again being considered above their own.

In this less than benign environment, and despite Peter's belief that there was 'not a symptom left of his sickness' and that he was as 'good as gold', David did not flourish as he might have done had he been in a restful situation while he continued to confront those unresolved conflicts raised by the psychiatrists. In fact, returning to the care of a father who, in his own words, wished to teach David 'his lesson', whatever that lesson may have been, put him once again under intolerable strain and great emotional conflict.

'The doctor said it was the father's fault, and the father said it was the doctor's fault,' David says with a somewhat derisive laugh.

It was an impossible position for David. While the psychiatrists had led him to explore the concept that his father was responsible for his inability to remain stable, they had also allowed him to return to Peter, and the same unchanged environment where they believed his anxieties had originated.

Given that factors which perhaps had been responsible for his condition had been aired and probably reinforced, the only possible prognosis in these circumstances could be that, in time, his condition would worsen.

Once back home, David was in the hands of a man who, albeit no doubt unwittingly, can only have added to his already overloaded emotional turmoil by telling him, out of his own exasperation and frustration, that he had destroyed the family.

Placed in the invidious position of having to accept either that Peter was right and the psychiatrists were wrong or vice-versa, and without a mediator to assist in resolving the conflict, David's situation was unbearable. Back in the pressure situation of demand and command yet again, all his old anxieties resurfaced.

After having fought his way free to sweet liberty, to have to go home again was soul-destroying frustration for David; worse was the knowledge that he was now powerless. The ultimate blow was being thwarted in his craving to perform his beloved music at the level of excellence he had acquired at such torturous cost to himself.

For a time he toed Peter's line, trying to satisfy his demands while at the same time attempting to hold fast to his own hard-won sense of personal identity, although his grip on that was tenuous. It seems that during this period David himself resorted to emotional intimidation. He insisted that all his clothes be sent to the dry-cleaners and demanded that he be allowed to practise through to the early hours of the morning when and if he felt like it. As there were two pianos in the house, the original Rönish which Peter had bought, and a Concord piano purchased by Margaret while he was studying in London, he would play either at any time, day or night, when the mood took him.

Margaret recalls that this was a very difficult period for her parents, 'especially my father'. However, in mid-August Peter was obviously reasonably encouraged by David's efforts to fit back into the home, for he wrote to Margaret, in Israel: 'David has improved since he has been home immensely. I think he's better now than he has ever been before.'

A month later he again wrote to Margaret:

About David, you can be sure I will not let him hurt me like he did before. I had made up my mind at the time when I saw him in hospital that I will try to pull him out of the mess he was in and to hell with the consequences . . . I was confident enough that I could make a real good job of him all the way round, and it was all very promising till he got mixed up with another woman and bang everything was lost down the drain again.

Once again David left home, this time for a very brief period. This liaison between David and 'another woman' appears to have been a rather unsuccessful attempt by David to establish a personal relationship and reaffirm his independence by taking control of his own life. Unfortunately he chose a partner who was as unhappy and as emotionally unstable as himself, and the affair broke up almost before it began. David was forced to return home. One can only imagine his distress and his sense of defeat and failure. In an undated letter posted to Margaret in late August or September 1975, Peter wrote of yet another of David's attempts to break free, this time with a restaurant proprietor:

Now about David . . . he's got already mixed up with another woman and she promised him to adopt him as a son and he took to it like a fish to the water and immediately dumped me in the rubbish, but this is not all, as I think the woman led him up the path . . .

David can offer no explanation as to why Peter would have written to Margaret that this woman wanted to adopt him. This is a period he cannot discuss at length because the mention of these relationships upsets him greatly. Like his time in Graylands Hospital, it is too 'painful' for him to talk about. The woman in question, however, offered David the pianist virtuoso much: he was able to perform nightly in the restaurant — and playing to an audience is what sustains him. She also promised to give him a piano in lieu of wages. He kept it until 1986, when her son asked for its return after learning that David had later been given a grand piano. David responded without hesitation. 'Why not? I have the best piano in the world.' When David was given his piano from the restaurant, a Beale, he had three pianos to practise on any time he liked.

On 26 October 1975, Peter wrote to Margaret:

> David is no trouble now, and he's surely glad to be home, and is following every instruction I am giving him. I now have decided to put him on the violin full time so as to keep him out of mischief, but personally speaking I doubt very much if he will ever be right again, but whatever is going to be is going to take a long time for sure, and he will always be susceptible to breakdown on the slightest provocation, and his mental capabilities are no more than a child of 7 years of age, and I am afraid that not much can be done in this respect.

It seems the intolerable stress had become too much for David and he had unconsciously or deliberately chosen to regress to an earlier period in his development. Perhaps Peter had at that time adequately identified David's emotional level but not his mental level, for David possesses intelligence and academic knowledge far above the average.

David was, as Peter wrote, giving him 'no trouble' and was demonstrating that he was 'surely glad to be home and following every instruction'. He had reverted to that time when nothing was demanded of him — and he wanted nothing — but to learn the piano. To be as a child: a classic case of regression.

A month before his death on 29 December 1975, Peter wrote to Margaret:

> David is more of a problem to me now than ever before, and I don't think I will ever solve it. I must find him a job of any kind . . . by the way David may take Clare, or in other words his wife, to court about getting his property and I will let you know how things are getting along.

Margaret is unable to shed any light on whether David did institute court action to recover his diplomas and the music scores which he had collected at great expense while he was studying in London, along with the medal presented to him by the Queen Mother which he won while at the college. It seems that David's attempts to recover these things, which are of great sentimental value to him, came to nothing. In 1984 David's second wife, Gillian, and journalist Kirsty Cockburn, whose unstinting efforts contributed enormously to the establishment of the career David now enjoys, visited Clara in the hope of persuading her to return these articles. Sadly for David, this effort also failed.

It was Peter's belief that he could 'cure' David by the right mixture of deep breathing, correct nutrition, exercise and positive thinking. David says, 'Daddy thought he could cure everything with water, milk and Farex [baby cereal].' If this was his diet while he was being 'cured', then it isn't surprising that his mental state deteriorated further. It is a diet scarcely suitable for a young child, and certainly not adequate for a convalescing twenty-eight-year-old who didn't need the added stress of being undernourished. Margaret, however, disagrees with David's comment. She says: 'Peter loved Farex, so he offered it to us;

may have been part of the meal but certainly not only the meal. The average Helfgott meal included soup, meat (frequently lamb chops), cooked vegetables and salads.'

Margaret thinks that when Peter accepted that he couldn't succeed in curing David, it broke his heart and that somehow this contributed to his death. However, Peter had had a number of heart attacks before the coronary occlusion which caused his death. Clearly, too, the prolonged stress and sorrow he had been subjected to would not have helped his condition.

Louise also believes the so-called 'constitutional crisis' of 11 November 1975, which resulted in the dismissal of the Australian Labor Government by then Governor-General Sir John Kerr, upset her father so much it accelerated his decline. Twenty years later the dismissal still stirs heated debates. Then and now, devotees of democratic socialism regard Kerr's action as the Queen's Australian representative as unconstitutional and unfair. Peter held strong political beliefs and respected the much loved Gough Whitlam, whose dismissal many Australians took as a personal affront.

After Peter's death David wrote, on 2 January 1976, to Sir Keith Falkner once again. This time it was quite a long letter and despite Peter's claim to Margaret that David's 'mental capabilities' were 'no more than a child of 7 years of age', the letter is not the expression of a juvenile mind.

Dear Sir Keith,

It was terrific of you to write, and I appreciated it very much. Your letter came at a time of mourning, as my Pop passed away recently.

Well, life is cruel, and it's no use crying too much. He was a super human being, and I wish you could have met him, but unfortunately it was not to be.

As you know we are Jews, and we will be mourning him in services for seven days. And life has to go on, in spite of sorrow. We are holding our

Festival of Perth soon; and then the season starts again. Artists appearing this year are Brendel, Measham, Ameling, Kawamura, Snaderling, Aveling, Ponti, Berglund, Wallez, Eros, Wilkomirsk and Kocsis. So it should be a good season.

If you see John Lill could you give him my best regards, Sir Keith; also Phyllis Sellick and Margot Hamilton.

Did I tell you; I have the chance to come to England this year with some wonderful people. Time will tell. I am lucky with my family, who back me up to the hilt; and that's the way it should be. It's no use crying over spilt milk; the main thing is to stay determined!

All my best regards for 1976 which I hope will be happy, healthy and joyful for you and yours.

I am going for an audition at the ABC soon, and am really resolved to do well. The programme is: Bach/Busoni's Organ Toccata, Beethoven's 'Pastoral' Sonata, Chopin's Polonaise Fantaisie, Rachmaninof's Prelude in G minor and Albeniz's Leyende. I am hoping for good results. Also I have seriously tackled the violin over the last few months; perhaps one day soon I'll go for an audition on this instrument too.

We have practically our own conservatoire here at home; what with brother Les on the fiddle and piano, me on the piano, fiddle and composition; and before we lost Dad on the piano and composition. We have a piano accordion, a mouth organ, numerous violins which Leslie makes, and three pianos.

My brother is a fantastic fiddler and is coming to England this year. If you like, I will give him your address and he will contact you. Sister Louise writes brilliantly, and has had an article on Rock published. Margaret, another sister, is in Jerusalem at Mt Scopus, while Suzie is at the WA Uni. Could you please give my sincere regards to Mr Stainer; and I will be writing as well.

I am glad you still remember my Rach 3! Unfortunately the chance to play it out here hasn't come yet; but I'm still hopeful. It's a handful, that concerto!

The weather here is very warm at the moment, just the opposite to England I suspect. I hope you and your wife have a wonderful time at Abani.

Yours truly
David Helfgott

After Peter's death Rachel went to Melbourne to spend some time with her relatives, leaving David in the care of Louise, who was then seventeen, and Leslie, who was twenty-seven.

While the letter to Sir Keith indicates David's optimism and does not suggest he was disturbed, Peter's death must have created David's final confusion by leaving him, as it were, rudderless, like a child who suddenly found that there was no-one to please and no-one to direct him. Worse, David, having abdicated all responsibility for his every action to Peter, had now lost the ability to resume an independent life. More frustration, more intolerable stress. What better way to cope with his confusion and frustration than to become as a child?

Little wonder, then, that on 21 March 1976 he was readmitted to Graylands. Louise simply could not care for him. This must have been a heart-wrenching, distressing decision for her, but what other choice did she have? In fact, without Peter, the father, the autocrat, but still the carer, there was no other choice.

22

Lost and Rediscovered

It is not certain on what date David was discharged from Graylands for the second time, but it appears to have been some time in May 1976. Therefore, he must have spent the greater part of three months there, possibly longer. Other details covering this period are not available from the family, nor from David, who refuses to talk about Graylands. David did not go home following his discharge. Instead he took up residence with a Mr and Mrs Price in the Perth suburb of Gosnells, where accommodation had been arranged for him by his friend the restaurant proprietor who had given him the Beale piano. The Prices, according to David, were her friends.

On 21 June 1976 his divorce became final.

During the time he stayed with Mr and Mrs Price, David occasionally walked the 20 km from Gosnells to South Perth to visit Rachel. On one of these visits he recalls that Rachel closed all the blinds and refused to answer the door. In reference to this, David says, 'It was a long way, a long way. But mustn't kvetch, mustn't kvetch.' It is clear the incident upset him.

After a few months the Prices came to the sad realisation that they were unequal to the task of caring for David. Having reluctantly reached this decision, they took him home in the belief that Rachel would take care of him. Rachel did not respond as they had anticipated. Instead David recalls that she met their request with, 'You would do this to me!' Rachel later told Gillian Helfgott that she didn't understand David and that she had been frightened because she hadn't known what to do.

In all fairness to Rachel, one must concede that caring for David at that time was a difficult assignment even for those with the wherewithal to do so. It is also important to recognise that Peter's death had left Rachel disorientated and adrift in a void of confusion as she struggled to establish her life alone and make decisions for herself without Peter's help.

Regardless of what view one takes of motherhood, it was unrealistic to expect a woman who had accepted her husband's direction as to what kind of apples she should buy to suddenly be capable of taking care of a person like David and know how to respond to his complex needs. When Mr and Mrs Price brought David home and Rachel found herself unable to meet the demands of the situation, she decided to admit David to Graylands for a third time, on 16 September 1976.

Only a few years before, David had been applauded and praised by London's music critics when he had thrilled an audience of 8000 classical music lovers with his performance of the Liszt Piano Concerto in E-flat Major at Royal Albert Hall. From the time of his return to Perth there had been no real performances, no serious audiences, no applause to confirm his worth. Given his bewildered state of mind, he must have believed he had been rejected by the people of his city because of his failure to achieve their expectations.

One cannot begin to imagine David's sense of final rejection and utter desolation when he found himself confined in Graylands yet again. For a time during this period of hospitalisation David became progressively more introverted, refusing to relate to anyone, which isn't surprising, given that his trust in everyone, including his mother, had probably been destroyed.

David says, 'I used to lie there wondering, if I had gone to America, where the music bounces off the walls, as Stern said, if I would ever have been in hospital.' It seems obvious that David identifies this first frustration of his ambition as the reason for his mental condition. David says: 'I was sick when I went into hospital but I was really sick when I came out.'

However, three months later, the receipt of a timely card from Sir Keith Falkner helped to assure him that he was still remembered, at least in London. He wrote to Falkner from Graylands on 7 December:

> Dear Sir Keith,
> I received your card and made haste to reply! I am still in hospital; but I try to get some good practice in now and then! I am thrilled that you still remember the Rach. Concerto! I haven't given up yet; and I run through the Rach. Concerto when I'm in the mood! I have Chopin's Mazurkas, and Schubert's Impromptus, and I often play them. I would bring some more music, but I'm scared that it would get lost! On the pop side I have Simon & Garfunkel's hits, the 'Sounds of Silence', 'Scarborough Fair' etc. ('Bridge over Troubled Waters' is another!)
> Dear Sir Keith, once again my sincerest wishes to you and your wife.
> All affection always.
> David

Slowly David began to progress until he was able to leave Graylands now and then for short periods: he hadn't given up. On one such occasion he was taken to St Luke's Church, Maddington, to enjoy a musical outing by one of the church choir members. David, as usual, was drawn to the piano. After he volunteered to turn the pages for the pianist, Mrs Dorothy

Croft, who was also a piano teacher, she realised that he knew something about music.

For several months after, Mrs Croft visited David in Graylands. According to her, after several visits she and David had formed a firm relationship. The doctors at the hospital were encouraged by signs of David's continuing improvement, eventually giving Mrs Croft permission to take him home for weekend visits with her family. From that point David took part in small concerts at St Luke's Church, eventually gaining the confidence to play with the Karrinyup Musical Society under the direction of Frank Arndt, who had been David's first music teacher.

Margaret and Leslie share the same wholehearted opinion of Dot Croft: 'Dot is a warm, caring and extremely kind person. She was genuinely fond of David and instrumental in helping him on the long road to rehabilitation. She visited him regularly in hospital, bringing him tidbits and presents, invited him to her house, gave him free use of her piano, found venues for him to begin playing again, and also found a few pupils for him whom he taught at her house.'

Margaret continues: 'When I first met Dot and asked her how she came to visit David in the hospital, she told me that she had once seen David attend a concert, and that he was hardly recognisable as the young genius she had once heard and knew about. It broke her heart to see him in such a condition. Dot decided she would go to the hospital and visit him to cheer him up, encourage and support him as much as possible. She was extremely kind to David during those difficult years. In fact when David met Gillian, Dot was "dropped" by David, after all those years, without warning, which caused her extreme anguish.'

On 19 April 1978 David was discharged from Graylands for

the third and final time. For the next six years he lived at Gildercliffe Psychiatric Lodge at Scarborough, a half-way house just outside Perth. Descriptions of Gildercliffe differ. Dr Chris Reynolds does not recall any detail which would suggest that Gildercliffe was any better or worse than any other institution. He reports that the grounds were well kept and pleasant and that the hostel itself was clean and kept in reasonable order. He rebutted a claim that the air was permeated with the acrid smell of stale urine, saying 'I only remember the horrible smell of stale cigarette smoke in David's room, it was revolting!'

At Gildercliffe, accompanied by shouts of 'Shut up, David!' from other inmates who didn't want to listen to classical music, David chain-smoked and played, using the music to hold on to what little remained of his sanity, practising up to ten hours a day on an almost unplayable piano in his room.

His brother Leslie regularly visited him there. It was Leslie, a kind and caring man, who bought David a television set of his own and generally tried to provide him with some homey comforts.

Late in October 1983 Reynolds, who was part owner and self-styled musical director of Perth's Riccardo's Wine Bar, discovered, by happy circumstance, that David was looking for work. In an article which later appeared in *Music Maker* magazine, Reynolds told how he had first met David when they were both students at Leederville Technical College in 1965. At that time Reynolds, with a seven-year career as a merchant navy deck officer behind him, had been cramming maths in the last two weeks before the final examinations, hoping to matriculate to the medical faculty at the University of Western Australia.

He recalled David as being 'more solidly built then, bespectacled, stooped and clearly "different".' With his own need to study, he took very little notice of David. However, he did remember hearing talk of David's outstanding pianistic virtuosity and imminent departure to further his studies in London.

In 1983, Riccardo's, presenting as it did modern jazz, opera, blues, folk and classical music, was considered to be ten years ahead of its time for Perth. Presenting new artists and finding artists who were prepared to play in a wine bar was no easy task. Losing a performer at the eleventh hour constituted a crisis. It was the loss of Riccardo's regular Saturday night pianist which brought Chris Reynolds and David back together after almost twenty years.

After Reynolds had tried unsuccessfully to find a pianist to do the Saturday night fixture, he remembered that the drama teacher and actor Jay Walsh had told his son Jamie to tell him that David was looking for work. Reynolds thought it was a long shot and that as David was a concert pianist he wouldn't play in a wine bar, even if he *could* contact him. Still, he was desperate, so he decided he had nothing to lose by trying. The only Helfgott listed in the telephone directory was Rachel. By chance David happened to be at the house, and by an even greater chance, he answered the call himself.

Reynolds recalled David's ready agreement and his offer to play for nothing, which made him think that times must be tough for concert pianists. He usually paid artists performing at Riccardo's $40 for a three-hour engagement. However, in view of David's reputation, he suggested a fee of $80. This David accepted, and they made arrangements for Reynolds to pick him up at eight o'clock on the Saturday night.

When Reynolds called to collect David at Gildercliffe Lodge he was stunned: 'I could hardly believe it was the same man I had seen all those years ago. He was squinting through bottle-bottom spectacles, very stooped, almost cowed and nervously chain-smoking. He was carrying a broken-handled briefcase stuffed with music.' He — and the diners — was even more shocked when David, who appeared somewhat anxious, sat down at the upright piano and arranged his dog-eared, coffee-stained sheet music, which consisted of singalong charts and Christmas carols.

Two articles about David by journalist Hugh Schmitt, who heard him play at Riccardo's, were responsible for the ultimate rekindling of public interest in David in Western Australia and around the continent. One was titled: 'He got by with a little help from his friends' and appeared in the *West Australian* of 17 December 1983. The second appeared in the *National Times* of 6 to 12 January 1984, and was titled: 'A master pianist returns to the stage'.

Schmitt recounted the story of David's first performance at Riccardo's, as told to him by Chris Reynolds:

The sensitive virtuoso sat down at the piano, his gaunt frame hunched over at the shoulders as his long, slim fingers toyed with a few notes.

Leering mischievously through bottle-lensed spectacles at his expectant audience, he started playing with two fingers.

There were some giggles from patrons who wondered what was going on.

Reynolds listened with disbelief to the meaningless sounds from the piano and the mockery coming from a group of young people at the table nearest it. His mind was working double time trying to figure out a way to get David away from the piano and out without causing himself, or David, too much embarrassment.

Then, at the crucial psychological point, which Chris believes he had timed perfectly, David exploded into a blazing rendition of Rimsky-Korsakof's 'Flight of the Bumble Bee', seeming to use more notes than Korsakof, 'the cause-of-it-all', as David puns, ever put into it.

Gerald Krug, director of Western Australia's opera company, was among the drinkers and diners who froze, glass or cutlery in hand. As the music faded they rose to their feet as one with a salvo of thunderous applause. Shortly after, Krug said, 'The man is a genius musical talent, his technique is equal to the greatest in the world, it is an unbelievable talent.'

That night David played for four hours straight without a break, chain-smoking cigarettes clamped between his teeth, drinking coffee after coffee interspersed with numerous glasses of orange juice. Chris says: 'It seemed as if he was determined to play everything he had ever studied in one sitting, for fear that he might never get the chance to play again.'

From that night he began to play at Riccardo's three nights a week. Chris, horrified at David's situation, took him from the misery of Gildercliffe Lodge and placed him in private board with a family. The ABC programme 'Nationwide' picked up Schmitt's *National Times* story, putting to air its own account of the David Helfgott story in January 1984. The 'Nationwide' story was followed in July by a piece produced by Kirsty Cockburn for the Nine Network's 'Mike Willesee Show'. Viewers of the Willesee programme were privileged to hear, and see, David's first public appearance for thirteen years performing a complete concerto with orchestra.

Jan Shepherd, in an article in the journal *Music Maker* of September–October 1984, was as spellbound by David's magic as James Penberthy had been twenty years earlier:

> Winthrop Hall has seldom seen such a huge crowd as that which turned out to hear David Helfgott with the Nedlands Symphony Orchestra perform the Rachmaninof Second Piano Concerto.

The atmosphere was electric even before the concert began. The audience included regular concertgoers, of course, but there was a whole new group there, people who had succumbed to the charms of the predominantly romantic music played by David at Riccardo's Wine Bar and were anxious to hear him play in a concert setting.

After covering the obvious improvement brought to the Nedlands Symphony Orchestra by its new conductor, Henryk Pisarek, Shepherd continued in her praise of David:

We all know the Rachmaninof, and David Helfgott gave it all the lyricism, sensitivity and passion we had come to hear.

The orchestra provided a sensitive accompaniment and the audience responded with great warmth to the whole performance. At the end they rose to their feet to applaud, but the most awe-inspiring part of their reaction was the silence which followed when they returned to their seats in respect for David, as they searched for another way of showing their tribute.

Much had happened in David's life between playing the 'Flight of the Bumble Bee' and Rachmaninof's Second Piano Concerto. Fate had brought him Gillian, the second Mrs Helfgott.

23

Chris, David and Gillian

David was brought to Riccardo's Restaurant and Wine Bar by his friend Dr Chris Reynolds. It was Reynolds who held out his hand to David; encouraged and supported him while he made the step from the bleak obscurity of an institution into the light; and gave him something even more valuable, the dignity of employment, which had been stripped from him during the years he spent in the depths of his own personal abyss.

Gildercliffe Lodge was peopled with sixty other tortured souls of whom few, if any, were devotees of classical music. It appears that although the administrator of the Lodge received requests for David to perform in public during the seven years he lived there, he did not grant him permission to take the engagements. Reynolds feels that the only reason for this was that the administrator may have felt public performances would be too stressful for David.

David's experience as a boarder in the family home Reynolds moved him to was less than successful. He later told Reynolds he had been charged double rent but had not told anyone for fear of losing his accommodation. There were other problems. David told Reynolds that the steak Chris brought for his dinner on a number of occasions was never cooked for him but instead eaten by the family. His association with the family came to an end when he was accused of ruining the refrigerator, which Reynolds was then expected to replace. Chris says the refrigerator was very old and 'David swore he had nothing to do with its demise,' which he believes was true. He formed the opinion that David was being 'ripped off and badly mistreated', and took him into his home, taking up the responsibility for his welfare and medical care.

Gillian Helfgott says: 'David denies that he was mistreated in any way. He said that they were very kind to him, let him play the piano day and night, got books from the library for him. He also added, "I should never have left there and gone to live with Chris".' This is a somewhat confounding statement, in view of David's comments when he wrote to Gillian of Reynolds during the first days of their romance: 'He has given me a chance to live and work again', and that it was wonderful to be living with Chris 'in my own room, a beautiful piano and good food'. Gillian acknowledged the importance of the friendship when she wrote in a letter to Dot Croft in May 1984:

> I have the most enormous respect for Chris and having lived in his home for four weeks, I know of his deep caring for David, the great amount of time he has spent in helping him, his generosity and that his main concern is for David's rehabilitation.

In the same letter Gillian wrote, 'I hope you will understand from my comments that I can see the manifestation of Chris' faith and care and to me the final outcome must be bigger than personalities.'

It troubled, even annoyed Reynolds that David refused to eat at the table with him. 'Bugger him,' he says he thought. 'If it's good enough for me to iron his clothes, cook his meals and generally look after him hand and foot . . . it's good enough for him to eat at the table with us!'

David told Chris he was too ashamed to eat at the table for the simple reason that he had forgotten how to use knives and forks because cutlery had not been provided to the inmates during the seven years he spent at Gildercliffe Lodge. As a result, he said, he and the other inmates were obliged to consume their food by tearing it apart with their bare hands and stuffing it into their mouths with their fingers! In light of the fact that David had told Mrs Luber-Smith years before that he couldn't use knives and forks because the Helfgott household was devoid of cutlery, it seems obvious that this was a story which David employed because he preferred to use his fingers. According to Gillian, David now says there were knives and forks at the Lodge! David also seems to have an aversion to sitting at table to eat his meals. Louise recalls that he did not eat at the table with her and Leslie, preferring to starve all day, then raid the refrigerator at night when they were asleep. 'No one kept David from eating at the table; he simply did not want to participate with his family, nor with Clara's.'

Reynolds says, 'David is "different". He is an eccentric genius whose genius has been mishandled. In my opinion, if David had not gone to the Royal College of Music but to the Julliard School of Music, New York, he may never have become a psychologically unclassifiable conundrum.'

It would be a gross understatement to say that David was a handful when he came into Reynolds' life, and quite unnecessary to say that giving him the care he required would have been a full-time job for a team of dedicated people. It would also be an understatement to say that Reynolds did his best to fulfil David's needs. He not only cared for David psychologically and physically as his physician, he also ploughed in a superhuman effort, as his manager between September 1983 and April 1984, attempting to re-establish his career. Reynolds' involvement did not end in April but continued for a long period afterwards. Because he believed in David's future, he spent hours travelling from place to place knocking on doors in an effort to get him engagements in 'establishment venues'. He invited journalists and numerous opinion leaders in the music world to Riccardo's to listen to David play, hoping that this would lead to his being offered recitals. All this was not only time-consuming but costly, for naturally the food and wine consumed by these people were 'on the house'.

Despite the fact that Riccardo's was packed most nights when David played, and despite the money Reynolds poured into the place, the venture did not work out. The difficulty of attempting to continue his medical practice, run Riccardo's, and look after David at the same time, ultimately contributed to his losing Riccardo's, his home, his practice, his self-esteem and his faith in people generally, and brought him to the brink of bankruptcy. And it took its toll on Chris's emotional and physical health for a long time.

When Reynolds met David again in 1973, after not having seen him for eighteen years, his stooped figure and cowering demeanour led the doctor to the conclusion that David had a pathological fear of rejection and was greatly depressed. He adds that it was David's courage in managing to carry on that moved Reynolds to help him.

His years in the institution had left David with a habit of saying to anyone and everyone, 'You're the best . . . You're the best.' This habit continued while he was staying with Reynolds and playing at Riccardo's. Today, thanks to a concerted effort by those around him, he has managed to get back some sense of his self-worth, and no longer seems to find such a debasing posture necessary.

In *Music Maker*'s May–June 1986 cover story, 'The Party's Over', Reynolds tells honestly of the relationship between himself and David:

Naturally I realised David's great potential would help our ailing business. Where else do you get to hear classics on request? Particularly from a genius who chats to you while he plays, and in a wine bar?

I have never had any illusions about there being a trade-off between David and myself. Put simply, it was, you bring in the customers, I'll back your career as much as I can. But it has always been unconditional, without contracts and based solely on trust and friendship.

It was a friendship that grew stronger after he moved into my home and out of the lodge where he had languished for so many years, and a friendship that withstood even his disgusting habit of chain-smoking which didn't make for mutual understanding at times!

It appears that David had a different view of their relationship at that time. Gillian says: 'David definitely denies that the friendship grew stronger when he went to live with Chris. David was extremely difficult to live with at this time, burning the piano stool and being incredibly untidy. Chris was trying to do his medical practice, run Riccardo's and look after David. An impossible agenda. Let us not think for one minute that the friendship grew stronger; it was stressed to the limit.'

However, the alliance exceeded a 'trade-off' based on reciprocal benefits. Reynolds estimates that over the three-year period during which he was closely involved with David he spent an incalculable amount of money trying to re-establish David's career. He bought two pianos, one a grand for David to use at Riccardo's to replace the upright piano, the other for him to use in his home; and expensive music scores to replace those David had lost or which he said Clara had kept. There were many other direct expenses, as well as others not so tangible, such as the high cost of neglecting his medical practice and his business.

Reynolds says he was subjected to pressure from many areas and for months to keep Riccardo's open. 'I was faced with Hobson's choice: either keep it viable until David was firmly back on his feet or close and face the unacceptable prospect of David possibly having to return to care, something I refused to consider. Of course the arrival of Gillian, despite my fears that she would bite off more than she could chew, did ease an enormous burden off my shoulders.'

Chris had met Gillian Murray, a fifty-one-year-old divorcee and mother of two children, Scot and Sue, then both in their early thirties, while on the cruise ship *Oriana*. He and a friend had decided to take a holiday cruising the Pacific, which, as he said, for an ex-merchant seaman seemed a little peculiar, a busman's holiday! On board he met Gillian, whom he described as a 'flamboyant blonde'.

Gillian is a respected astrologer, now one of the few honorary life members of the Federation of Australian Astrologers, as she says 'the highest award an astrologer in this country can receive'. She was working as the *Oriana*'s Esoteric Arts and Body Language lecturer, demonstrating her skills as an astrologer, numerologist and Tarot reader. Neither one knew anything about David at that time; neither did Chris know that Gillian would eventually become an influence in his life.

David had been playing at Riccardo's for about three months when Gillian renewed her acquaintanceship with Chris at the bar in November 1983. Well along the way to regaining his confidence and virtuoso skills, David had already created something of a classical music cult, attracting a large following of loyal devotees. There were, of course, nights which were poorly attended and it was on these nights that Reynolds would bemoan the fact that if it were in Sydney or Melbourne, not Perth, the restaurant would be packed each night. Most evenings when David played at Riccardo's, his adoring courtiers would be gathered around the piano lighting his cigarettes, or fetching him numerous cups of heavily sugared coffee, all of which made him more hyperactive and kept him playing classics on demand until midnight, closing time. Each night after Riccardo's closed David would relax and enjoy a cigar with a glass of port before Reynolds drove him home.

Then as now, David's energy, warmth, gentleness and his passionate love of life and people, so vividly expressed in his music, cast a spell over all who heard him. Regardless of what or where he plays, no barriers exist between himself and the audience. Today, even from the platform, David still has that indefinable rapport with his audience which has been said to give a concert hall the intimacy of a cosy nightclub.

His brilliance was recognised not only by the Perth classical music lovers who frequented Riccardo's just to hear him play but also, as Reynolds said in the March–April 1985 issue of *Music Maker*, 'A lot of prominent musicians from overseas, concert musicians, have seen David at Riccardo's and raved about him.'

That November Gillian, who was in Perth for a five-day visit to establish a branch of the Federation of Australian Astrologers, was introduced to David by Chris as 'a most unforgettable person'. It was when David played Rachmaninof's Third Piano Concerto, hardly the music one expects to hear in a nightclub, that she 'felt a strong karmic bond' with him.

Gillian describes herself ten years ago as being 'more glamorous than I am today. I was reasonably well travelled, sophisticated, a very "glittery" woman.' Indeed, even now she has a great love of bright colours, sequins, very large earrings, bulky necklaces and bracelets. David and Gillian's present home is also an expression of Gillian's colourful, forceful, 'quadruple Sagittarian' personality, with superb highly glazed dinnerware, gold-embossed ruby Venetian glass and other unique decorating accessories.

Right from the start Gillian, some sixteen years David's senior, found herself being questioned by people who were curious and suspicious about her interest in David. She says, 'No-one could understand that I loved David as a person and they couldn't understand what I was doing with this strange young eccentric.' Gillian believes that because she presented an extroverted, glamorous image to Riccardo's patrons, some responded to her with enormous scepticism and plain rudeness. Often she would be asked, 'What's your angle? What are you after?'

Gillian says David proposed to her on 1 December 1983. She does not say what her response was. Before returning to Sydney, she asked Chris, as a medical practitioner, whether it would be acceptable for her to write to David. According to her, he said he thought it would be not only acceptable but desirable, as David was crying out for someone to take an interest in him on a personal level. Over the following weeks Gillian sent David letters, postcards and small gifts from the various ports of call made by the P&O cruise ships and whenever possible she telephoned him for a chat.

In January 1984, on a cruise, a fellow esoteric lecturer, a clairvoyant, did a reading for Gillian. According to Gillian the clairvoyant told her there was a very important person in her life who would 'manifest very strongly'. 'She said, "The thing I notice most about him is his hands. I don't know what he does but he does it in the most incredible way." This woman also said, "He almost has a Christ-like quality. He has a great simplicity of selflessness about him." ' The clairvoyant also predicted that Gillian would marry this man.

Gillian says David had asked her to marry him the second time he saw her. 'I must say I felt this amazing bond with him. It's not the sort of thing that happens in everybody's life. It was just destiny.'

During 1983 a number of astrologers, who knew Gillian had been living alone in Sydney for a year, had been watching her horoscope and predicting that something 'momentous' was about to take place in her life. After every trip she would be asked the same question: 'Did you meet Mr Right?'

In Gillian's words, 'I felt like a jumbo jet on the runway waiting for flight control to tell me when to take off. When I got off the plane that December my daughter knew something important was about to happen, as I did. As soon as I met David I knew he was going to be part of my life.'

The subject of David's medical treatment at this time is a difficult one, on which Gillian and Chris Reynolds hold quite different views. During the time Gillian had been corresponding with David she had done some astrological predictions for him and also for Reynolds. Sending her findings to Chris, she told him that she was very worried about David: she believed he was going through one of the 'great challenges' in his life. Hugh Schmitt's January 1984 *National Times* article quotes David as saying: 'I feel I can now do without psychiatric treatment and have stopped taking the drugs that were prescribed for me. I'm feeling better every day.' David also told Schmitt, 'I have never been happy in my life till now.' Gillian believes that David's happiness was the result of her regular telephone calls and letters.

Gillian claims that David's medication had been dramatically reduced and that this had an adverse effect on him, bringing about a 'great challenge'. Reynolds says that when he checked the bathroom cabinet in David's room he was horrified to find a large assortment of prescription drugs which David was taking without supervision or understanding of what each was for or when to take them. 'When I asked him what each was for, and when he took them, he answered "Golly, Chris, I don't know."' At that time both Reynolds and David faced a great challenge: Reynolds, to reduce the number of drugs and sort out those which conflicted with each other and, having done so, to find the right dosage to stabilise David's condition; David, to survive the process. Chris says: 'Gillian knows that balancing David's medication is a fine art and she also knows that David can often refuse to take medication, making his condition difficult to monitor.' Without re-admitting him to hospital, which no one wanted, least of all David, it was a 'trial and error' process. To help him with the problem Reynolds consulted with the psychologist who had handled David's case in Graylands.

At this time, and shortly after drawing up David's and Chris's horoscopes, Gillian says she received a telephone call from the clairvoyant she had met on the ship, telling her to return to Perth if she could because David was 'going back into the foetal position'.

It is not unusual that the sudden withdrawal of antidepressant or other psychotropic medication from a person who has depended on these drugs for their continuing stability can precipitate a rapid relapse or worse. However, as Reynolds says, it was necessary to manipulate David's medication in order to establish a maintainable balance. 'What could I do? On full dosage he was spaced out; on too little he fell apart. At least I did try to achieve a balance.'

After referring to his medical notes about David, he says: 'I reduced the dosage over a period of time. The thing with David was his chaotic state of mind. It was very difficult to control both the dosage and compliance. He did regress for about a week, but I increased his dose and he was okay.' He observes that the interesting thing about that period was that 'Everyone knew best how to manage David; however, none of them had tried living with him or even sticking with him.'

It was after the clairvoyant called that Gillian says she realised she loved David, something which had occurred to her while watching the ABC 'Nationwide' programme in late January 1984. 'It was a very strange experience, realising you are in love with this very, very unusual man on the television set!'

The next day Gillian rang her daughter, Sue, to tell her this. Some time during the conversation Sue asked her why she loved David. Her answer sums up the reaction most people have to David when they get to know him: 'He changed my vision of the world a great deal, and the beauty of the world; and he touched many things in me and I feel much better for knowing him.'

It was then, she says, that she realised that the clairvoyant's call was very important because it 'was tying in with the astrology'. Because of the clairvoyant's claim that David was enduring a harrowing experience, Gillian decided to approach Reynolds with an offer to fly to Perth to care for David while he took a holiday. Concerned about how he would accept her offer, she selected a Tarot card, which indicated that she would be rejected but should be patient. She says he reacted as she had anticipated, telling her that he was able to cope.

Chris, however, has a different version of these events. He says that he 'would have been happy for anyone to take David off my hands at that time'. He acknowledges that his girlfriend Pippa was a great help, and also that there was a family who took

David out a couple of times a week. Dot Croft also took him occasionally. 'Otherwise I was left on my own and I was a lousy cook.'

Two days later Gillian says she drew another Tarot card, the Chariot, which, as she loosely interpreted, 'naturally meant move forward'. Again she telephoned. In her account of this, all she said was, 'Oh, Chris, it's Gillian,' and he answered simply, 'I'll come and meet you at the airport.' (Chris, who is not a man of few words, finds this amusing, 'I can't imagine that was all I said, it doesn't sound like me.') Gillian's daughter, Sue, offered to pay her airfare to Perth.

At that stage David was an enormous handful for Chris to care for, burning holes in the piano stool with his cigarettes and creating general havoc by leaving mess all over the house. Chris was beginning to sag under the weight of the responsibility of looking after David, carrying on with his medical practice and running Riccardo's.

During this time Gillian and David built up a strong rapport, and Gillian began to make serious plans to leave Sydney to be with him. She says that although Chris thought it was an excellent idea, he was also concerned for her and the possible problems she would have to face, not least of which was David's desire to please everybody. Speaking as Dr Reynolds, he pointed out to her that, given David's driving need to be loved and to love everybody because of his deep, ingrained fear of rejection, it was possible that he would never be able to love her, or anyone else for that matter, above all others.

Gillian told Chris she understood this. She also said that she had no idea on what level their relationship would be, whether she would be 'a housekeeper, a mother, or a lover', just that it was part of her 'destiny' to be there.

Destiny? Or the self-fulfilment of the clairvoyant's

predictions? Whether or not one believes in astrology and clairvoyants, one immutable fact remains: David drew Gillian to him like a magnet.

In April 1984 Gillian moved into Chris's home, sleeping in a single bed with David in the Reynolds sleep-out. She left behind, in Sydney, a car and ten packing cases that were to follow her to Perth at a later date. Chris says that he 'selfishly, I suppose, could see Gillian taking a weight off my shoulders'. Himself a divorcee, when talking about this time he remarked with a laugh that David and he living together 'was like a mutual survival course'.

Although David was living with Chris, he still made the occasional weekend trip to Maddington to visit Dorothy Croft. In view of his continuing, though reduced, personal relationship with Dot and in recognition of the invaluable help she had given David during a most difficult period in his life, when there was virtually no other support and encouragement, Gillian thought it appropriate to make contact. She telephoned Dot to let her know she was coming to live in Perth to look after David. While Mrs Croft acknowledged that Gillian's plan could only be good for David, Gillian says she followed up by saying, 'The Lodge was such a good place. Chris was very wrong to take him away from there.' Chris, who has often questioned his own role in bringing David into the spotlight of public life, has made the thoughtful observation that 'this may eventually prove to be correct. The thought has crossed my mind many times.'

Under the circumstances it is not difficult to understand how Dot Croft may well have experienced some distress over these changes at a time when David was beginning to regain some emotional stability and emerging out of obscurity to again receive public acclaim. As Gillian publicly acknowledged in a letter to the *Comment News* newspaper, her friendship and her 'encouragement of his musical genius', which had extended over almost seven long and difficult years, 'was indeed a blessing'.

At the time Gillian moved to Perth, neither Rachel nor Dot had seen David for a number of weeks. Chris had found it necessary to contact both women and ask them if they would at least see him once a fortnight. By unfortunate coincidence, Gillian's arrival coincided with one of David's pre-arranged weekend visits with Dot.

Gillian recalls her distress upon learning this: 'I'd just left everybody in Sydney and here I was on the other side of the continent. It was incredibly difficult. I thought, well I've got to come to terms with this. So all night I talked to the universe, Big Daddy, whatever you want to call it and battled with my sadness and sense of "What have I done?" Because it was so incredibly difficult, I thought, well I've got to come to terms with this. So in the morning I said in all truthfulness to David, "Go and have a happy time with Dot for the weekend." About half an hour or an hour later the phone rang. It was Dot's daughter, who very rudely said, "Tell David not to come!" I thought, that's interesting, I battled the thing with myself and freed myself of it, then it didn't happen!' The same sequence of events was repeated a few weeks later. David has not seen Dot since.

Quite some time later Gillian and Dot met by accident at Rachel's home when Gillian had called there to give Rachel tickets for one of David's recitals. Gillian recalled their meeting as unpleasant. According to Gillian, Mrs Croft felt that she had formed the relationship with David for financial reasons whereas, as Gillian says, when she and David met his sole possessions were 'a cane basket, a worn-out transistor and $200'.

Chris says of this troubled period, 'We all did the best we could under the circumstance: Whatever happened, we all said, "We have to do the best we can for David." We all ran around like beheaded chooks while David indulged his passion . . . so who's the smart one?'

In May 1984 it became very clear that David and Gillian could not continue to live with Chris. Conditions were much too crowded, especially as Gillian wanted to begin astrology classes, for which Chris' house did not offer the necessary space and privacy. That month David and Gillian moved to a rented fibro cottage in the Perth suburb of Lathlain which they decorated and made into the first home they shared together.

24

Born Performer

Before Gillian moved to Perth, David had found another major supporter. The entertainment entrepreneur Michael Parry, well known in Perth for Michael Parry's Classical Concerts, in particular the Chamber Music Subscription Series, approached Chris Reynolds as David's manager. He asked if David could play a recital in June as one of a series of twelve subscription fixtures he was mounting between April and November 1984. Although Chris was concerned that David might not be ready to cope, he decided that, for David's sake, it was worth taking the chance.

At the time David was chain-smoking at least 125 cigarettes a day. He never had a cigarette out of his mouth except when he was drinking coffee or swimming in Chris's swimming pool. Gillian says it was imperative that David stop smoking for the sake of both his health and his image, which was not enhanced by a cigarette hanging out of his mouth while he played the romantic classics. During the sessions at Riccardo's, David's demeanour was more that of a jazz pianist than that of a talented classical pianist.

Chris Reynolds says Gillian bullied David into giving up the habit, though Gillian says this is 'untrue and offensive'. As David told the ABC's Caroline Jones in a radio interview with him and Gillian in 1987, 'I would be dead now if it were not for Gillian, I would have smoked myself to death.' In that same interview, when asked what were the major turning points in his life, he replied, 'Meeting Gillian, she brought sunshine into my life, she saved me.'

Taking the cigarettes away from David mouth made Gillian very unpopular with the female fans in residence at Riccardo's who had been pandering to his habit long before she came on the scene. Gillian began by persuading him to play the first piece of the night without a cigarette, until eventually he was able to play for the first half-hour to forty minutes without one.

The forthcoming Mike Parry recital signified David's return to the concert platform as a solo performer after an absence of twelve years. It was obvious that David had to work hard to bring himself back to concert standard. More importantly, he had to be able to complete the recital without resorting to cigarettes for psychological support.

Once more, then, David found himself in a stressful situation. Although he had Gillian's support twenty-four hours a day, and together they were determined he would walk out on the stage with dignity and play for forty-five minutes without a cigarette, it was a testing time for David. Between April and June Gillian and David jogged and swam, which reduced his smoking, kept him occupied and also contributed to his physical well-being. By the beginning of June, he had his smoking under control to the point where he could perform on stage without a cigarette.

This was a remarkable achievement and a demonstration of David's determination and courage. David told Martin Kingston in an interview titled 'Play It Again' for *People* magazine: 'I no longer need treatment. I need my cigarettes but I find swimming helps me relax, I don't smoke much when I swim.'

On 8 June 1984 David played his first professional recital to a full house at Perth's Octagon Theatre. For David, to walk out onto the concert platform after so many years and face the people of his home town, to perform and prove that he hadn't lost his nerve or his magic touch, was an ordeal by fire. Eight days before to the recital, a notice inserted in the *West Australian* by Michael Parry announced in large, bold capitals that the David Helfgott concert had SOLD OUT. This was at once both gratifying and terrifying.

When David walked out onto the Octagon stage that night he was shaking with fear. Backstage, Chris and Gillian were doing the same, especially when he began the programme by playing at a frantic pace. A year later, in an interview with Chris for *Music Maker*'s March–April 1985 issue, Peter Laud wrote of the recital:

> 'He [David] received a mild dressing-down from Reynolds for playing too fast at his comeback. (At interval, mentor Reynolds told him to go out and do his job properly like a professional, to which Helfgott replied: "Golly, Chris, I will," and he promptly did.)'

Peter Wombwell, writing in the *Sunday Times* of 10 June 1984, reported on David's re-emergence onto the concert platform in an article titled 'Helfgott back with confidence':

> 'David Helfgott returned to the concert platform for the first time in many years on Friday night, tentatively to begin with but then, buoyed by a highly encouraging 'House Full' reception, fully regained his confidence.'

After a paragraph of salute to Michael Parry for his 'valuable chamber music subscription series', Wombwell continued:

> In this third programme of the series, Helfgott delved into the

romantic period with works by Chopin, Rachmaninof, Scriabin and Mussorgsky.

The Chopin opening revealed a nervous tension and here the tentative approach brought too heavy a hand, over-fast tempi and slight lapses in notation.

And it was with three of Rachmaninof's preludes, G major, G minor, and the popular C sharp minor, that he really settled to his task. He appeared more relaxed and produced some playing of extraordinary power and understanding with a keen sense of the rubato. This was emphasised in the C sharp minor which can be pedestrian, Rachmaninof came to hate it, but to which Helfgott brought a deep feeling of romanticism without gush.

Before the interval he interspersed Balakirev's remarkably athletic 'Islamey', chosen only by pianists whose command is well above average. Helfgott tossed this one off with all the aplomb of one who had received accolades from such as Daniel Barenboim, Isaac Stern and many others.

His post-interval offerings were Scriabin's exacting Etude in E flat minor and a totally convincing exposition of Mussorgsky's 'Pictures at an Exhibition'. The fun, the wit, the degradation and the grandeur were all there as Helfgott redrew the lines with infinite care.

The *West Australian* of Saturday 9 June, under the heading 'West Arts', was concerned less with the music and more with the man:

Perth pianist David Helfgott has many good friends and well-wishers, as the attendance at last night's Octagon Theatre recital amply showed. But once the seats are filled and the lights dimmed a performer must stand or fall by his own ability.

Mr Helfgott fully rewarded the faith that has been shown in him, and showed that the outstanding promise of his early years has survived the long illness which diverted him from an international career in music.

His individual style revealed great mastery, by turns magnetically powerful and serenely lyrical. There was a tendency at times to sacrifice stability for speed, and tempi were thus occasionally wayward.

In a Romantic-period programme Balakirev's 'Islamey', recognised as a pianistic tour de force, was thrown off without apparent difficulty.

His standing ovation from a delighted audience was well deserved and was as much a recognition of his courage as of his musicianship.

Chris Reynolds, interviewed after the recital for the *Sunday Independent* of 24 June said: Whether or not it will lead to a concert career is another thing, but here is a man who has beaten the system through his courage. The man is brilliant. He can play anything.'

Michael Parry, who had taken over David's management in approximately April 1984, was beside himself with delight. 'We will all remember that performance for many years to come. It will always be a very special memory for me.'

Previously, when David had played, gratis, excerpts from concertos with the Karrinyup Symphony Orchestra, his work had been marked by patches of brilliance and uninspired playing. However, in giving him the opportunity to perform as a virtuoso soloist, the Octagon recital confirmed both David's singular musical expertise and the fact that he is a born performer.

As David said recently: 'If you persevere, the hiccups get less; you've got to have hiccups before you can have a triumph. When it works it's bloody great! I reckon when it works, it's bloody great!' Philosophy from David is not unusual, but swearing is quite a new phenomenon.

David makes only oblique mention of the Michael Parry evening as one of his 'triumphs'. Although he has bowed to many emotional standing ovations and experienced many other 'triumphs' since then, the reception he received after playing Rachmaninof's Third at the Royal College of Music, in 1969, will forever remain in his mind as his first and greatest 'triumph'.

At the end of the Perth recital, when the last thundering notes of Mussorgsky's 'The Great Gate of Kiev' died, the audience went wild, standing up and cheering, crying and clapping. When I asked Chris Reynolds if he recalled whether David was excited by his tumultuous reception, he said: 'David is a born performer. His music is his life, not the applause. All I remember him saying was, 'Golly, Chris, golly!'

While David may have seemed to Chris to have lacked the ego to appreciate his own potential, it was clear to Chris and Gillian that the worst of his 'hiccups', his years in the psychiatric wilderness, although not forgotten, were behind him. Once again it was possible that he might achieve the international acclaim he deserved. David says he has always appreciated his potential. He says, 'One must not doubt one's genius.'

The Mike Willesee television piece on David's life included his performance of the Rachmaninof Second Piano Concerto with the Nedlands Symphony Orchestra in July, the month after his solo recital at the Octagon. At the end of this wonderful segment Willesee mentioned David and Gillian's forthcoming wedding, adding with a wry grin that David was issuing invitations to all Riccardo's patrons.

David and Gillian married in August 1984 in a civil ceremony in the garden of the home of Gillian's friends Mr and Mrs Brackley, in Applecross, Perth. Gillian and Barbara Brackley, also an astrologer, were close friends and together they established the Perth Academy of Astrology.

Woman's Day the following month carried an article titled 'Wedding bells for the piano man', which opened with: 'Never has a bride been kissed so many times by the bridegroom during the wedding ceremony. And rarely have wedding guests been musically entertained with such panache, also by the groom.'

Chris Reynolds gave them the use of Riccardo's for the wedding reception and supplied the wine. Friends Gillian and David had met at Riccardo's made the wedding cake. Gillian's children, Scot and Sue Murray, cooked the wedding breakfast. Of course, the bridegroom was in fine form at the reception, tossing off a classical 'set' which included Chopin's 'Tristesse' and Ravel's 'Ondine'.

When Chris reflects on the period preceding the wedding, he says: 'I was naturally suspicious, did not trust Gillian, and wanted to protect David. The sheer speed of events, the wedding, et cetera, had me worried . . . [but] . . . selfishly I suppose, I could see Gillian taking the weight off my shoulders. They seemed to be happy, and I was not David's guardian. Family members asked questions about the marriage, I asked questions too, but David was an adult. The consensus was, it was none of our business; neither it was.'

After their wedding the couple resumed their lives in the little fibro cottage in Lathlain. Gillian adopted a daily schedule aimed at improving David's health, and also to establish a sense of direction and purpose in his life. This routine incorporated six to eight hours of practice a day, two daily trips to a heated swimming pool, and playing at Riccardo's three nights a week.

The swimming sessions contributed strongly to David's well-being. When David is upset or disturbed, immersing himself in water and swimming for half an hour will restore him to a state of calm. Despite his unusual, splashy swimming stroke, he is a very strong swimmer. Equally at home in still water or a lively surf, he has been known to swim for hours.

In the absence of a piano, David still finds security in the water. I vividly recall an occasion when, together with Kirsty Cockburn, her partner George Negus and George's mother Dorothy, my husband and I met for dinner with Gillian and David at a riverside restaurant. David, perhaps threatened by unfamiliar surroundings and with no piano to retreat to for security, stood up at the table and in a very loud voice announced to the startled assembly, 'My father castrated me.' He then took himself off into the night to swim in the river estuary.

The assembled company thought he was experiencing emotional distress. Leslie Helfgott says David's exclamation should not be taken literally (which it was not) nor as a reflection of how David feels about his father's treatment of him, but was more likely an attention-getting device. His disappearance for over an hour brought us out into the dark to find him. Of course when we did he was swimming powerfully up and down the river as if he had only just entered the water, from which he emerged calm and relaxed. This was more than could be said for the rest of us, who, apart from Gillian, had never experienced such behaviour from David before.

After their marriage, although Gillian had given up the bulk of her astrology work to concentrate on David's rehabilitation, she continued to hold astrology classes each Saturday afternoon, conduct astrology talks for ABC Radio 6WF on Friday mornings and maintain her private astrological consultations. The loss of income as the result of surrendering some of her astrology work, and the expense of supporting David's smoking habit, meant life was very trying for Gillian — and would continue to be so for a long time.

25

Back on Top

David's return to the concert platform began in June of 1984, with his recital at the Octagon. In the early months of 1985, one of Riccardo's regular patrons asked Gillian what kind of piano he practised on at home. Surprised to learn that David did not have a concert grand, the man promised to buy him one.

The *West Australian* on 21 March 1985 ran a photograph of David smiling broadly, leaning on a gleaming grand piano. The accompanying article by Hugh Schmitt was entitled 'A grand surprise for a virtuoso'. David had returned home to find installed in his living room a $20 000 Yamaha C7 concert grand, tied with a huge white bow and with a card wishing him well. On top of the piano was a huge basket of flowers and a bottle of expensive wine for Gillian. The businessman and winegrower Malcolm Jones had been true to his word at Riccardo's. He and his wife Deirdre and their children, who had given David the piano 'to show their appreciation of his music', were waiting in another room to see his reaction. David did not disappoint them: 'I feel like I'm walking on air', he said. 'I've never owned a grand piano in my life.'

Fortunately, by the time David received the piano, he and Gillian had been able to rent a larger house at South Perth, which backed onto a park and looked out across the Swan River to Perth. Not only was the house large enough to accommodate the baby grand, it was in an ideal position for David, allowing him to jog in comparative privacy and to swim in the river. On many occasions the water police, who knew David, would pull along side to remind him to stay clear of ferries plying to and from the city.

It would be an understatement to say that David's life had taken yet another upward turn. An article titled 'The love that reclaimed a lost genius' appeared in New Idea magazine on 24 August 1985, a few days short of his and Gillian's first wedding anniversary. Journalist Pauline Lee wrote: 'At first glance the couple might appear to be strangely matched ... David the introverted genius; Gillian, an astrologer and vivacious divorcee with two grown children.' Gillian was quoted as saying, 'Even the most hardened cynics say our marriage was made in heaven. Ours is one of those rare cosmic loves few people are lucky enough to experience.' David too was carried away with joy: 'I have finished with the drugs and now Gillian is helping me to cut down on my 150 cigarettes and 25 cups of coffee a day. I no longer need those props. With Gillian I am in heaven.'

David continued to play at Riccardo's throughout 1985 and perform solo virtuoso recitals in Perth and surrounding areas. Once again he returned to his teacher Alice Carrard, a true friend who appreciated his musical ability and loved him dearly. Alice gave him lessons to sharpen his technique and polish those finer points which over his years away from the piano had become a little wayward.

Early in 1985 Chris Reynolds, ever confident that David would take his place on international concert platforms, discussed the idea of his going to Europe for some 'fine tuning'. Chris planned to go to Italy later that year, 'armed with tapes, cassettes, videos and a fat file of newspaper clippings', to promote David. However, airfares and an extended sojourn in Europe and the United Kingdom were as prohibitively expensive then as they are now. Owing to his growing financial problems with Riccardo's, Chris never did get to Italy. It became necessary for him to pass the plan on to David's manager at that time, the musical entrepreneur Michael Parry who had become his manager in 1984.

The only possible way possible for David and Gillian to make the proposed study tour was to apply for a grant from the Arts Council of Western Australia, which had replaced the Music Council of Western Australia. Michael Parry had not long returned from England, where he had found Professor Peter Feuchtwanger, an internationally acclaimed master musician renowned for his master classes. Parry believed Feuchtwanger was the perfect choice to work with David. On David's behalf Parry made the application for a grant to the Western Australian Arts Council. At the time he was told that applicants were assessed solely on their ability. However, although he met the required criteria, David's application was rejected on the grounds that he had received a grant to go to England in 1966; there seemed to be a suggestion that it was not the preference of the Arts Council to give a grant twice to the same person. In fact, David had received a bursary, not a grant. In any case, according to Gillian the 1986 Arts Council grant was then awarded to the young pianist who had received it the year before.

It was not to be the first time that the establishment would turn its back on David. To this day, apart from the bursary, David has never received one cent of government money to assist his comeback and has been given almost no exposure by the ABC. Mike Parry recently observed: 'Strangely, he's not counted as a serious professional musician by many of his peers.' Parry believes this is partly based on David's ability to generate income and to draw a crowd. For many, his performances are an entertaining introduction to the classics.

Parry may well be correct. Perhaps the Australian musical intelligentsia does resent this unusual and eccentric man who has rattled their ivory towers by introducing classical music to the populace. David can be proud that through his unique ability to communicate through music he has cast a wide net, showing that 'classical music' is not the sole province of an elite group. Unlike many other pianists of note, David is such a popular performer that he now has no need to supplement the Helfgott income by giving lessons.

It has been a long, hard, awe-inspiring climb for David, one that has required not only all his determination to regain some of his old expertise, but great courage to overcome the difficult memories which continued to haunt him. The climb would perhaps have been longer and tougher without the generous monetary assistance given to him by a West Australian mining magnate, Russell Smith, at a time when he needed to resume his studies.

1985 and 1986 were the middle years of the biggest boom in Australia's west. Lavish mansions appeared along the sides of the Swan River. Becoming an art collector, patron of the arts or philanthropist was popular among the newly wealthy, and many artists benefited, in the process possibly conferring social respect upon their patrons.

Shortly after Christmas 1985, David was engaged by a mining company to play for a corporate function at the Merlin Hotel, Perth. While David played Gillian chatted with one of the company's executives, mentioning that David had hoped to go to Europe to study but his application for a grant had been refused. The man could not believe that David had been rejected. Excusing himself, he left Gillian briefly, only to return shortly after: he had spoken to Russell Smith, the owner of the mining company, and Smith wanted to give David $10 000 for his trip. The only thing Smith asked for in return was a photograph of himself presenting David with the cheque.

The *West Australian* gladly obliged, and the photograph appeared with a caption implying that because the Arts Council had rejected David, the mining magnate had pulled out his personal cheque book to assist him. Russell Smith acted spontaneously and generously, donating not $10 000 but $12 500.

David and Gillian could now make plans to go to London in June 1986 to join Peter Feuchtwanger's master classes, and eventually to tour Europe. Apart from the master classes there was another important aspect to the trip. It was time for David to go to London and lay a ghost or two by returning to the scene of his first great triumph — and of what he had felt to be his failures.

It was true that David had outgrown the wine bar and restaurant circuit. Over three years, he had made about 400 performances at Riccardo's. Knowing it was time to move on, however, did not make parting with Chris Reynolds, Riccardo's and the friends he had made there any easier.

Leaving Riccardo's marked the opening of yet another chapter in David's life. Unfortunately the same could not be said of Riccardo's. Dogged by financial problems to which the Labor government's tax package and the Perth casino's monopolistic 24-hour liquor licence had contributed heavily by 'reducing the turnover to a trickle', Chris Reynolds was forced to accept the inevitable — Riccardo's would have to close. In a desperate bid to forestall closure, some of the staff worked without wages, those who had taken jobs elsewhere arriving after work in business suits to serve in the restaurant. When the lights of Riccardo's were switched off for the last time, Chris, having refused to accept bankruptcy as an option, was destitute, literally 'down on his uppers', living in a boarding house where the rent was $30 a week. He faced the grim prospect of a long haul to pay off his creditors, which he ultimately did without help from anybody.

'I was saddened that we had to close, Riccardo's cost me the earth emotionally and financially, but I learned an awful lot about myself along the way. So it all balances out,' Chris says. 'And let's face it, if Riccardo's helped David Helfgott get started again on his career, then it was all worthwhile.'

The period David spent at Riccardo's was undeniably a unique and invaluable time in his life. Gillian herself says that without Chris and Riccardo's, David would not be able to do what he does today. Sir Frank Callaway confirms this, saying that the role Chris played by restoring David's self-confidence at a time when he needed it most was invaluable. Sir Frank comments that Chris's contribution to getting David back on the concert platform was well recognised in Perth; Chris says that it is the people of Perth themselves who should be acknowledged in David's reemergence. While David may have slipped from their memory and into obscurity when he first came home from London, it was they who were responsible for bringing him back. 'There was a strong undercurrent of support for David — they remembered his playing when he was a boy. It was this support which filled the Octagon and the Winthrop Hall and every other venue. The Octagon trustees allowed David to use their precious Bosendorfer, use of which other pianists were denied, because they remembered his fantastic ability.'

Chris also points out that no-one should forget the contribution made to David's comeback by Gerald Krug, then the musical director of the West Australian Opera Company and the West Australian Arts Orchestra. He says: 'The West Australian music fraternity knew David's music was chaotic then but Gerald stuck his neck out when no one else would: first in 1984 when he worked with him in recording, for broadcasting, the Rachmaninof No. 1 with the WA Symphony Orchestra and then again in 1985 with the Arts Orchestra when he performed Tchaikovsky's No. 1. It's a damn shame', he adds 'that Gerald was ignored, he was a professional. He was the best qualified person in the Helfgott camp to select the music for David's public performances. But everyone thought they knew what was best for David — to hell with the professionals!'

Chris recalls attending the last of a series of three farewell concerts given by David at the Octagon Theatre on the eve of his and Gillian's departure for a concert tour of Australia's eastern states, before they left for Europe. These concerts were arranged for David in order that he could undertake a study trip, which was, in effect, the culmination of all the plans that Chris, Mike Parry and Gillian had made for David.

On the morning of that last concert, fate made a pass at dealing Chris a terrible coup de grace that could have ended all his difficulties, including money problems. He was involved in a car accident in which he only narrowly escaped being killed. 'It seems there are times when the gods are never satisfied and the challenge to survive against outrageous odds is merciless,' he says of that time.

Because Chris was so committed to repaying his creditors, he forced himself to do a full day's work after the accident. Then he went straight to the concert from work with a friend. Badly shaken, in need of a shave, limping and in considerable pain, he was to find on arrival that the dress was far from casual, with Gillian 'aglitter and gilded' for a gala occasion. (Gillian herself says, 'I am sometimes criticised for dressing up for recitals.')

Acutely aware of his appearance and feeling, as he says, 'broken', Chris hoped desperately for anonymity but at the close of the concert he was called to come forward. Embarrassed, he limped to the front, urged forward by cheers and applause in recognition of the support he had given David over the years. Exhausted and burnt out emotionally, Chris could not rejoice. He 'felt hollow', although he knew, 'If nothing else, for once in my life, I had achieved something of value for another human being — this ingenuous soul who seems to be touched by the supernatural.'

David performed for the last time at Riccardo's on 9 May 1986. It was the end of an era. David and Gillian gave Chris an air ticket to Europe. As Chris says it was impossible for him even to think about using it. 'I was committed to pay my way out of bankruptcy. Although Gillian had suggested I could share some of their accommodation, the ticket was quite useless to me. I might have been able to get to Europe but what was I expected to use for money to support myself once I got there?' Because Chris was desperate to reduce his debt, he did as Gillian suggested and cashed in his ticket.

The weekend before their departure from Perth to begin their European tour, David and Gillian were interviewed by Keith McDonald for *The Western Mail Magazine*. It reported that David had cut his smoking from 130 cigarettes a day to eighteen, and reduced his coffee intake from twenty-five cups to four. McDonald described David, then thirty-nine years old, as 'thin, stooped, balding and wearing thick glasses', and 'talking non-stop, even when Gillian was answering questions.'

In a brief encapsulation of his 'lost' years David was quoted as saying: 'It's a miracle I survived. I say that to myself all the time. I lost so many years. I had no confidence.' Gillian reaffirmed her dedication to David and his career: 'He is one of the few romantic pianists in the world. They are all too clinical but David has the passion and the romanticism. I have no doubts that he will reach his full potential.'

In answer to McDonald's questions about David's mental breakdown, Gillian denied that the pressure of his London studies had caused it. 'It's too complex to explain in an article without hurting people, but they were personal problems rather than professional problems.' She also said that being David's 'domestic manager' was a demanding job which meant that she had less and less time for astrology. 'David's career is really moving into top gear, by 1988 astrology will be a hobby. I will then be working full-time for David.'

Referring to her love for David and her interest in spiritual matters, Gillian revealed that she believed that David 'now had a concept of universal love, a divine love. It's the greatest power on earth. I knew this sort of love would heal him. It's not my love as such.' Gillian took her nurturing role very seriously: 'Most geniuses need constant care. They need someone to look after the practicalities of life for them. I see David as the orchid and I am the hothouse. A rare orchid needs a hothouse.'

On 19 June 1986, before going to England, David and Gillian flew directly to Russia from Brisbane after David had completed his tour of the eastern states, which was a huge success, with all the concerts sold out. Apart from England the only other country David had really visited was Egypt in 1966, on his way to the Royal College of Music.

Like his father's before him, David's passion for Russian music is intense, and he had been brought up with an interest in Russian culture. It was possible, in 1986, for David and Gillian to walk around Moscow and Leningrad in safety. To be able to saunter around Leningrad's streets and byways, where Tchaikovsky, Rimsky-Korsakof, Borodin and Prokofiev had walked, was for David an encounter with friends. In Moscow David was in his element browsing through music shops and purchasing editions of Russian music. Gillian says, 'It was just wonderful to see him absorbing it all. He was grabbing armfuls of these experiences and just hugging them to him.'

After meeting Professor Feuchtwanger and spending three weeks studying with him in London, David spent two weeks in the professor's summer-school master classes in Sion, Switzerland. Gillian attended both the private lessons and master classes with David: 'Peter Feuchtwanger was not only a great teacher but became a very dear friend and he and David developed a special rapport. I attended all the private lessons and master classes and this gave me a new view of the structure of music and its meaning, which has opened my perceptions greatly.' When Michael Parry chose Feuchtwanger as the perfect teacher to draw out and highlight David's qualities, he demonstrated his acute awareness of David as a musician and as a unique individual who would only benefit by learning from a kindred soul. According to David and Gillian, Feuchtwanger believed that there must be unity between life and art, between body and spirit, between technique and expression, without egocentricity and egoism. Feuchtwanger also taught that music is always more important than the performer; and that there is no room for outbursts of eccentric temperament which can only be detrimental to the music. The music must be allowed to speak for itself.

Feuchtwanger believed that the basis for optimal functioning is total relaxation. He taught his students to sit low at the piano, which allows the forearm to 'hang in the elbow', instead of being held with muscular effort. Further, he insisted that the face remain relaxed, as tension in any part of the body can disturb the freedom of other movements. Feuchtwanger also invented his own exercises, which only needed to be done a few times each day. The focus was not on the sound produced but on the fingers, hands and arms. His aim was to prepare a situation in which the ideal positioning of the hand and the arm for each motion would be carried out automatically, unconsciously. The desired sound would happen by itself, as the logical result.

Given David's usual state of tension, Feuchtwanger's educational methods were perfect. David was taught in the informal warmth of Feuchtwanger's own home, surrounded by twenty-five professional musicians who were still coming to master classes. The emphasis on natural expression and relaxation released the wellspring, carrying David to the heights of phrasing and structure and putting him in touch with the meaning and beauty of the music.

The time the Helfgotts spent at Sion was one of the most important periods in David's life. In Australia, David's eccentricity had isolated him from the company of other musicians. At Sion he was accepted by his peers without professional jealousy, which in the highly competitive musical world is exceptionally rare. So impressed was Feuchtwanger by the brilliance of David's mind and so moved was he by his playing, that he told Gillian he believed David was a reincarnation of one of the great masters.

On the last evening at Sion, David played the Liszt Ballade No. 2, 'La Campanella' and the Scriabin Etude Op. 2. The response from his peers, generated by respect and affection, was memorable and moving. After he had finished playing David took Feuchtwanger up onto the platform with him. Feuchtwanger declared that he could not teach David anything else: 'I hesitate to use the word genius but in the case of David

Helfgott I am happy to — he is without doubt one of the greatest musicians I have ever come across.' Feuchtwanger left the stage with tears in his eyes.

Gillian recalls: 'The transformation and the joy and the excitement that we felt . . . the way the students just stood in awe of David! The thing I found so incredibly interesting was they were students of high calibre, quite a number were earning their living from music, they were professional people who were still coming to have lessons with Peter who was a very charismatic man, a very fine teacher. But when David played — and this is unusual — they all rejoiced with him and they were over the moon about his playing. You know, there wasn't one ounce of jealousy, resentment or competitiveness. I made this comment to one of the students at the end of the course and he said, "Gillian, he's in another dimension to us. How could we possibly be jealous of that?" '

At that time David was pouring out his soul in the big Liszt works which are so beloved of European audiences. The demands on David when he plays are obviously emotional as well as physical, for he responds to every note with real affection. Always individual, never cursory, he shapes each phrase with spiritual energy. He creates crystalline poetry from Liszt's 'Fountains of the Villa d'Este'. With head bent, shoulders rounded, arms and fingers throbbing with the mood of the music, he brings powerful, feverish dimensions to Liszt's *Funerailles*, a work which evokes the death of Chopin as well as those of friends lost in the Hungarian Revolution — a work which aptly expresses the turmoil of the times. Liszt is David's favourite composer, with Rachmaninof a close second. Once, when I congratulated him on an especially spectacular rendition of Liszt's 'Mephisto' he answered, 'Well I reckon it was alright, pretty cheeky too.'

The Helfgotts' visit to Europe turned into a 'grand tour', introducing David to Switzerland, France, Austria, Italy, Yugoslavia, Hungary and Germany. He and Gillian visited the medieval cities of Sienna and Padua, saw *Aida* in the Arena at Verona, and enjoyed dining beside the Grand Canal in Venice. Along the way David gave some minor recitals in Vienna, Munich and Bonn. Bonn proved to be one of the highlights of his career. The German audience responded to his playing with standing ovations after almost every piece he played and at the close of the recital he was recalled for six encores. Gillian believes that the Germans probably respect David's genius more than any other nation.

The peak of the tour was undoubtedly a visit to Budapest, one of the most beautiful cities in the world, for the Centenary Liszt Festival. Here David played in Liszt's home, now a museum, performing 'La Campanella' on Liszt's own piano. According to Gillian, as quoted in the *Bulletin* of 14 April 1987, 'The people couldn't speak English but they were clasping their hearts. An old bearded man thrust money into David's hands.'

After Europe the couple returned to London. Gillian recalls, 'We were staying in this wonderful Rudolf Steiner Lodge in Hammersmith. There was a doctor/osteopath who said to David, "You really have got to do something about your smoking." ' Previously he had been told by Perth doctors that the top of his lungs was badly affected, and that if he kept smoking it might very well kill him. On 4 November 1986 David gave up smoking while they were waiting at Heathrow Airport to board the flight home. Gillian said to him, 'David, wouldn't it be great fun if, when you got off the plane, you weren't smoking any more?' David replied, stubbing out his cigarette, 'Okay, darling.' And has never lit one since.

Gillian says she was aware then that taking David's cigarettes away from him completely might cause him 'an enormous fear', but in place of the cigarettes, 'he had loving care and the inspiration of getting back on the concert platform'. Gillian also suggested that David might like to have a cigar after a recital if he felt he needed it, which he did occasionally over a period of approximately a year.

Since that first visit to Europe, David has become a firm favourite with European audiences and returns there every year. He is particularly popular in Denmark and Germany. In Bonn, the Helfgotts stay with their friend Esther Friedman, who is a keen supporter of David's work. Gillian and David met Esther while she was running Professor Feuchtwanger's master classes, staying with her during that period. Gillian says, 'She is just like family and we love her so dearly.'

In both Denmark and Germany, critics are effusive in their praise of David's work. The man who has been most influential in David's popularity in Denmark is Nils Ruben, his Danish manager. Nils, also a very fine musician, had also been a student at Professor Feuchtwanger's master classes. He and his wife, Charlotta, a violinist with the Copenhagen Philharmonic Orchestra, have both been extremely supportive of David and as musicians appreciate his abilities.

Nils first heard David play at Bonn; eager to hear more of his work he travelled to Munich, where David was to give a recital. Then, in 1988, he travelled to Denmark just to hear David play again. At this time a lasting rapport was established between the two men. When Gillian casually asked Nils where in Europe he would recommend they spend a spare ten days, he suggested that they come to Denmark, where he would hold a concert in his home for David. A newspaper journalist who attended the recital wrote an article on him which appeared in the *Politiken* newspaper. From that time David's popularity in Denmark soared.

Since 1990 Nils Ruben has worked to arrange tours and recitals for him in all parts of Denmark. He writes: 'Wherever David has played, the love for him as a person and genius musician has been overwhelming. The reviewers in the leading Danish newspapers have compared his playing with both Horowitz and Glenn Gould. People attending the concerts have in words and letters told me of their unique experiences. Having come to know David both as a musician and personally, and being given the possibility to work with him as his personal manager in Denmark, has been one of the greatest adventures in my own life as a musician.'

Each year when the Helfgotts tour Denmark they stay in a lovely little cottage owned by Nils's father on the Sound, which looks across the water to the lights of Sweden. Gillian emphasises the value of Nils Ruben's contribution to David's career in Denmark and all over Europe. 'He's [David's] played in so many different parts of Denmark — he's got a higher profile there than anywhere else in Europe, and this is due to Nils's complete dedication. Nils is such a fine musician himself, he knows what David is doing. Without Nils and his beautiful wife Charlotta and his parents, we couldn't tour Denmark, they have opened up the whole country to David.' David's 1995 recitals in Denmark were an outstanding success. According to Gillian, hundreds were turned away and David was 'mobbed like a pop star' by people wanting to buy his CD (produced in Denmark by Rapp Records in 1994).

In the same year David and Nils forged their close association, was also the year David again met Sir Keith Falkner, whom he had not seen in twenty-seven years. Over the years David had kept in touch with Sir Keith, sending him Christmas cards and notes. Sir Keith and Lady Falkner were impressed that Gillian and David had driven across England from where they were staying with friends in the Malvern Hills ('Elgar country') to Norwich, to make the visit. However, as Gillian says, it was so important for David to met with Sir Keith once again that they would have driven twice the distance to do so.

After lunch Sir Keith asked David to play for him. David played Liszt's 'Dante' Sonata (Apres une Lecture de Dante) and the Liszt Ballade No. 2 in B Minor. Given David's affinity with Liszt these were perfect choices. Gillian recounts, 'At the end Sir Keith leapt out of his chair in great excitement, saying, "David, this is what music is all about!" ' The reunion after so many years had been emotional and the farewell, as one might guess, was equally poignant. Gillian recalls Sir Keith, a tall and very dignified man, had tears in his eyes when saying goodbye to David. He told David how grateful he was that they had been reunited and how overjoyed he was to find that the essence of David's gift had not been lost since his college days.

Apart from Gillian and Chris Reynolds, perhaps the person most responsible for David's comeback is the television journalist and producer, Kirsty Cockburn. Kirsty's interest in David's career and life has helped him to gain public exposure which would have been much more difficult without her enthusiastic support and hard work. Kirsty's efforts to get David television coverage resulted in the Willesee segment and several later appearances on Channel Nine's Midday Show with Ray Martin. Gillian acknowledges that Kirsty's support has been of inestimable value to David. She says that the Ray Martin segments made him a household name from Perth to Sydney to Kunanurra, where a bus driver, having seen David on the show, leaned out of his bus to yell: 'Good on you! Keep on playing, David!'

Since the time Kirsty met David ten years ago she has worked tirelessly to help his career, assistance which has cost her considerable time, effort and emotional distress. Kirsty herself has done much research on David and is also writing a biography, which, as she says is 'stalled at the three-quarter mark'. There is only so much a mother of two lively boys with enquiring minds can do, while also directing and administrating Negus Media.

After David and Gillian moved from Perth to the Promised Land, Kirsty, still aiming to increase David's public profile in New South Wales, regularly wrote press releases and contacted journalists about his work. In addition, after much time-consuming effort, she successfully negotiated a recording contract for David with EMI; the resulting CD was nominated for an ARIA Award. Both she and George gave the Helfgotts accommodation while their home was being built — even going as far as buying a piano for David.

At this point it is worth remembering Chris Reynolds's observation that everyone runs around after David like decapitated chooks while David does exactly what he wants to do. Whether David plays, as he says, 'like an angel' on his off days, or as he says, 'like the God of Gods' when he is at his best, somehow people do fall under his spell, especially when they see and hear him live in concert, or at one of the many recitals Gillian arranges for seventy-five or more people several times a year at their home. David, for whatever strange reason, is something of a Pied Piper who somehow, without apparent intent, effortlessly takes captive the time and energies of everyone he touches. He doesn't appear to be interested in what the critics say, or do not say, about him; but he has been known to remark, with his peculiar laugh, 'You're slaving for me!' when some personal favour is being done for him. David takes everything in his stride; after all, the only thing he wants to do, I believe, is live in his own world and play his beloved music. However, it takes the love of many people at many levels to make David's world go round.

26

Who is David?

After an absence of twenty-five years, David returned to play at the Royal College of Music in October 1994. He had performed only twice in London since his traumatic departure all those years ago.

My daughter Vanessa approached Isla Baring, the chairman of the Tait Memorial Trust, with a proposal for the Trust to sponsor a recital by David. The Trust, under the current patronage of Dame Joan Sutherland and Lady Viola Tait, was formed in memory of Sir Frank Tait and his brothers. The Tait brothers played an important part in the establishment of theatre and the performing arts in Australia. It provides funds to promote the careers of some of the many talented young Australian musicians and performing artists studying in the United Kingdom. Through Vanessa's involvement, The Trust agreed to sponsor a concert at the Royal College of Music. The Trust's efforts in obtaining the sponsorship of the Australian and New Zealand Bank, their generous provision of wine and food, and access to their mailing list, set the stage for a gala occasion. Gillian was delighted: at last David would play again at the Royal College of Music. (A year later, Vanessa was also to organise a performance for David at Australia House.)

On Tuesday 25 October 1994 David gave his performance at the College in the presence of His Excellency, the Hon. Neal Blewett, High Commissioner for Australia. This time he did not play the Rachmaninof Third Concerto but gave a virtuoso recital of Mendelssohn's Andante and *Rondo Capriccioso* Op. 14, Beethoven's Sonata Op. 53 ('Waldstein'), Liszt's Ballade No. 2 in B Minor, Etude de Concert No. 3 (*Un Sospiro*), Paganini's Etude No.3 and Liszt's *Apres une Lecture de Dante Fantasia quasi Sonata*. Like his meeting with Sir Keith Falkner, this event must have been a milestone for David.

David continues to tour successfully together with Gillian, both in Australia and internationally, delighting audiences everywhere. And yet we are left to puzzle over the eternal question: Who is David?

It is only possible to conjecture why David has become a 'manic eccentric', as some people describe him. We cannot attribute this solely to his background, his experiences in London, his medical treatment, or his music. The man we see is the product of all these factors and no doubt some further unknown ones.

At Graylands, David said he was often drugged and at one stage was 'deprived of my music', the thing he lives for. There were pianos in the other wards but David says he was forbidden to play because it was thought that music had contributed to his breakdown. Instead he was forced to bind books, which can only have intensified his frustration.

'It wasn't the music's fault,' David says. 'When I was playing well, I was also well. The worst thing about being incarcerated in those places was there were no performances. They punished you if you didn't co-operate, but you punished yourself anyway with the mental illness. It was a vicious circle. It was a terrible place to be. Who would want to be mentally ill?'

Margaret Helfgott does not agree that David was not allowed to play the piano. She says that staff members and other patients at the time, as well as their brother Leslie who visited him at Graylands, recall his frequent playing there. She does agree that David was not at liberty to perform whenever he wished, due to hospital schedules and rest periods.

Discussing this period, David has said, 'It was very sad. The point is, the institution is really in your mind; the torture chamber is your own mind. It's hard to improve there. For twenty-five years no-one really gave a damn whether I lived or died, no-one really cared for me. It was a long, long time in the wilderness.'

At first I thought that David was being extreme when he said no-one had really cared for him for twenty-five years. After a calculation or two, I have come to the conclusion that he dated this period from that time in 1961 when Peter refused to allow him to go to America, the time when David says 'the fog' began. Once again Margaret cannot agree with David's view, writing that 'Peter adored him and did the best he knew how for him for all of his life. Rachel often cried about David even though she didn't always understand him. We all cared.'

Today David says, 'I reckon I'm lucky to be alive, exceptionally lucky to be alive. Nothing is really lost. They say what you are can never be destroyed.'

If you saw David as a child, a clever child, and concluded that he was a blessed being without ego, you would be very wrong. In his own words, 'One must not doubt one's genius.'

Does David's ego transcend the 'I'? Is he not driven, like most of us, to achieve for his own gratification? His ego seeks recognition, naturally enough, responding to applause. It also seeks tears which show him he has truly touched you in the only way he knows how — with music. As David says, 'It's not just the notes, it has to be more than the notes.'

Alice Carrard in her wisdom prefers to see David not as a child but rather as an artist whose ability to communicate is best expressed through music.

Neville Cohn, a music critic, says, 'He has naturally the kind of agility that anyone aspiring to a concert career would probably mortgage their soul to emulate.' Kathron Sturrick, who studied at the Royal College of Music with David under Cyril Smith, vividly describes David's mastery and recalls how he would play on request the most difficult pieces from memory for his fellow students at parties.

Cohn says, 'When he tackles things more technical than emotional, he demonstrates extraordinary agility and accuracy at breakneck speed. He is phenomenal.' Sturrick, however, recalled that when they were in London his gift transcended mere technical capacity. She especially recalled David's playing of Balakiref's Islamey.

Some music critics wax lyrical over David's interpretation of the work. Most find words inadequate to describe the astonishing skill of his playing, not only in terms of dexterity but in the meaning he gives to what, in less capable hands, could amount to little more than barren keyboard pyrotechnics. Despite his 'abnormality', David is hailed as a genius by a number of respected musical critics around the world. In Tokyo he performed a rhapsody written for him by a Japanese composer before an audience of two thousand people in Tokyo. In Albania, he successfully performed the Rachmaninof No. 2 Concerto in 1993 after not having played this piece since 1984. It was a performance which went to air almost unrehearsed, as a result of a misunderstanding by Albania's Radio and Television

Orchestra. Gillian reported in the *Arts West Magazine* of November-December 1993: 'David's performance was quite outstanding. It was one of those nights when everything falls into place and David was at his virtuosic best. He was given a tremendous ovation and the celebrations went on into the night!'

There is no doubt that David does have singular intellectual gifts, heightened creative, interpretive powers which find their full imaginative and instinctive expression through his heart and his hands. He is not accepted by every music buff as the pianist extraordinaire. There are many who love his work and those who hate it. In Europe critics have compared him to great pianists such as Richter, Horowitz and Arrau. Others find his tendency to hum or sing occasionally while he is playing somewhat off-putting, in some cases, sufficient to make them walk out of his recitals.

When Neville Cohn speaks of David's playing not as a critic but as an individual, he says he often feels a nagging tension. Can David sustain it? Can he keep control? Cohn says, 'It's this fantastic brilliance but one always wonders is it going to survive intact.' Yet it does.

Chris Reynolds feels that there is something supernatural about David and his music. He tells of how he once asked David if he saw the notes when he played.

David replied, 'Golly, Chris, no. I see forests and rivers and fields and things.'

'But how do you know where to put your fingers?'

'Oh,' replied David, 'they just seem to know where to go.'

As Chris said, 'Work that one out.'

At times, David seems to have something of Liszt's spirit. The French musicologist Alfred Leroy, quoted in the *Larousse*

Encyclopedia of Music, said of Liszt: 'With the descriptive and narrative element there is closely linked an emotional and emotive psychological element, an intuition which links the real with the eternal.' Leroy might well have said the same of David's musical outpourings, especially when he plays Liszt.

There is undoubtedly something supernatural about the way David communicates through his music. More than three years ago, as I sat beside him at the piano, he played Chopin's Funeral March, which Gillian said she had never heard him play before. In fact she had not realised that he knew the piece. After he finished he put his arm around me and said, 'I played that especially for you.' It had been a stunningly emotional performance which made me cry. I thanked him saying that, while I appreciated it, I would have preferred something a little more cheerful. But once again he put his arm around me, saying simply, 'I played that especially for you.'

The following week my father died. I do not believe that David's playing of the Funeral March was a coincidence. David had sensed my father's imminent death and the only way he had of communicating this was was through the music.

Is this a mind in chaos? No, David is simply an enigma, the true mystery within a mystery: eccentric, whimsical, intriguing, exceptionally intelligent, at times wilful, irritating and frustrating, in tune with the unknown.